20 SECRETS TO SUCCESS FOR

NCAA STUDENT-ATHLETES

Ohio University Sport Management Series

Dr. Heather Lawrence and Dr. Norm O'Reilly, Series Editors

20 Secrets to Success for NCAA Student-Athletes,
by Rick Burton, Jake Hirshman, Norm O'Reilly,
Andy Dolich, and Heather Lawrence

*Alternative Models of Sports Development in America:
Solutions to a Crisis in Education and Public Health,*
by B. David Ridpath

20 Secrets to Success

for NCAA Student-Athletes

SECOND EDITION

Rick Burton

Jake Hirshman

Norm O'Reilly

Andy Dolich

Heather Lawrence

Foreword by Stan Wilcox

Afterword by Christopher J. Parker

OHIO UNIVERSITY PRESS

ATHENS

Ohio University Press, Athens, Ohio 45701
ohioswallow.com
© 2018, 2021 by Ohio University Press

Printed in the United States of America
Ohio University Press books are printed on acid-free paper ⊗ ™

Library of Congress Cataloging-in-Publication Data
Names: Burton, Rick, author.
Title: 20 secrets to success for NCAA student-athletes / Rick Burton, Jake Hirshman, Norm O'Reilly, Andy Dolich, Heather Lawrence ; foreword by Stan Wilcox ; afterword by Christopher J. Parker.
Other titles: 20 secrets to success for NCAA student-athletes who won't go pro | Twenty secrets to success for NCAA student-athletes
Description: Second edition. | Athens : Ohio University Press, 2021. | Series: Ohio University sport management series | Revised edition of: 20 secrets to success for NCAA student-athletes who won't go pro. 2017 | Includes bibliographical references.
Identifiers: LCCN 2021011268 (print) | LCCN 202101269 (ebook) | ISBN 9780821424643 (paperback) | ISBN 9780821447505 (pdf)
Subjects: LCSH: College athletes—Education—United States. | College athletes—United States—Life skills guides.
Classification: LCC LC2581 .B87 2021 (print) | LCC LC2581 (ebook) | DDC 378.1/98—dc23
LC record available at https://lccn.loc.gov/2021011268
LC ebook record available at https://lccn.loc.gov/2021011269

Contents

Foreword

It wasn't until eighth grade that I developed a fierce feeling of confidence that I was destined to play basketball at the high school varsity and collegiate level, and potentially professionally. At that time, I truly did not know all that it would take to reach each of these heights. But the experience of playing for a first-time coach who had just completed his undergraduate degree as a student-athlete at Dowling College on Long Island was exciting.

Joe Pellicane, my eighth-grade coach, trained and managed our team as though it were a college team. The conditioning and discipline, combined with the defensive mindset that was a cornerstone of his strategy, catapulted our team to a one-loss season. (And it is worth noting that the one loss was avenged in crushing fashion in a late-season rematch.) One of the most significant things I recall Coach Pellicane teaching our team was how to play one-on-one and team defense.

The first couple weeks of practice, we never touched a basketball. We just conditioned on the court and did defensive slide drills. Our workouts were like nothing I had ever experienced, and at the end of one specific practice, I recall more than half of the team, including myself, discussing quitting the team. We felt we couldn't take any more of the pain that came with the physical conditioning. I remember one evening lying in bed and screaming because it felt like I had cramps in every muscle of my body. Needless to say, by the end of that season, we were all in such great shape that we felt invincible. That we could take on any team, at any level, and beat them.

What really set me on the path to a collegiate athletic career was the feeling Coach Pellicane instilled in me at the end-of-the-year class assembly. I was sitting with classmates as Coach recapped our season and called each of my teammates up to the stage to receive his end-of-the-year participation recognition award. It appeared he had finished calling up the entire team but had forgotten me.

At that point, Joe began talking about an individual whom he deemed the catalyst for the team's success, the hardest worker day in and day out. He read out individual players' playing statistics (none of us even knew individual stats were kept at that time). Then he called my name and motioned for me to join my teammates on stage as the team MVP.

To this day, that was one of the most significant moments of my life.

It was the point I knew I could be successful in this sport and wanted to prove to my family and friends that I could be successful in life. I began to seek guidance from Coach Pellicane as to what it would take to become a collegiate athlete like him. Our team went undefeated as ninth graders; then it was on to high school, where I became a three-year starter on the varsity team and we eventually won the New York state championship.

It was Coach Pellicane who provided me with my first book on all I needed to know about the collegiate athletics recruiting process. Along my high school journey, I became one of the top guards in the country. I was admitted to the best summer camp where all the college coaches went to see the top players in the country, and I played at different all-star basketball events around the country.

Hundreds of recruiting letters poured in, and I took my five permissible official visits and a few unofficial visits. I finally narrowed my decision to three institutions, Rutgers, Syracuse, and Notre Dame. It was time for me to make one of the most important decisions in my life. I knew it was a decision that was going to be all mine and that my parents and high school coach would support me.

I ultimately chose to attend the University of Notre Dame for the following reasons:

1. It had almost a 100 percent graduation rate for its basketball team.

2. The few individuals that left Notre Dame early to play professional basketball were coming back in the summer to take their remaining classes to graduate.

3. I wanted to play with and against the best in the country.

4. I wanted to benefit from national TV exposure, and Notre Dame basketball was one of the few teams in the nation at that time offering that spotlight on an annual basis. Plus, the UCLA–Notre Dame basketball games were among the most watched games (at that time) in the country. That rivalry happened because Notre Dame had broken the eighty-eight-game winning streak of John Wooden (one of the winningest coaches in history) in 1974, just before I arrived at Notre Dame in 1977. Those games were featured on national television every year, much like the North Carolina–Duke games today.

As I mentioned, I entered Notre Dame in the fall of 1977 as a wide-eyed, naïve freshman living away from home (on my own for the first time) for an extended period. From the hustle and fast pace of New York to the mellow, slow pace of the Midwest. If I would have had access to a book such as *20 Secrets to Success for NCAA Student-Athletes,* my four years at Notre Dame would have been so much easier.

I had no idea how to create a student-athlete plan, no full understanding of what being a student-athlete meant, and no vision for a success wheel. I followed the path of my upperclassman teammates. I observed what they did wrong and what they did right. I also listened to the advice of my coaches and academic advisors. So as a freshman my student-athlete plan and success wheel came from my teammates, coaches, and academic advisors. That plan included attending classes, then playing pick-up ball in the evening, and going to the dining hall for dinner after. After dinner came class assignments for a few hours, then socializing with teammates and dorm mates into the late evening.

Notre Dame was unique in that it required all students to live in on-campus dorms unless you were married. Then, you either had to live in on-campus married student housing or an off-campus apartment. Notre Dame had no coed dorms, fraternities, or sororities and created a rule precluding male students from being in a female dormitory after a certain hour and vice versa. The term used for these restrictions was "parietals." You could get expelled from school for breaking parietals.

Freshman year was an eye-opener for me from an academic perspective. I would see the thousands of students on campus only when changing classes or going to the cafeteria for breakfast, lunch, or dinner. At all other times, the campus had just a few students walking on the quads, a very eerie feeling. I soon learned that when the quads were empty, the students were in their dorm rooms studying for classes. That was foreign to me, as I expected most of the students would be outside socializing.

My academic goal as a freshman and sophomore was to be eligible to participate in practice and competition. Before the NCAA even had eligibility rules, Notre Dame had its own academic eligibility requirements. You had to complete twelve hours a semester with a 2.0 GPA. So that was my goal each semester of my first two years. My first semester, I put in the same effort I did in high school toward my academic studies.

I was in for a shock as basketball practice started and we had our first team meeting with our academic advisor regarding our midsemester grades. Including me, there were five freshmen on the team. Professor DeCicco was the head of our academic advisors and the head coach of the fencing team. He would always jokingly threaten us with one of the foils or sabers if he heard we were not attending class or doing poorly. Needless to say, I had a number of foils and sabers pointed at me during my freshman year.

As Professor DeCicco went around the room and discussed with my teammates what their midsemester grades were and which classes they needed to focus on and improve in, he left me as the last person to discuss grades with. He looked at me and said: "Stan, four Ds and an F. We have some work to do here. I believe we can drop the class that you are failing in and work on those Ds for the remainder of this semester and get them up to Cs." He indicated if we could do that, I would be all right. It was very embarrassing, but an eye-opener for me.

If I had not worked hard in the classroom to get those Ds up to Cs, I would not have been eligible to play. Fortunately, with tutors, study hall sessions, a time-management plan that I worked out with a professor, and a cutback on social time, I was able to do just as Professor DeCicco said. I turned those Ds into one B and three Cs and was eligible to play in the fall.

At Notre Dame, you were required to take fifteen hours per semester to stay on track to graduate. With permission from our academic advisors, we could drop to twelve hours for one semester of the year. However, if you did drop to twelve, you were required to come to summer school and take six to nine hours of classwork. During my career, I was in summer school practically every June.

As I reflect upon my collegiate athletics career and compare my experiences with the *20 Secrets to Success for NCAA Student-Athletes*, I see how valuable the information in this book is for student-athletes and how it could have helped me had it been written about forty years earlier. For example, it really did not dawn on me that I likely would not have an opportunity to play professional basketball until a freshman named John Paxson was moved in front of me in the point guard rotation during my junior year. By the time we were in the NCAA tournament, I saw little to no playing time. It was at this point I realized that I had not been prioritizing my academic studies the way I should have. This is when I realized I was not getting as much out of Notre Dame academics as I was putting into Notre Dame athletics.

That was the year I became a serious student. The academic-athletic balance all collegiate athletes must strive for is well established in this book. In fact, I used the same story later in my athletics administrative career whenever I would speak to student-athletes about how important it is to have balance in their collegiate athletics careers. This is what collegiate athletics is all about. An opportunity to continue playing a sport you love while pursuing an undergraduate and, in some cases, graduate degree. If you do not balance the two, then you could lose out on the most important thing no one can take away from you: academic knowledge and a degree.

I truly wish I had come to that realization during my freshman year and used all the tools addressed in the *20 Secrets to Success* throughout my collegiate athletics career. Not to say my career after intercollegiate athletics was unsuccessful, but what if I'd been able to better apply myself during my time at Notre Dame? I might be a brain surgeon today.

I am so thrilled to be able to share my experience as you embark on reading this book. Please understand *20 Secrets to Success* will help propel you far beyond your wildest dreams, just as this opportunity to participate in a sport you believe in and love so much can also propel your career in life through the education you obtain from your institution.

Stan Wilcox
Executive Vice President
of Regulatory Affairs
NCAA

Acknowledgments

As a group of authors, we are thrilled that this book, a longtime passion for a group of former student-athletes, has received enough attention and use to justify a second edition. For the first edition, we learned that writing a book requires the input, support, and expertise of many, with a second edition requiring even more! Even with a dedicated core writing team of five authors with varied backgrounds and experiences, a topic as vast and complicated as this book's necessitates the contributions of many others. We are fortunate to have received input from about sixty external contributors in updating this second edition. Their experiences, perspectives, and advice played a vital and significant role in the compilation of this book.

We would also like to acknowledge Ohio University Press, the many universities and athletic departments that adopted our book, and the long list of students who have helped us put together the content required, including Kevin Fagin, Arek Olson, and Sierra Shafer. Special thanks also to Margie Chetney in the Department of Sport Management at Syracuse University and Lorry Weaver at the NCAA.

Within the book, the names of interviewees are noted when they are quoted or when their input was included. The interviewees come from many backgrounds, including former student-athletes, coaches, athletic directors, sport administrators, other professionals, and former professional athletes. For this second edition, we have spoken with some of the same interviewees, who have given updated responses, and we have recruited new interviewees as well. Ultimately, we sought more diversity and inclusiveness in our selection of interviewees and perspectives throughout the book. All of the interviewees, along with their sport and school if they are former student-athletes, plus their current title, are listed in Appendix C at the back of the book. We would like to express our most sincere appreciation for their support, time, and expertise, which informed and helped shape this book.

The second edition of this book was written during the COVID-19 pandemic, a biological event that has impacted the world at a level unseen since the influenza pandemic of 1918–19. Collegiate sport was hit particularly hard, with seasons lost, scholarships compromised, the Final Four canceled, homecomings held online, and so much more. Despite its negative effects on college sport, the pandemic has firmly emphasized to us how amazing and wonderful the student-athlete experience is and how it is worth cherishing.

Finally, all five of us would like to expressly thank our families, friends, and colleagues who supported the long nights, big pushes, and tough conversations that are always required in the process of writing a book of this nature. Reflecting on the impact the first edition has had, we feel our time invested in this project has more than paid off, and our goal remains one of helping student-athletes achieve success in every facet of their lives.

Introduction

When business author Stephen Covey wrote his landmark text *The 7 Habits of Highly Effective People* in 1989, he drew from more than twenty-five years of observing what made leaders successful. That book has never been out of print, and we suspect a major reason is Covey provided simple, straightforward advice built around just seven habits. Covey believed businesspeople, future leaders, and students could become more efficient and accomplished by simply reading his book.

As a group of authors, we wanted to emulate that concept but do so for a very specific audience: the collegiate student-athlete. We believed we could assist high school seniors getting ready to go to college and NCAA student-athletes already enrolled at a university . . . including the ones who sometimes learn the hard way that when the final horn sounds, life after college beckons.

Listen, we get it. Many NCAA athletes dream of playing sports professionally or competing at the Olympics, but few realize that dream. For everyone else, a primary postcollege intention is simply to find success and contentment. That's why this book is a handbook. It's been specifically written for the locker room, dorm room, house off campus, cafeteria, bus, plane, or study hall. It will also work in the classroom if you have a really boring professor. Its purpose is to help student-athletes and their parents make better decisions.

The reason we want you to read this book is because there is a rushing reality bearing down on you. Let's start with the basics: Competing as an intercollegiate student-athlete means enduring a rigorous schedule of practices, classes, labs, tutorial sessions, weight training, road trips, and academic counseling. And as this book went to press, we expected NCAA student-athletes would have the right to start a business and leverage their name, image, and likeness (NIL). That's essentially three full-time jobs.

So, let's be clear. We want this book to work for every type of NCAA student-athlete. Not just students whose families have gone to college for generations. It should also help student-athletes whose grant-in-aid schol-arship makes them the first ever in their family to go to college. Very importantly, we wanted this book to benefit student-athletes of all backgrounds. Similarly, we want this book to serve not just students who have grown up in a highly developed American system of sport (that is, Amateur Athletic Union teams, elite travel teams, private sport academies) but also the thousands of international students who are recruited to play for NCAA schools. These students must adapt not only to the myriad rules by which NCAA athletes are governed but also to the hard task of living in a new country.

But why stop there? Every individual is unique. Readers vary by personality, height, weight, intelligence, hobbies, sexuality, prior accomplishment, race, religion, socioeconomic status, gender identification, country of origin, historical association with higher education, and types of foods enjoyed (or disliked). And those are just a few of our differences. In fact, we've gone out of our way to recognize how every NCAA student-athlete is different and faces numerous physical, emotional, social, spiritual, and mental health challenges during their time at college.

Mental health is not to be taken lightly. The NCAA's Chief Medical Officer, Dr. Brian Hainline, who is responsible for running the NCAA's Sport Science Institute, has been tireless in telling athletic administrators, athletes, and parents that understanding and supporting student-athlete mental wellness (as well as addressing sexual assault and interpersonal violence) are mandates for the NCAA as well as for all of the NCAA's member institutions.

Like mental health, diversity and inclusion are also foundational issues for anyone who participates in the college sports experience. As one sage noted, diversity is getting invited to the party. Inclusion is getting asked to dance. Many student-athletes of various racial and ethnic backgrounds, nationalities, sexual orientations, genders, and religions feel their recruitment and subsequent invitation to the NCAA party failed to acknowledge their identities.

Most student-athletes will make their way through college and find individuals like themselves. But not everyone gets comfortable in every situation. Following the horrific social injustices witnessed during 2019–20, when Black men and women like George Floyd, Ahmaud Arbery, Breonna Taylor, Elijah McClain, Jacob Blake, and numerous others were shot, murdered, or killed by police, social tensions rose dramatically. These deaths and the systemic racism behind them are also part of the NCAA landscape. We want everyone who reads this book to find value or to be provoked to think differently about their goals, aspirations, and on-campus reality.

To draw upon the work of the acclaimed writer and social scientist Malcolm Gladwell, author of the seminal book *Outliers* (2008), the difference between those who succeed and those who fail is "not something expensive or impossible to find; not something encoded in DNA or hardwired into the circuits of [young] brains." What those who fail lack is "something that could have been given to them if we'd only known they needed it: a community around them that prepared them properly for the world."

You, the reader, may or may not have enjoyed great support, encouragement, and endorsement at home. Either way, most readers of this book will need to adapt to a new setting (college) and then to actively find a supportive community. We hope this book is a literary version of that process—a simple book that provides insight, advice, and counsel, much of it from others just like you, who made the same journey.

Why tell you this? Because when your time at college ends, you'll find that 99 percent of all NCAA student-athletes will not become full-time professional athletes. The end of college is the end of the elite sports experience. What follows is the start of a new chapter: your professional life.

So, how do you prepare for what comes next? How do you leverage your strengths and minimize weaknesses? The answers are in this book. We created chapters so any student-athlete can browse or skim our secrets quickly. You don't have to read it sequentially or in one sitting or during any specific semester. Rather, use this book the way you use Wikipedia, searching it when you need an answer quickly. In other words, this is a quick-reference self-help book for elite student-athletes with limited free time.

We believe most student-athletes arrive at their goal of playing intercollegiate sports because of a great deal of hard work and discipline that produced both athletic and academic success. To help you build on those accomplishments, we wanted to make this book flow, starting with the first secret of creating and following a student-athlete plan that leads to a successful future.

From there, nineteen more secrets follow. They have all been written by our team of five authors, including four former collegiate athletes, two of whom captured championships; a university faculty athletics representative; a dynamic young scholar; and an executive who worked his entire career in professional sports. We worked together to make this book easy to read and understand.

The NCAA and its member institutions face the ongoing challenge of doing more to support student-athletes. Student-athletes, however, must "own" the act of preparing for their future. Choosing a major with your advisor, attending classes, and launching your professional career is up to you. Simply said, whatever you put into it is what you'll get out of it. This book gives student-athletes a wealth of information needed to positively influence individual outcomes.

In the NCAA's promotional materials, student-athletes proudly proclaim the tag line "There are over four hundred thousand NCAA student-athletes, and just about all of us will be going pro in something other than sports." If most student-athletes believe that claim, then most student-athletes should take advantage of our twenty secrets.

But don't take that from us. Thumb through this book and notice the athletic directors, coaches, and former players who kindly offered advice to make sure student-athletes succeed. We wrote this book with you in mind. All student-athletes are welcome in this book and all are acknowledged. Collectively, we are here to help you out and to encourage you.

We sincerely hope these pages unlock the mysteries contained and camouflaged on college campuses. We are confident these "secrets" can make you more successful in college and far beyond your current campus. We wish you all the best.

The Authors
January 2021

How to Use This Book

NOT SURE HOW TO GET THE MOST OUT OF THIS BOOK
(OR WHERE TO START)?

If you are a high school student-athlete hoping to play collegiate athletics, please read chapters 1–11 first.

If you are a high school senior, check out chapters 12–20.

If you are a college freshman or sophomore, check out chapters 1–11 and 15 first, then 12–14 and 16–20.

If you are a college junior or senior, check out ALL the chapters.

If you are a college graduate, check out chapters 13, 14, and 16–20.

And as a special request to everyone, please review the recommended readings and other resources (found in Appendix B) for your ongoing benefit. Importantly, we would like to draw your attention to Appendix A, which is full of student-athlete data completed by the NCAA and Gallup that will help inform you as you follow the secrets.

Secret 1

Create and Follow Your Student-Athlete Plan

THE SECRET IN A FEW WORDS

There is an old saying that failing to plan is planning to fail. Sure, it's a simple twist on a few words, but the second part of the saying is where the big outcome rests. No plan means you fail. For many that word "plan" is probably mysterious or simply a hassle. Most of us remember in elementary school having to produce an outline that used roman numerals, capital letters, and arabic numerals. Many of us thought it was stupid to be forced to outline a report on birds or the state of Tennessee. Why couldn't we just start writing the report? The reason was that "the plan" (that is, the outline) would make writing the story so much easier. For student-athletes, the creation of a plan, simple or otherwise, is a massive determinant in achieving post–athletic career success.

CREATE AND FOLLOW YOUR STUDENT-ATHLETE PLAN

When we asked Oliver Luck, former Executive Vice President of Regulatory Affairs at the NCAA, about career planning for a student-athlete, he succinctly said, "The backup plan is going pro in your sport." Yes, a leader of the NCAA who played in the NFL is suggesting that a career in pro sports is Plan B. Plan A is your life path based on your academic choices.

Steve Cobb, who was the Director of the Arizona Fall League from 1993 to 2018, said, "It is important to have a plan as an athlete, a roadmap. If you don't have a plan, you aren't going to get to where you want to be. And you can have the best game plan of anyone, but if you don't have the right people supporting you or around you, your plan won't be as effective."

Wise words from these two executives are ones to take to heart, and an indication that you should probably start your plan now.

Most young adults arriving on a college campus as recruited student-athletes (or walk-ons) have both specific and vague goals. And the source of these goals has likely come from life experiences, role models, parents, or peers. Commonly held objectives for freshman student-athletes entering college include the following:

List No. 1

1. Impress the coaching staff and earn "playing time."

2. Beat out others on the team and emerge as a "starter."

3. Take advantage of the university's training facilities to help achieve Goals 1 and 2.

4. Make new friends and settle into college life.

5. Figure out how to balance athletics with academics and a social life and eventually graduate.

6. Make sure to take care of mental health and consistently make good decisions on sleep, food, socializing, and interpersonal relationships.

Unfortunately, for most student-athletes, there are several other desirable goals that never get stated or are formulated so vaguely that they don't register until late in an athlete's senior year. Those goals look a lot more like this:

List No. 2

1. Identify a professional work career that seems exciting and will sustain the lifestyle I want for the many years after I finish playing my sport.

2. Graduate in four or five years with a degree in a major that will enhance the procurement and enjoyment of my future professional career.

3. Graduate with honors or a GPA that will impress future employers or make admission to graduate, medical, or law school possible.

4. Take advantage of every single athletic department and university/college offering that makes me more accomplished and more functional for life after college.

5. Build an individual brand that resonates with teachers, administrators, the media, and future employers.

6. Join professional groups on campus or attend professional presentations that facilitate the development of a well-rounded individual and not "just" a "jock" or athlete.

7. Take advantage of the travel opportunities related to my sport and get to know the different cities and countries I might visit. Get out and explore.

ROB SMITH

(former student-athlete, now Head Baseball Coach at Ohio University)

I didn't have a plan, and I was very misguided early on in the process. I had some struggles, and I didn't really get things going until after my first year in school. I learned how to start prioritizing things like my academics, because the baseball wasn't hard to prioritize.

I was also the first person in my family to graduate from college, so academics wasn't a highly emphasized thing in our house, and I got buried early on because of that.

The plan component is probably more important than the goal-setting component because you can't reach your goals without a plan. It's important to understand what your tasks are and what needs to be done to execute them. As Herm Edwards, former NFL star, would say, "a goal without a plan is just a wish." The plan is far more important than the goal.

If all you are concerned with is the endgame with no real process, then more often than not, you will fail. If you're like the 99 percent of us who walk on the planet who can't just show up and play, or have great skills without training as much, you must think about the process.

You already know which of the two lists above you naturally gravitated toward. And, granted, as a seventeen- or eighteen-year-old landing on a college campus for the first time (carrying the weight of an athletic scholarship and the pride of parents, guardians, or an entire "village"), the reason you were recruited as a student-athlete was because of your athletic skill. So, logically, it makes sense to "stick to what got you here."

But here's what makes that natural inclination to simplify tricky. Media coverage of student-athletes around you will reveal many starters or prized recruits who believe they will go pro in their sport. Since they believe they will go to the NFL, NBA, WNBA, NHL, MLB, MLS, LPGA, PGA, WTA, the Olympics, the Paralympics, or the Pan American Games, their goals rarely go beyond numbers 1–3 in list 1. So their goal-setting is simple. Get noticed, get media coverage, get drafted/selected. And the faster the better.

But here's the biggest secret of all that we'll keep repeating in this book: 99 percent of all collegiate student-athletes will never play professionally or represent their country in the Olympic Games.[1] Yes, some will . . . and there is nothing wrong with keeping that particular dream alive . . . but if 100 percent believe they will play professionally and 99 percent will fail at that ambition, then a key secret for the 99 percent is to hedge your bet (even just a little) so you have a safety net for the day your ACL tears or the coaching staff starts taking playing time away from you. If trends hold, on average you have a good sixty-ish years to live after you stop playing a high-performance sport.

The idea of a safety net for college athletes is a well-supported idea based on previous research in the area.[2]

College (in general) covers four years, from late August of your freshman year to May or June of your senior year. That's about 1,365 days between the day you arrive on campus and graduation. Call it approximately 195 weeks. If you are an elite athlete, you may train, practice, or compete in your sport during each of those weeks. But how much will you put into preparation for the week after you graduate and realize you aren't going back to College Station (Texas), Collegeville (Minnesota), or State College (Pennsylvania) that next August?

This is where planning comes in. The building of the safety net. It is the effort you put into everything other than your sport. Sure, there are a lot of hours that will disappear. If you average eight hours of sleep for 1,325 days, you will lose 441 days (more than 14 months) sleeping. That's right, 33 percent of your college career will be spent sleeping. Eating won't take up another year but it will fill entire months when all the hours are added up.

And how about your sport? If you average four hours a day (every day) in pursuit of your goal of more playing time, you will lose close to 220 days. The bottom line? There is less time than you imagine available for establishing and actually accomplishing that "other" priority of postgraduation career success.

So how do you create a plan that lets you master this initial secret?

The very first thing to do is to really understand your schedule. Many around you will assume you are not disciplined enough to set a schedule that fits your long-term goals . . . or even the goals of your head coach. That's why forces beyond your control will set practice times, conditioning times, eating times (training table), class times, study times (mandatory study hall), injury rehabilitation times, and sometimes even bedtimes.

All of a sudden, one thing missing in your calendar is free time. This is a hard realization for many and it often comes as a surprise to learn that one day you wake up and realize there is no time to hear a guest speaker on campus or to join a campus organization featuring a topic or profession that interests you. The choice has been made for you. Classes, practice, eat, study, sleep. Repeat for seasons on end.

This is not to say that you won't have any free time at all . . . but free time is often not "free" and it is sometimes the hardest time to spend wisely. So, a part of this first secret is learning how to schedule your free time to plan and accomplish the bigger-picture goals you want to achieve.

One trick is developing lists of things you want to do or see. Lists are also fun because you can throw them away as soon as you make them or carry them around for years. Lists can be created in spare time, boring time, while eating, or, as some driven people do, as soon as your day starts. They can be "Must Do" lists or "Dreaming to Do" notations. Here are a few types of lists to consider:

- Places I Would Like to Visit on Vacation

- Places Where I Would Like to Live

- Dream Jobs

- Books I Would Like to Read

- People I Would Like to Meet

- Potential Mentors I Should Connect With

- Musical Acts I Want to See before I Am Thirty

- Ten Celebrities I Would Invite to Dinner

- Cars I Would Like to Fix Up and Own

- Hobbies I Would Like to Have

- Grad Schools I Would Consider Attending

- Meals I Would Eat if the Zombie Apocalypse Was Starting in One Week

- Locations Where I Could Outlast the Walking Dead Zombies

Your "Dream Jobs" consideration may be the last thing most readers would construct, but in reality, should probably be among the first. Instead, responses such as the ones below are something you may catch yourself saying . . .

- I don't have a dream job. I've never thought about that.

- I want to own the Dallas Cowboys or get hired as the general manager of the New York Rangers.

- My dream job is to work for _____ but I know I could never get them to hire me.

- None of my dream job companies recruit at my university.

- What do you mean by dream job? Do you mean like working for someone cool or just doing a task that's easy?

- What's the difference between a dream job and a dream company?

- Dream jobs don't exist. That's fantasy talk for people who believe that if you follow your dreams, you can be happy. Where I come from, there are no dream jobs. Just stupid jobs.

For some, the "Dream Jobs" list would include the following companies:

- Apple or Samsung
- Google, Amazon, or Netflix
- Facebook or Twitter
- EA Sports, Activision, or Riot Games
- The NFL, WNBA, MMA, WTA, NASCAR, LPGA, or USOPC
- Nike, Under Armour, Puma, New Balance, or Adidas
- Microsoft or Dell
- Dick's Sporting Goods or Abercrombie & Fitch
- New York Liberty or the LA Clippers
- ESPN, NBC Sports, CBS Sports, or FOX Sports
- Disney, Sony, or Marvel Studios

As you can see, the list can feature many potential careers, but the power of the list is that it functions as a vehicle for imagination, creativity, and accomplishment. The old adage that "it won't happen unless you write it down" is true for many and is a strong rationale for lists and plans in general.

One list that is not shown in the many already suggested above is this:

What I Want Out of My Four Years at _____ University.

As an exercise, try making such a list in which you limit yourself to only ten achievements. Then let's see if the hypothetical list we created here (during our imaginary freshman year) would have any similarity to something you might create:

1. Graduate in four years with a 3.5 GPA.

2. Get hired by Nike to work in an area connected to my sport.

3. Make friends with at least four professors who are intellectually stimulating and committed to my success through introductions and networking.

4. Become a member of at least one campus organization that has nothing to do with sports.

5. Participate in an overseas course that is either a semester abroad or a shorter study tour in another country (less than twenty-one days).

6. Give back to my sport or college community by coaching or using my team's access to less-privileged individuals.

7.   Make three lifelong friends who will be there for me when times are tough (and for whom I will be there when they need me).

8.   Get real about how much I will owe in college loans or in appreciation for those who helped me get through college for free.

9.   Read four books that were not assigned but that will stretch my imagination or stimulate my intellectual curiosity.

10. Dominate my friends in video games such as *FIFA, Madden, Fortnite, League of Legends,* or *Call of Duty: Black Ops.*

Bonus: Cure cancer, walk on Mars, get my screenplay purchased, record demo tracks with Beyoncé

Again, you should see that the creation of the list is not hard, but committing to the plan that will deliver the itemized outcomes requires long-term awareness. The other piece in the puzzle is figuring out how to evaluate progress toward your various goals. When students start their freshman year, graduation seems light years away. Four years. At least 120 credits. So many term papers and final exams.

Sheesh. It's hard, then, to write "Graduate in four years with a 3.5 GPA." But if that is the goal, the 3.5 GPA allows for semester-by-semester evaluation. Like an athlete, you will have either exceeded your goal or missed it. If you are ahead, you make plans for leveraging that success. If you are behind, you need to make adjustments. GPA is a great example of the kind of thing to evaluate since it is measurable semester by semester, course by course.

Football movies are famous for their stirring halftime speeches in which the coach convinces the players to put their first half mistakes behind them, to overcome their distrust of each other, to block out the distractions of the crowd and "win one for the Gipper" or some other clichéd personage (how about the speech in *Rudy* or inspirational words said to Michael Oher's character in *The Blind Side*). Sometimes players get chewed out at halftime. Sometimes players get the silent treatment. But invariably, the announcers covering the game, witnessing a great comeback, suggest that adjustments "must've gotten made at halftime and would you look at how this team is responding!"

You should feel the same about your ability to adjust. Traditionally, school years are usually broken into semesters (two) or quarters (three) and after final exams there is a point when you know your GPA for the grading period and therefore for your academic career so far. You know whether you are meeting NCAA academic progress requirements, are eligible, are likely to get announced as having made the Dean's List, or maybe have a shot at making an All-Conference Academic list.

If your grades aren't what you want, then adjustments must be made. Perhaps your adjustments include one or more of the following:

- Paying more attention to course details
- Skipping fewer classes
- Changing studying habits
- Working with different tutors
- Studying with different friends
- Allowing more time for homework and test prep
- Making more time to meet professors and getting to know them
- Asking for help earlier in the semester
- Making a commitment to do better by working harder
- Allocating more time to studying

Perhaps, as you read this, you have never had, nor expect to have, grades that fall below your expectations. If that's the case, you can move on to any of the other items listed above in the "What I Want Out of My Four Years at _____ University."

The second bullet point is getting a job at Nike, and while we randomly selected that particular company, the goal can be evaluated just like grades. If you want to work in athletic apparel and equipment when you graduate (or technology, media, medicine, or music), the same approach to accomplishment can be evaluated regularly (and often with the help of a list that is focused on the goal):

- Whom can I meet from my desired industry this term?
- What did I read about my desired company this month?
- Who at my school knows someone working in the field I want to enter?
- How can I get networked to an employee at my dream company?
- What more did I learn about the field I want to work in?
- Will I be ready for a job interview (or internship opportunity) if one suddenly materializes?

Interim measurable goals could be a class project opportunity, a consulting project, a practicum, or an internship with that company or one in its field.

CHAPTER SUMMARY

One of the most important secrets to learn during your time in college is how to create a plan for success that leads to a desirable outcome. It is not as simple as creating random lists (although that can certainly help) or banking on the hope that things will fall into place for you. An essential element is establishing concrete goals and having a true desire to accomplish those goals and then "checking them off." This is what will lay the foundation for you to position yourself for career success.

ERIK PRICE

(Associate Commissioner at the Pac-12 Conference)

I think it's very important to have an academic plan, do internships, and travel during the summer. Traveling exposes you to new perspectives and provides you with new experiences. You don't necessarily have to have a plan that is divorced from being an athlete, such as coaching, training, or strength and conditioning. I have seen a lot of student-athletes be successful and go into ancillary careers such as those. Every student-athlete should have two paths that they want to follow that are not "playing sports" related, so that the last time you suit up, you are not in a crisis afterwards. For example, one of the most important parts of your plan is graduating, and having a graduate school plan because advanced degrees are what help you get the jobs that you can sit in for life, generally speaking.

Goals may change and dreams may get upended . . . but failing to plan is planning to fail. Why let that happen when a little effort can set anyone on a path to a much more fulfilling future?

Secret 2

Understand Who a Student-Athlete Is

AUTHOR VIEWPOINT—DR. NORM O'REILLY

I was fortunate enough to be a student-athlete during both my undergraduate degree (Nordic skiing at the University of Waterloo) and master's degrees (swimming at the University of Ottawa). Although they are two major Canadian universities, Waterloo and Ottawa would be the equivalent of Division II colleges in the United States (from an athletics perspective). Both have formal and resourced athletic departments and a full slate of sports, but scholarships are low, facilities sufficient (but not great), and ticket sales for events low or nonexistent in some sports.

I believe I was successful as a student-athlete: getting named an Academic All-Canadian twice, requiring both academic and athletic success. Life as a student-athlete was challenging, to say the least, and full of sacrifices, mostly on the social front. Parties missed, events declined, hanging out with my roommates at a minimum.

As an undergraduate student, in a challenging science program, I was very focused on individual learning (lots of studying) and a large amount of class time: fifteen hours in class and fifteen hours in labs. Five days a week of classes, including late-Friday-afternoon labs. As a graduate student, less class time but enormous responsibilities as a teaching assistant, as a research assistant, and in my reading.

As an athlete, I focused efforts on competing and performing at a high level. My sports were both individual but with training and competition as part of a team. Between fifteen and twenty-five hours per week training and at least ten weekends away each academic year for competition, sometimes more. 5 a.m. practices regularly. Friday night practice. Saturday/Sunday morning practice. Late nights at the gym. Team meetings. Coach consultations. All on top of challenging academic schedules.

I don't believe my experience is atypical for most student-athletes.

THE SECRET IN A FEW WORDS

Secret 1 told you to follow a plan. This is vital to the student-athlete or really to anyone with any objective at all. This leads us to Secret 2, which will give context to your plan. You are a student-athlete. Being a student-athlete is a special experience, and a privileged one. Yes, a small percentage are super-privileged and may go professional, but this book is not for them. It is for you, someone who will live four years of your life in a unique way. Like Spider-Man and Peter Parker, you've got a double role, even a double personality.[1] And, you need to be very good at and focused on each.

On one hand, you are a high-performance athlete. Respected by other students, under massive pressure from your coach and teammates, fortunate to have a scholarship (in many cases), and surrounded by support structures that few athletes of your level outside of the NCAA can even dream about. On the other hand, you're a student, one of more than nineteen million college students in the USA, a learner making your way in the world, trying to get ahead, and seeking a job one day. You have to approach each role separately, find time for each, and be successful in each. Get poor grades and you are off the team. Bad performance on the field, no more scholarship. Yes, your privileged role is coupled with a lot of pressure. And, wow, you get to do this for four amazing years. Many of those nineteen million would change spots with you in a heartbeat. So, the secret is simple: know who you are, relish it, and leverage it to the max. It will be, for many if not most of you, the best years of your life.

UNDERSTAND WHO A STUDENT-ATHLETE IS:
A STUDENT-ATHLETE OR AN ATHLETE-STUDENT?

This book and the secrets within it are written for student-athletes who will not go pro. Several of the authors of the book were athletes in this situation. The gender of student-athletes is a factor to consider because—although male and female athletes alike rarely manage to become professional athletes—there are statistically more opportunities (though still very few) for male student-athletes, so female student-athletes often have a better understanding than their male counterparts of the reality of being a typical student-athlete.

There are many contexts comparable to this reality. Think about music, where very few who dream of performing professionally ever establish a career as a professional musician. And, of those who do, few achieve the success they dreamed of. The same can be said for fashion designers, authors, journalists, and artists. Although some do "make it," most need to find another path to a sustainable career and a life outside of their passion.

As a full-time student in college in the United States,[2] you are one of nineteen million. However, as an NCAA student-athlete, you are one of fewer than five hundred thousand. Yes, only one in thirty-eight students in the USA has the status you do. You are special. You have earned privileges.

However, with great power comes great responsibility.

So, "special" and "privileged" are coupled with "pressure" and "risk." Let us explain.

The path for most student-athletes in most sports is similar (and we're quite certain you can relate). As a high school student, you were likely the big fish. Academically you did very well (or well enough), and athletically you were a star. You won championships, you captained your team, other teams in your district feared facing you, the media attention in school and local publications piled up, and you've got boxes of awards, medals, and honors that most of your friends covet.

Yes, you were a big deal. And, because you were that big deal, fortune shone on you and you got the chance to become an NCAA student-athlete. Perhaps you're a Division I, Division II, or Division III recruit. You might be on a "full-ride" scholarship or you might have "walked on" and barely made the team. Whatever the path, you delivered the academic and athletic credentials to become a one-in-thirty-eight student-athlete.

Very cool. You have the "power." But, the pond just got bigger. You're still a big fish but with a lot more swimming to do! And let's be clear, there are fish bigger than you. There always are.

So, what exactly is the great responsibility you face? Well, it manifests itself as pressure, and it has multiple sources:

1. *Your parents (grandparents, guardians):* You are the apple of their eyes, they brag about you at their local curling club, golf club, favorite pub, and with their friends. They have likely invested in you over the years (athletically, academically, and even financially) to help with your training and your studies. They may also be the type of parents who exerted pressure on you to perform. And, even if they don't directly exert any pressure, the perception of such is likely there. If you need clarification on this point, just imagine what would happen if you failed two classes one semester, lost your scholarship, and got kicked off your team. How would you tell your parents (or grandparents or guardians)? How hard would that be? How disappointed would they be?

2. *Your friends (who are not teammates):* Your core social group, your high school group of friends, will love you no matter what, but you've likely built your image and your "self" around being a star athlete, and now a student-athlete, so that expectation is there. You'll feel the pressure here if anything starts to slip . . .

3. *Your college coach:* You were likely comfortable with your high school or club coach as you developed, but now you're in college. Your coach likely recruited you, selected you over others, and helped you get that amazing scholarship. But now put yourself in your coach's shoes. College coaches are fired often; turnover is frequent and the pressure on them to win is extremely high. This pressure is transferred to the athletes (you), who often feel a need and a pressure to perform "for their coach."

4. *Your college teammates:* Again, back home, in high school or club, you were likely with your buddies or boy/girlfriends. Now, you're with a bunch of teammates, some older than you, some competing with you, some who may rely on you for their success or who may hope you fail so they can play more. Some teammates will probably become lifelong friends and may even have the same academic major as you. Other teammates may not. They may be rivals or live a completely different life (in a different academic program). Whether friend (counting on you) or foe (wanting to take your playing time), teammates will be a source of pressure as well.

5. *Your partner (if you have one):* This is a relationship that we will delve into in much detail in a later "secret" in this book, but it is one to be cautious about. Either a relationship from home or a new one at college is a source of major pressure and can compromise any student-athlete who must already live two lives. Only a very supportive partner can work, even if that partner is also a student-athlete, and even then, this is a source of stress.

6. *Your hometown media:* If you are from a city of more than a million people, you can skip this one. But if you represent a small hometown, this is a big commitment and an important responsibility. You could find, like one of this book's authors who comes from a town of fifteen thousand people, that you remain a media personality in your town's local publications many years after your athletic career. This manifests itself in pressure to represent your town, pressure to continue to perform for and contribute to family and friends, and time pressure from the requirements of setting up calls, giving interviews, responding to questions, and maintaining a social media presence.

7. *Your athletic department:* Off-the-field commitments will come
    from many sources in your university's athletic department.
    Media interviews. Pep rallies. Athlete councils (like SAAC). Team
    meetings. Anti-doping seminars. Marketing. And much more.
    Be wary of these commitments: they are "time-eaters" and bring
    their own political pressure.

These seven sources of responsibility (aka pressure) are certainly not an
exhaustive list, but they are ones we believe will affect almost all student-
athletes. Depending on your particular situation, you will have other sources
of responsibility (for example, a part-time job, a sick parent) and pressure
(for example, a need to travel home, sleep deprivation) that you need to deal
with.

MAX DITTMER

**(former swimming student-athlete at the University of Iowa,
now Principal at CORE Office Interiors)**

My parents for the most part were hands-off and supportive for whatever/
whenever I needed them. I can't imagine the extra pressure added if they
weren't the way they are, and I am thankful for that.

Academics were never a problem for me personally, so as long as I was
maintaining good grades as expected, I had almost no conversations or
pressure from my parents about the academic side of things. However, the
pressure from them was put on me at a young age to maintain good grades.
Therefore, the pressure of getting good grades just became an internal
pressure.

The pressure I received from athletics was more just wanting myself to
succeed and be happy. I was always very positive, and never negative. I never
felt any pressure from anyone else's end if I didn't succeed or do as well as I
hoped.

My friends didn't add any academic or athletic pressure, but more social
pressure. I always got the "come out with us," "skip practice," or "go to
practice hung over." From the coaches' standpoint, it depends on the coach,
but for the most part they were supportive in both areas, but definitely they
were more focused on the athletic side.

For academics, the coaches would give me relative accommodations, but
practice/competitions for the most part trumped all. Everything else should
be scheduled around these. I remember receiving pressure during finals
weeks from coaches for missing practices when we were on "break" and
"no required practices" to allow for academic focus during finals week.
Essentially you would be shamed for missing unless your test was during
finals. That was hard to deal with. For swimming, there was lots of pressure

to perform, but never negatively stated if you performed bad, just positive reinforcement when you performed well.

Teammates would pressure me to just stay eligible, that's it. Athletically, there was pressure and expectations to perform well, come to practice and try hard. If you were slacking for any reason, your teammates would let you know about it.

The hometown media for Iowa didn't have any backlash academically because the swim team had a great GPA, and athletically, it was mainly positive because we were never under the scrutiny that a football or basketball team would be under. But, the swim team constantly improved over my four years, and I do know that there was some media backlash in later years after I left with all the new facilities and a small decline in performance.

The pressures from the athletic department were definitely vocalized more on the academics side than the athletics. Our academic help was need-based in the sense that if you sustained above a 3.0 for consecutive semesters, you did not have to log study hours, but if you were below you would need anywhere from four to twelve hours a week. For athletics, not a huge showing from the AD for swimming. During the fundraising years for the new pool, it was more noticeable, but being a non-revenue sport, we were not the main focus so expectations weren't as big as for other revenue-generating sports.

Even for the most successful student-athletes, life is challenging and full of sacrifices.

To delve further into the student-athlete role, we interviewed Anson Dorrance, currently the head coach of the women's soccer program at the University of North Carolina, and the winningest women's soccer coach of all time. He agreed with the special status of the student-athlete and emphasized the importance of realizing the opportunity and how fragile it can be. He emphasized that "there are so many things you can that will derail you if you have ambitions academically and athletically but also in terms of character development." Each of your sources of responsibility must be planned for and managed in the context of the "double objective" of academic success and athletic excellence. Clearly, Secret 1 relies on understanding Secret 2!

So, what can you do? What is Secret 2 really telling us?

From our perspective, there are five things you need to do.

1. *Realize that you are special and fortunate.* The opportunity to both continue to progress your life (that is, study toward the pursuit of a career) and concurrently be a high-performance athlete in arguably the top sport development system in the world is an experience to cherish and one you will miss (and often talk about) when you are older. The combination of your two lives will help you build character. Embrace the student-athlete status role and

put your focus on those two outcomes, little else. Dan Butterly, Commissioner of the Big West Conference, explained very clearly why you want to realize the unique student-athlete role.

> Student-athletes continue to be outstanding leaders. That has not changed over the years. There are tremendous traits student-athletes have that they often undersell on their resume or during a job interview. Team building, how to deal with adversity, excellent health and wellness, leadership traits and a zest for success. One of the great trends I have seen from this generation of student-athletes compared to previous student-athletes is how they venture outside their own sport, come together with student-athletes in other sports, and have created a significant voice and leadership group not only to make the NCAA better, but by leading, they will make their generation better too. When I was an undergraduate, I heard student-athletes from other teams often complain about all the great resources football and men's basketball received. Now, many of those same benefits are available to all student-athletes because of the voice this generation of student-athletes has put forth.

As Butterly emphasizes, the successful completion of your plan (Secret 1) and deep understanding of the privileged role you are in (this secret) will launch your career.

2. *Be a student AND an athlete.* Many student-athletes in the "other 99 percent," even though they realize that a professional career or Olympic opportunity is not probable, still view themselves as athletes first and not as a student. If you know you will not play professionally, you must view yourself as a student first (or at least tied for first) in all things and all activities. Glenn Schembechler, NFL scout, provided the following support:

> High school athletes who earn a college scholarship aren't getting it for the right reason. Many high school athletes don't identify themselves as students first. They see it as this opportunity for just sports, with school on the side; as opposed to getting school paid for and getting to play sports. You need to identify yourself as a student first because you need to have a realistic outlook on where you are going to go after playing sports in college.

However, what Schembechler outlines is much easier to say than to do. So, you must make being a student as important as (if not more important than) being an athlete. A balanced approach is highly recommended.

Schembechler supported a couple of specific points that we want to emphasize within this secret. The first is related to the choice of major or degree or area of concentration. Often, as student-athletes, you are so focused on sport and competition that you just want "a degree." You may not think about where your interest is for a career postcollege. The focus is on picking some classes that fit your training schedule and will allow you to graduate in four years.

But if that's the case, you are not spending enough time thinking about what you should be taking in order to set yourself up for a career postgraduation. Student-athletes are often too busy to meet with an advisor or to get to know a professor, or to even consider who their favorite professor is! Setting yourself up for success after college needs to be a priority. You need to find your passion outside of your sport. Schembechler agreed and gave some great advice: "Find something that you are passionate about so that you can wake up and give a 100 percent effort to it each day. If you aren't passionate, you are going to fall behind quickly in anything you do."

This advice is very appropriate, and following it is not beyond the time or resources available to any student-athlete. Before your season starts, or on a quiet weekend, spend some time thinking about what you love, what your favorite class is. Then, get to know a professor or two (or four!) in that area, get some advice, and get into the program you are interested in (one that ideally has job opportunities). And, in this effort, reach out to family members, friends, and others who know those areas, have connections, and can help advise you on great choices.

The second piece of advice we'd like to emphasize is the vital importance to get work experience during your four years as a student-athlete. Of course, this is easier said than done, given your busy schedule of academics and athletics. Schembechler advises that you have to "take advantage of the opportunities to do internships and other experiences so that you can dip your toes into the industry of focus." This is a key point. To get ahead in most fields today (engineering, business, health professions, technical, etc.), the more experiences you have on your resume, the better you will do and the more competitive you will be for jobs.

Quite simply, four years of being a student-athlete cannot compete—in most cases—with a well-prepared graduate who is not an athlete but who has a practicum, two internships, an independent study with an expert in the field, and related summer jobs. This is not to say that one path is better than the other, but just to underline the reality that a student-athlete faces at the end of senior year. So how do you do this? How do you fit these practical experiences into your busy life? Well, a few pieces of advice.

First, you need to network with the right people, inside and outside the university. Inside, this includes career coaches, advisors, faculty members, researchers, and administrators (including deans and support staff). These are people who have your best interests at heart, contacts in your field, and a mandate to help you. But they won't be able to help you unless they know who you are and unless you ask. Get to know them, attend events, join clubs and student organizations. Sure, you have to balance this with your training and competition, but that is no excuse. You have off-seasons, downtime, days off, and free time. The trick is to replace some of the "useless" activities like watching TV and playing video games with positive ones. Instead of going out one night, join a student club in your area of interest. Instead of sleeping in one day, go to a career fair. These are very simple choices, with very significant positive outcomes.

Second, figure out what you want to do. As noted earlier, meet with advisors, professors, and more. Find a mentor. Connect with a professor. Meet a graduate student. But take that a step further and include this in your plan from Secret 1. Write down your career choices. Your "dream job" (in real life, not as an athlete) postgraduation. Outline what you need to do to get competitive for that job at graduation and go do it.

3. *Be responsible for building your own character.* When you are trying to balance the pursuit of academic success and high-performance sport, it becomes difficult to focus on other elements of what it takes to be a successful person. Some student-athletes have these traits and high-quality characters but many do not. The legendary women's soccer coach at UNC, Anson Dorrance, provided the following response when we asked him about this:

> From my perspective, the definition of student-athlete is that this is part of a process to become a better human being. A critical quality I think most of us overlook when we are evaluating a student-athlete is character development. . . . The main priority for someone coming into college as an athlete is to develop his or her character and there are some fantastic benefits to that. I think there is a direct correlation between developing your own character and having a successful athletic and academic career.

Dorrance went on to explain that it is you, the student-athlete, who needs to take responsibility for your own character development:

> Student-athletes are supervisors of their own development. They get to guide their own development and obviously most critically, their character development. They also are the supervisors of their own academic world and their athletic world as well. . . . [It] is very critical for any [student-athlete] to understand their opportunity to shape their own future based on the standards they set for themselves. The responsibility they take for themselves.

Practically, what Dorrance advises is very important. You need to take responsibility. You need to plan for your career. You need to do the research to determine what career path (major, courses, internships, etc.) is best for you and will get you a job after graduation.

HILLARY NELSON

(former softball student-athlete at Arizona State University, now Trainer at Positive Coaching Alliance)

Some people enjoy expectations and some people don't enjoy the added pressure. I would say, for those that do, use it as confidence. Your coach or your parent, whoever is putting those expectations on you, they think you're capable or else they wouldn't be asking you to do this. If they are starting you in a big game, it's because they know you can be successful. I never met a coach who tried to lose. So, if they're putting you in there, take it as a really big sign of confidence and enjoy it. Enjoy that pressure and go out there and show them that they were right, prove them right. If you don't enjoy the expectations, try focusing on smaller goals. If the expectation is to pitch a shutout game against the big rival, try focusing on winning every inning or winning each batter or winning each pitch. I want to throw a curveball outside. Did I hit that spot? No. Okay, I lost that pitch, but let me win this next pitch. Focus on those small things that you can control, just like your effort on each play or that positive attitude that will help you keep your mind off of the bigger picture.

---

4. *Be career focused.* This point builds upon the others and is quite simple. Think about your career, alongside your training and

competition goals, as a focus of your plans, your choices, your efforts. It is about planning for life after graduation right from the get-go. It is about understanding why joining a student club in your area of interest is better than a night of television each week. In his interview, Schembechler captured this point clearly: "As a student-athlete, you need to realize that you are going to have to change your mindset to be ready for a career. It's all a matter of who you associate yourself with that allows you to change that mindset." In order to accomplish this, he advises that you "have to study what the market is like of the industry you want to go into."

5. *Maintain relationships outside your sport.* When you come to college as a freshman on scholarship, it is very easy to build your entire social network at college around your team and your teammates. You will spend a lot of time with them, and often you won't have any close friends from high school who are nearby. Chris Dawson, a former student-athlete, and Associate Commissioner at the Pac-12 Conference, explained this very clearly:

> I think student-athletes can best prepare for the transition out of sport by making sure that when they're still an active athlete they maintain other relationships and other interests to the greatest extent possible. If your whole world is your team, which is very easy to do when you're a college athlete, then you lose your support system when your athletics career is over and you lose your sense of identity. I think that the transition can be smoother when you understand that it's going to happen to you at some point. It's going to be a different point for different people.

CHAPTER SUMMARY

The three things you can take out of this chapter (if you remember nothing else from what you just read) are these:

1. Have an understanding of who you are and what opportunity you have in front of you. Focus on the NOW with the future in mind and the past in the rearview mirror.

2. Build your character and take responsibility for your actions. As Jim Rohn once said, "You must take personal responsibility. You cannot change the circumstances, the seasons, or the wind, but you can change yourself."

3. Rise to the challenge, don't let the pressure get to you, focus on your career, be a great student, and create relationships outside of the teammates you are with 24-7.

Secret 3 Learn What Name, Image, and Likeness Means for You

THE SECRET IN A FEW WORDS

The NCAA world has changed significantly since the first edition of this book came out in 2018. One of the most notable modifications has been the arrival of legislation granting student-athletes a benefit commonly known as NIL (name, image, and likeness). Although the NCAA did not approve initial NIL legislation in January 2021 as scheduled, as of this writing student-athletes are expected to receive (with certain conditions and limitations) the right to generate their own revenues via their name, image, and likeness. Therefore, we have written this chapter with the assumption that, when you read it, these rights will have been granted.

This secret is designed to let you in on the complexities of NIL, and share what benefits you, as an athlete, may come to enjoy. The bottom line is that for most, NIL will have a unique impact on your financial situation or life.

LEARN WHAT NAME, IMAGE, AND LIKENESS MEANS FOR YOU

Okay. Settle down. Although NCAA-approved legislation allowing student-athletes to monetize their NIL is a historic rules reform and a huge win for you, now comes the hard part. You need to holistically understand what NIL is, what you gain, what it may cost, and how to keep up with the rules as they evolve.

Understanding what NIL is and is not would be a good first step. The NCAA provides the following context for student-athletes: "Most simply, 'name, image and likeness' are three elements that make up a legal concept known as 'right of publicity.' Right of publicity involves those situations where permission is required of a person to use their name, image or likeness. For example, no permission is required for a newspaper to publish a photo of an athlete playing in a game. The legal copyright would belong to the photographer, not the person pictured."[1]

Suddenly, your "brand" is likely on the open market, and you are wondering how it will benefit your bank account while you try to avoid creating another coming-of-age college athletics headache. What exactly does it mean that something you have always had (your name, image, and likeness) is now available for you to leverage? Haven't college students who could act or play guitar always held this right? How is it that playing music or deejaying in a club wasn't constrained but attending school as an NCAA athlete was? We won't debate the old rules here . . . or the fact most traditional college students historically didn't try to run businesses while earning college degrees. They took courses, had an active social life, attended NCAA games (as fans), possibly worked part-time jobs, and graduated. That was their reality.

But that changes with NIL legislation. Student-athletes are suddenly allowed, if not encouraged, to start small businesses built around the person in the mirror. That's significant and no small undertaking. First, depending on when you read this, you could be among the first wave of NCAA student-athletes to receive NIL privileges (or opportunities), which are so complex you may have no idea what any of this NIL shouting and hollering means.

Second, having NIL rights does not mean you hit the jackpot and local or national companies have decided to throw money at you. What 99 percent of student-athletes have received is a "right" to leverage their NIL. Rights are different from free money. And leverage, without getting into B-school definitions, requires work and planning. Think about it. You have the right to work hard at your sport, but it doesn't mean you will start. You have the right to want a pizza, but more than likely you will have to call someone and give them money in order to get it delivered. So, first off, rights are different from results.

Third, while having a right can create opportunity, it can also create obligation. You have the right to sell your name, image, or likeness to anyone who will pay you for it, but you will then have to deliver something for that money (your time, your expertise, your image, your name). That is the obligation part. You must then manage those agreements as a small business and deliver what you legally promised to provide. Let the previous sentence sink in. Monetary transactions (for services rendered)—and we are referring only to those in which the athlete gets paid—will essentially make you a business (an entrepreneur), and any income you earn will be taxed by the state and federal government. Additionally, the "O" word (we'll say it again: obligation) means you may quickly find yourself dealing with agents, boosters, demanding retailers, accountants, lawyers, and unwanted hangers-on.

LEARNING THE ROPES

You can figure this all out, but you can't enter the NIL era blindly. Not long ago, the privilege of competing in college sports meant you served two groups: your coaches and your professors. If you didn't keep your grades up, you couldn't play for your coach. In many cases, if you didn't play well for your coach, your place on the team was at risk (and possibly the continuation of your scholarship). It meant you continually fought a two-front war, and both "battlefields" (even with tutors and position coaches) were pretty demanding. For some student-athletes, sports demanded upwards of thirty-five hours a week, and academics chewed up almost as many. Tight time management, short sleep schedules, and lots of pressure kept it all together. Throw in a social life (with or without the team) and you were stretched thin on time and energy to please everyone.

With NIL rights, you can face additional individuals who may or may not have your best interests in mind and lack a thorough understanding of NIL. Friends, family, and maybe even distant relatives might tell you about the amazing opportunity you have because you can finally cash in on all those years you spent making yourself into an NCAA student-athlete. These well-meaning supporters often believe, whether you are a scholarship athlete or not, that there is a long list of companies lining up to give you money just for being you. They might even pass judgment on your intelligence if you aren't choosing between cashed-up suitors. They may tell you on day one that something is wrong. In fact, their attitude could be "As of today, money should be falling from trees for you. You've got NIL now. Why aren't you getting some?"

That's where we need to start. You have a right . . . but you do not have a fully grown magic money tree. The soil might have been tilled and some fertilizer sprinkled for you to plant a NIL tree, but the ground you're standing on needs a lot of cultivating. If seeds are in the dirt, you have to water them and protect them if you want to bring home a financial harvest. The analogy of planting and harvesting may be a bit much for some of you (too old school) but consider this: if you don't stay on your sports team, your athletically related NIL rights are pretty much worthless. If your college cuts your sport (as big schools like Clemson and Stanford did with multiple teams), your NCAA NIL rights no longer matter. If you don't remain academically eligible, your athletic NIL rights are greatly diminished (or meaningless). In other words, you must understand the landscape in front of you. You can make money from your name, image, and likeness, but you also have to start farming. That takes effort and work.

MORE RULES AND YOUR NIL BRAND

The year 2020 was incredibly difficult. It unfolded with momentous social unrest, COVID-19, remote classes, canceled games, truncated seasons, a bitter presidential election, and constant uncertainty. On the bright side, 2021 began with nationwide vaccination programs and a return to normal competitive NCAA seasons by August. Even if 2020's pandemic issues are resolved by the fall of 2021, many things are now different because of what you faced and learned in 2020.

One positive outcome of this time could be imagining how you can monetize your social media platforms, convince car dealerships to feature you in their advertising, and, for many, return to your hometown to leverage your celebrity status by coaching or giving clinics. These opportunities never existed before. Along the way, you will see media outlets use words like "preemption" (a federal law covering NIL vs. state laws), "guardrails" (limitations of where NIL applies, such as gambling), and "amendments" (ongoing changes due to legal action). NIL "rights" also vary. As of this book's publication, these laws are all still being worked out by the NCAA, your conference, and local, state, and federal governments.

What all of this means is that outside forces (your state senator, your athletic department's compliance officer, the NCAA) will demand you pay attention to all of the requirements they are imposing. The NCAA wants you to understand what is allowed and what isn't. For example, if a drug is banned by the NCAA, you can't endorse it. If your athletic department has a deal with Pepsi, you might not be able to work with Coke (since it is a competitor brand). You have NIL rights but there will be "guardrails."

Along with these guardrails, there are more rules. Understand that businesses must comply with multiple rules. As NCAA student-athletes already living with a fat rule book, you know about the real ones and the unwritten ones. Don't take this business premise lightly. As a fledgling entrepreneur, you are governed by team rules, athletic department guidelines, university codes of conduct, NCAA regulations, city ordinances, state laws, tax codes, and federal legislation.

That's Business 101 (or Real World 101), and for you to leverage your NIL, you have to stay "real." If you skip practice to make money via a NIL side hustle, you are guaranteed to have problems with Coach. If you rarely play but are a great teammate, NIL earnings may not come your way . . . and complaining about it may make you unpopular with teammates who find it easier to leverage their NIL. Long-term, feelings of inequity can lead to bitterness if you are unable to leverage NIL. That could impact your entire athletics experience in a negative way. If this starts to happen, seek out support from mental health professionals, because you are way more than just the value of your NIL. Remember, many of you previously signed national letters of intent binding you to your school in return for benefits such as tuition, housing, meals, team apparel, medical care, game tickets, books, tutors, cost-of-living expense money, and away-game per diems. For the vast majority of NCAA student-athletes, those *assets* are much more valuable than any amount of pocket change you can make with your NIL.

Additionally, depending on your school, athletic conference, or NCAA division, some student-athletes will find their school is helpful when it comes to NIL, with services ranging from providing rules education to actually helping you leverage your NIL. At other places, there may be little support.

To paraphrase George Orwell's famous book *Animal Farm,* all NCAA student-athletes are about to find they are theoretically equal but some will undoubtedly be more equal than others. Some athletes will already have preexisting fame or play sports that attract more spectators. Football and basketball usually draw bigger crowds than swimming and cross-country. Men's sports often get more media coverage than women's sports. Recognize also that some student-athletes score points or goals, anchor winning relays, or set records. This happens while others "set the table" for them or rarely get on the field or court.

It's also important to note that some student-athletes have a head start because of their existing influencer status on social platforms. Some student-athletes are funny and creative and approach gaining followers as competitively as they approach their athletic performance. Others simply don't like social media or have not engaged in it before. Whether it was intentional to develop a following, it's likely the numbers will matter. It may not seem fair, but with NIL you must understand the ground you are tilling. To reap NIL benefits, you must tend to your personal garden . . . all while fitting in with your team and staying strong in the classroom.

This is a long way of suggesting you learn the rules, acquire a true understanding of who you are athletically, recognize the varying values tied to certain sports, and master the skills needed to build your NIL brand.

THE BUSINESS OF NIL

Let's switch gears a little and walk through a few more specifics of NIL in action. Let's assume that you, while excelling in the classroom and performing as a top athlete on your team, are ready to leverage your NIL. Suppose you are contemplating signing NIL deals with local car dealerships, serving as a social media influencer, or creating coaching clinics back home. Most of those initiatives may need to involve contracts requiring you to perform specific services that differ from earning grades or helping your team win. Studying and scoring points are agreed-upon "contracts" with professors and coaches but are nonbinding in the legal sense. For example, your performance at practice or during competition will vary based on your physical and mental health, playing time or events entered, the opponent, time of year, weather, and degree to which you stay laser focused on competing that day.

In the business world, failure to perform can destroy a business. If you are uncomfortable with bratty nine-year-old children and lose your temper easily, coaching clinics may not be for you. The word will spread quickly about your "style" in a negative way. If you despise public speaking, are uncomfortable in front of a camera, and can't remember your lines, you may not get many commercials. If you don't understand or like social media, forget to post when you mean to, have uninteresting feeds, or don't get many people to follow you online, becoming a social media influencer may not be for you. This is not meant to dwell on the negative but rather to serve as a reminder to get honest with yourself about where you can excel and where you should avoid trying to make a few extra dollars.

Most readers of this book will see themselves as accomplished, physically fit, relatively smart, and fun to hang out with on weekends. Playing an NCAA sport makes those assumptions easy to suggest because, as someone between the ages of seventeen and twenty-three, you are amazing and you have worked hard to make a college team. Earning a spot on a college athletic roster means an athletic department is already featuring you on its website and team media guide. Parents, guardians, and professors are telling you your whole life is ahead of you and because you are on your way to earning a college degree (while playing a demanding sport), you can become anything you want.

Student-athletes' smarts, sociability, and accomplishments give many of them degrees of well-earned confidence their non-student-athlete classmates lack. And now you have NIL rights! It means you can start making money; everyone says you should. That's great if you are honest about the time commitment needed to chase those dollars and if you promise yourself you will investigate what words like brand, leverage, privilege, rights, right of publicity, opportunity, obligation, forces, preemption, guardrail, amendment, permission, rules, assets, contracts, business, and rights (again) mean.

You are now a formal brand and hold the potential to create the business of YOU. That's incredibly exciting, especially as one of the first college athletes ever to do so. But don't fall into the trap of thinking anyone owes you money simply because of who you are. What's coming at you requires work. There are now nearly five hundred thousand individuals able to start small businesses, and many of them have been hearing from family and friends to "get after it." That encouragement will bring out agents and others (think roommates and sport management students) who will offer to make all the arrangements so you can stay focused on school (getting your degree) and your team (winning). They will want a percentage of whatever revenue their design, plan, or scheme generates.

These third parties (such as agents) usually mean well, but they are primarily thinking about themselves and how to make money off of you. That is how they see their job, and to them there is nothing wrong with "using" you to make money. They see *you* as the money tree.

Your job is protecting you. Remember the Under Armour advertising slogan "Protect This House"? Well, that is Job No. 1 for you. Agents and agencies generally understand business, contracts, payments, taxes, rules, and the law better than you do. That requires you to remember YOU are the business and in charge of YOU (as a business). YOU decide how you (as a business) run. Start by getting smarter with experts you can trust. We (the authors) would like to think we've armed you with foundational knowledge, but you'll need more sources, and checking various websites will help when it comes to better understanding NIL.

STRATEGIES FOR EVALUATING AGENCIES IN THE NIL ERA

Dean Jordan (Managing Executive of Properties and Media, Wasserman)

The ability to exploit name, image, and likeness rights brings exciting new opportunities for student-athletes to pursue and consider. While the size and frequency of those opportunities may vary depending on their market and sport visibility, all student-athletes have opportunities to take advantage of their NIL rights. For some, entering the NIL marketplace may seem overwhelming, especially when trying to balance academic and sport participation obligations. To the extent allowed by the NCAA, a student-athlete may consider working with an agency to review and evaluate opportunities, provide guidance, and serve as a representative in dealing with third parties. There is no doubt that many agencies want to take advantage of this new market, but all agencies aren't created equal. An agency with experience across multiple industry business segments can be an asset in negotiating a highly competitive marketplace. The following are some important things to consider when evaluating an agency relationship:

1. Good Personality Fit

   - An agency and its team will be your representatives, advisors, and voice in the marketplace. In addition to being comfortable that its experience matches your needs, you also need to feel a personal connection with the group. If there is anything that makes you uneasy, you may want to reconsider that agency despite positive attributes it may have.

   - Don't hesitate to ask who at the agency will be your primary contact and representative and who will be assisting them. Ask for their plan and vision for representing you. Confirm the agency will also assist you with any NCAA and school compliance-reporting processes and obligations.

   - Establish expectations for both yourself and the agency. While NIL opportunities are exciting, make sure the agency is fully aware of the parameters for NIL activities that you will consider. Consider your academic time requirements and your sport's competitive activities schedule when determining the amount of time that you are willing to spend on fulfilling any NIL obligations.

2.   Agency Representation Agreement

- Make sure you fully understand the terms before signing an agency agreement; seeking advice from legal counsel can help.

- The representation agreement should not require you to have any obligation to work with the agency beyond a set period of time upon which you mutually agree but not beyond the completion of your collegiate eligibility.

- The scope of the agency's representation should be clearly defined and include specific services and assistance being sought by you (for example, the agency's representation is limited to personal appearances and intellectual property only).

- In general, refuse any terms proposed by the agency that could limit the flexibility to exploit your rights in the future or bind you to the agency beyond the initial term.

3.   Knowledge of NCAA Rules and Understanding of Your Sport

- It's your eligibility at risk if the agency violates NCAA rules. Additionally, the agency should understand the rules regarding the usage of your school's intellectual property in your NIL efforts. Confirm its knowledge.

- While there are basic NIL opportunities for all student-athletes, to fully exploit the potential NIL market in some sports, it may require unique knowledge and experience from working in the sport.

- For student-athletes with Olympic aspirations, exploiting NIL rights may provide the ability to continue competing collegiately while pursuing Olympic dreams. An agency with experience working with Olympic athletes will be advantageous in understanding specific Olympic markets.

4.   General Business Negotiation and Applicable Subject Matter Experience

- Ask for examples and references to understand the agency's experience in negotiating basic business terms such as sponsorship, social media participation, personal appearances, or radio, television, or other media programming participation. The agency should demonstrate an understanding of your NIL value in applicable categories and markets, both with and without your ability to use school intellectual property.

- If you are presented with more advanced NIL opportunities, what experience does the agency have in more specialized areas, such as literary publishing or intellectual property licensing, or in opportunities such as shoe and apparel deals?

- Does the agency have experience in negotiating terms and value for unique compensation structures that may be proposed, such as value-in-kind or equity?

5.   Credibility in Calculating "Fair Market Value" (FMV) for NIL Rights

- The exchange of FMV for student-athlete NIL is central to the NCAA's approval of NIL exploitation, and it's important that your agency have credibility in this area.

- Making certain the agency has knowledge of current market data metrics and demonstrated experience in calculating FMV will ensure the student-athlete is receiving a fair deal and will also provide reputable support if the FMV is questioned by the NCAA.

- Basic valuation capabilities must include linear media platforms, digital and social media, and intellectual property.

6.   Personal Brand Development and Positioning

- Developing and positioning your personal brand is a key component in driving value along with creating and aligning NIL opportunities.

- The agency should have experience in advising clients on brand growth and be able to demonstrate specific examples of strategies that helped a client's brand stand out and achieve desired growth.

- The agency's brand-growth plan should also include an assessment of the platforms and causes which are important to the student-athlete.

7.   Experience with Digital and Social Media Platform Development

- A student-athlete's personal social media and other digital platforms will play an important role in a student-athlete's brand and ability to exploit NIL opportunities both present-day and beyond college.

- An agency should have demonstrated experience in developing social media strategies for athletes or other visible individuals designed to enhance the individual's brand image and social media following.

- Specific strategic capabilities should include posting subject matter and frequency, messaging tone, format (text, still or moving images), and interaction with followers.

8.   Ability to Facilitate Content Production and Distribution

- Unique content can enhance a student-athlete's social media and digital platforms. Given the time required to create even simple content, for creatively challenged persons, an agency with the ability to help facilitate content and creative assets can be a welcome resource.

- Consider an agency's in-house capabilities for, at minimum, creating and providing social media templates, graphics, and basic production editing.

- The agency should provide understanding and recommendations on how to utilize available campus production assets to further content creation efforts.

9.   Knowledge of School Multimedia, Rightsholder, Partners, and Integration Opportunities

- As of this writing, proposed NIL rules do not allow for a school to directly assist a student-athlete with exploiting NIL rights. The rules do not, however, prohibit a student-athlete from working with a school's third-party multimedia rightsholder on integrated marketing opportunities.

- An agency that has knowledge of school multimedia rights, established relationships with the multimedia rightsholder, and experience working with a school's official partners may provide an advantage in determining opportunities to integrate the student-athlete's NIL into those agreements.

- The possibility still exists for some form of group licensing opportunity to be created by schools for student-athletes which, if created, may also include the school's multimedia rightsholder. An agency's experience in this area will be valuable in advising a student-athlete on the benefits of participating in the group license.

Clearly, an agency relationship isn't required in order to exploit NIL rights. But for student-athletes who have multiple NIL opportunities, who are looking for assistance in developing their brand and opportunities, or who need assistance with a unique situation, an agency relationship can be a valuable resource.

You've got this, but there is plenty of work to be done.
All right, class dismissed.

NIL POSES QUESTION FOR NCAA ATHLETES: SHOULD I STAY OR SHOULD I GO?

Kaiden Smith (Appalachian State University Student-Athlete)

Originally published in Sportico on December 17, 2020,

https://www.sportico.com/personalities/athletes/2020/nil-ncaa-athletes-eligibility-1234618382/. Reprinted by permission of the author and the publisher.

Kaiden Smith graduated from Appalachian State in 2020 and is now a graduate student in communication/journalism. He is a strong safety on the football team, which has won four consecutive Sun Belt Conference championships. He graduated with departmental honors, submitting a thesis titled "How College Students Perceive the Representation of Women in Sports Media." He cohosts *The 135 Podcast* with teammate Thomas Hennigan, available on Apple and Spotify, and is also a senior sports reporter for his student newspaper, *The Appalachian.*

For a college athlete like me, this year has been anything but normal. Some differences are obvious to anyone watching on TV: the lack of fan attendance, the wearing of masks, and even social distancing on some sidelines.

But there are also behind-the-scenes changes, like the differences in how we meet, travel and eat team dinners before our games; the frequent COVID testing; our drastically altered academic schedules; and the constant reality of having your next game cancelled or postponed at any given moment.

All of this uncertainty won't end with the season, either. Because of the unusual circumstances surrounding the pandemic, the NCAA has decided to grant athletes another year of eligibility, which as a graduating senior has left me at an interesting crossroads. There's a laundry list of factors influencing my decision to leave or stay for another year, with the most interesting being the era of name, image and likeness (NIL) rights that will begin next year for college athletes, and the opportunities this will present.

Because of current NCAA rules, I can't use my status as an athlete to make money endorsing products, nor can I monetize my publicity using social media. If Sportico tried to pay me for this column, I couldn't accept it. But with NIL rights, that will change, making college players more like the professional athletes my age—people such as U.S. soccer stars Christian Pulisic and Weston McKennie, and even cheerleaders at the University of Oklahoma—who can profit off their fame.

When people think of NIL, they think of the big-name college athletes like Clemson's Trevor Lawrence starring in Gatorade commercials or signing a contract with Nike. But what does NIL mean to an athlete like me? I'm a safety at a mid-major FBS program who is less like Lawrence—a guaranteed millionaire when he turns pro—and more like the 99% of college athletes who exit the arena and move on to the working world after college.

Thankfully for me and most college athletes, there's a local market and fan base to tap into for revenue. My teammates and I may never be on a commercial during a CBS primetime football game, but we will be able to make a few bucks advertising and working with local businesses (restaurants, car dealerships, sporting goods stores, etc. . . .) in our college town.

But this only scratches the surface of the possibilities presented by NIL. One of the most fascinating and potentially lucrative aspects of this ruling will impact athletes like myself who are content creators.

I regularly publish articles and produce my own podcast, which has me wondering: Would the NIL ruling allow me to profit off of this content I already produce through sponsorships, advertising, donations or paid subscriptions?

One of the fastest growing and popular aspects of sports media is exclusive, behind-the-scenes content, which is in heavy demand and has been popularized by a multitude of programs like HBO's *Hard Knocks* or Netflix's *Last Chance U* or *QB1: Beyond the Lights*. One of my own teammates already makes documentary films about athletes and publishes them free of charge. Would he be allowed to tap into this market for exclusive content and earn money?

The opportunities in content creation for college athletes are endless. They could profit from an insider YouTube vlog, a live video game stream on Twitch, or even by creating and producing their own music.

Each locker room across the nation has journalism majors like me, and those majoring in other fields like public relations, advertising, video production and many more that equip them with the skills and understanding to take advantage of NIL rights.

I predict that over time college athletes will realize how much power and influence they have through NIL, giving them a lot of leverage in the near future. This could create some problems if it's not regulated properly. For example, what if athletes decide to not do media interviews or the personal story segments seen on sports networks, knowing that they could do the same thing independently or with their own teammates—and profit from it?

Naturally, the NCAA's ultimate NIL rules will also trickle down and impact high-school athletes, particularly top recruits in sports like basketball and football. Bronny James has 5.8 million followers on Instagram as a high-school basketball player: Is it in the NCAA's jurisdiction to regulate how he utilizes his platform financially before he is a part of the college athletics family? There are many questions that will need to be answered regarding high-school athletics surrounding NIL regarding matters like recruiting, working with agents, eligibility and more.

As time passes collegiate athletes will come to realize how in demand they are, which will force the NCAA to work cohesively with athletes to find some sort of balance. The NCAA cannot limit the creativity of college athletes just because they can suddenly profit from it, but the NCAA leaders likely will not want these students running media businesses that could potentially work against them.

Whether I decide to move on from college sports or stay one more year, it will be interesting to see how the first year and future years of NIL unfold. Change is coming soon, as college athletes across the nation will soon start cashing out on a payday that has been long overdue.

Secret 4 Ride Your Success Wheel

THE SECRET IN A FEW WORDS

Current student-athletes sometimes have trouble succeeding in both athletics and school.[1] Being a student-athlete is like having a full-time job to go along with school. The average person works forty hours in a week, and a student-athlete is putting in at least seventy-five hours of work a week in just school and sports alone. No one said it was easy, but a little help can go a long way. This chapter will provide strategies for how to succeed as a student-athlete and get set up for success in life after sports with your success wheel.

As we've said before, being a student-athlete is a privilege and also a choice. Student-athletes are among the hardest-working students on campus because of their dual commitments, but that doesn't mean they are held to lower standards academically. The institution and athletic department want to be known for having great student-athletes who can succeed in both academics and athletics.

RIDE YOUR SUCCESS WHEEL

If you are a student-athlete who thinks that you don't have time to put a 100 percent effort into both academics and athletics, you are wrong. Colby Targun, a former student-athlete at Texas State University, played both football and baseball for all four years. He now works for the NFL at the league's headquarters in New York City, and says, "Having the proper balance between academics, athletics, and social life is imperative to being successful as a student-athlete. All this while having attention [to] detail, organization, and a drive to succeed will make for a great experience."

Targun said he had three priorities as a student-athlete that led to his success as both a student and an athlete. He summarized his priorities: "Having my coursework completed in time and receiving good grades, performing on the playing field, and developing myself as a person overall (working on relationships, my future, etc.)." He remembers, "I was always working to get as far ahead as possible with my coursework, therefore allowing me to focus as much as I could on football or baseball, whichever season it may be." One of the greatest things he learned from his success was his "relationship skills in being teammates with [people from] all walks of life." He further emphasized that it "is important to be able to relate to anybody you meet in some way."

Targun advised student-athletes to "have an eye on the future, but also live in the moment. Don't worry about the next chapter so much that you miss out on your junior and senior year. Everything will work out eventually as it should if you are prepared."

THE STUDENT-ATHLETE SUCCESS WHEEL

In writing this chapter, we reviewed previous work in the area,[2] built on our own experiences and backgrounds, brainstormed, and developed our own version of a "success wheel" that you can follow and use to track your efforts and decisions as you progress through your experiences as a student-athlete. The following graphic depicts the wheel.

The success wheel, shown above, highlights the top ten aspects of how to succeed as a student-athlete. Each of these aspects, or spokes on the wheel, is discussed in detail in the following paragraphs. The core idea behind the success wheel is that each aspect builds on the others to cumulatively drive your success.

Priorities: Priorities are arguably the step where the success wheel starts to turn. It is extremely important that you prioritize your time—your most important resource. Sleep is incredibly important for an athlete's success, and you should aim to get an average of eight hours a night. That leaves, again on average, sixteen hours in a day to do everything else. Class and homework will take up a minimum of five hours a day. Training, practice, and competitions will occupy close to six hours on average daily. Eating, bio-breaks, and any other obligations get the leftover five hours maximum during the day. If you are dating someone or in a relationship, you need to make time for that person. Same with friends and social time with teammates. A social life is important, as well as any other extracurricular activities. If you want to be successful, having your priorities written out is a must. Prioritizing your time is crucial in becoming the best all-around student-athlete you can possibly be.

Relationship Building: Once you've set your priorities, building relationships that are key to those priorities is crucial in constructing a support system around what you are trying to focus on and achieve as a student-athlete. Aside from your family, creating relationships with coaches, teammates, professors, and friends is the minimum. Over the years, you will figure out the people you can rely on, trust, and go to for help. By building each relationship, you will gain support in the important areas of life. Developing relationships (for example, a favorite professor becomes a mentor) that create trust in people to seek advice from is extremely important in making educated decisions on important life, career, academic, and athletic choices.

AUTHOR VIEWPOINT—ANDY DOLICH

Teamwork, Leadership, and Trust

As athletes, administrators, executives, coaches, and fans across the sports world continue protests for social justice, we are reminded that without teamwork, leadership, and trust (TLT), the loftiest goals of any movement will fail. During this current surge of Black Lives Matter activism, this is more important than ever.

In my journey through the business of sports, I have learned that tactics without a coherent long-term strategy will not generate any systemic or lasting change. We are now living in what I call a "new different." And what do I mean by that? The powerful sports engine fueled by TLT is being revved up to create programs for positive change that will become more than words, individual actions, or media events.

Fox News talking head Laura Ingraham famously told NBA superstar LeBron James in 2018 to "shut up and dribble." James easily crossed her over and formed More Than a Vote in the spring of 2020. In partnership with other Black athletes, entertainers, and NBA venue operators, James and company organized, funded, and teamed up to push for mega–voting sites to accommodate in-person balloting amid the COVID-19 pandemic and political divisiveness that characterized 2020.

Some athletes have massive audiences and followings. James alone had more than 135 million followers on social media in late 2020. That's almost the same number of Americans as voted in the 2016 election. Even before the advent of social media, athletes have had a long and storied history using their expansive profiles to call broad public attention to societal ills. There have been many notable examples over the past century, including the following:

1. Track star Jesse Owens running to gold four times in the 1936 Summer Olympics in Nazi-controlled Berlin

2. Jackie Robinson of the Brooklyn Dodgers breaking the MLB color barrier in 1947

3. Sprinters Tommie Smith and John Carlos giving their gloved-fist protest—inspired by Dr. Harry Edwards's Olympic Project for Human Rights—at the 1968 Summer Olympics in Mexico City

4. Muhammad Ali refusing induction into the US Army in 1967

5. San Francisco 49ers quarterback Colin Kaepernick taking a knee in 2016

6. Elite athletes, including LeBron James, Matt Dumba, and the entire Atlanta Dream WNBA team, participating in Black Lives Matter protests in 2020 after the killing of George Floyd

7. Athletes and sports leagues calling a timeout based on the 2020 events involving Jacob Blake in Kenosha, Wisconsin

When these athletes and their resources team up across sports, they can play an influential and leading role in creating long-term systemic change.

As a student-athlete, you may not be a game changer on national television, but you have the ability to be an immediate difference maker today by using your education to make differences on many fronts. Pick a cause that fits your skill set, learn about it, and make a difference in your own way. Of course, this is much easier said than done, and the sports world has always been a bit disjointed with respect to working together as a powerful, united force for positive change.

Just look at all the different ways that sport, from Little League baseball to the NFL, is handling protocols and programs relating to COVID-19. How often do you see all the pro leagues, the NCAA, high school sports associations, and the major governing bodies for Olympic and Paralympic sports holding decision-making summit meetings?

As this book went to press in 2021, two major issues were facing not just organized sport but the entire world. The complicated fight to eliminate systemic hatred and achieve social justice continued, COVID-19 numbers were rising, and vaccines were not available to everyone to erase the ongoing pandemic.

Sport provides one of the last town squares of civility and unity in a divided world and can be an agent for meaningful societal change. TLT can make athletes, their sports, owners, league officials, and fans into a powerful force of nature in our country and around the world. As the future leaders of sport, with all the global energy and transformative powers it has, you all will shoulder the responsibility to be a proactive force of connectivity. Embrace TLT, for now is the time for dreams to turn into reality and change protests into policies.

Using Resources: Universities and colleges provide multiple resources for students, and you should take advantage of them. Again, these resources should align with your priorities and relationship-building efforts. The array of resources the university provides might include a tutor, librarian, mentor, career coach, psychologist, nutritionist, athletic trainer, or anyone else who is there to help you become the best student-athlete you can possibly imagine. The extra effort and time you devote to using these resources can make a huge impact on your college experience. You won't have all of these great "free" resources after you graduate, so why not take advantage of them now?

Mentors: An example of an ideal relationship (from a prior spoke [or leg] of the success wheel) is a mentorship relationship in which you connect to a key person who will help guide you through your decisions and life steps. Not everyone has a mentor, but we strongly advise you to work to find one. If you have more than one, even better. No two people have the same type of mentor and no mentor-mentee relationship is the same. Mentors are people who have experienced what you are going through and can offer advice or help for many situations. Mentors tend to be older than you, but someone who is just a few years older may be able to provide a more recent perspective on things. Depending on how the relationship works, age doesn't really matter. Find a mentor who cares about your personal development and long-term success.

Time Management: The previous elements all support the implementation of time management. Time management is the efficiency with which you use your time. It is important to any student in any context, but it is extremely crucial to a student-athlete. It sounds like such a simple aspect of life, but may be one of the hardest. Time management is a skill, and it can be acquired through experience. This is a skill that translates best into the working world, because it directly relates to priorities (that is, if you know your priorities, you can allocate your time) and use of your valuable resource of time (that is, the better your time management skills, the more efficient you can be with your efforts and the more activities you can fit into a busy schedule).

Organization: Organization may sound like a simple term (that usually gets overlooked), but it truly plays a large role in the success of a student-athlete. In the context of the wheel, once you know your priorities, relationships to build, resources available, and time plans, getting organized is a key next step. With how much goes on in one day, you must be organized in terms of where you need to be at certain times, and what is due and when. A calendar can be very useful, as well as utilizing technology for reminders and notes. Ultimately, organization helps you prioritize your activities and stay on top of what you need to achieve. A lack of organization will cause extra stress, missed deadlines, and possible tardiness. Being organized helps show responsibility and assertiveness, two important characteristics. And make sure you know what the difference is between time management and organization.

Motivation: Student-athletes must be motivated in the classroom, in the weight room, and at practice. Motivation stems from wanting to be successful, but the motivation must be for the right reasons. It comes from you, not your parents, your coach, or anyone else. The only person who can truly motivate you is yourself.

School/Sport Balance: As you build your plan for time, resources, mentors, networking, and other aspects, a balance between your dual objectives is important. Many coaches and administrators will argue about the relative importance of school and sport. However, the term "student-athlete" means that being a student takes priority over being an athlete. Today, we see a lot of "athlete-students." Don't be an athlete-student. Take pride in your education and understand your sport participation as a key aspect of the student experience.

However, regardless of what you think, stay balanced. Some readers may balance the two areas 50/50 and some may balance it 60/40 or 40/60. There is no "right" balance as long as you are aware of where your balance should be and where it actually is. Knowing that your high-level athletic career likely won't continue after you graduate, why wouldn't academics take priority?

Networking: Closely aligned with mentorship, networking is widely known to be one of the most important characteristics of success. More than ever in today's society, it is all about who you know, not necessarily what you know. As a student-athlete, you have more opportunities to network than any other student. You are automatically connected with alumni from your sport, as well as with coaches and administrators, plus their networks. Why not leverage those opportunities and network? Find out what they really do, how they got to where they are, and what you can learn from them about different career paths.

People are more likely to hire someone they know or share a common bond with, and the more people you know, the more connected you will be.

If one individual cannot directly help you, that person may know someone who can. Build your network of contacts and use LinkedIn to network as well. Networking is extremely important because it allows you to develop relationships over an extended period of time. The longer you can build a relationship with someone, the more that individual will be willing to do something good for you.

From the collective experience of the authors, we know that much of the above narrative sounds trite. If you find that many pieces of advice sound repetitive and obvious, that's because "trite is right." After many years in the sports business, we believe there is no such thing as a network that is too big. In 2016, one of us met an Olympic swimmer who was about to graduate from college. She was interested in looking into career opportunities in sport business. Her swimming network was extensive, but her network outside of swimming was small. We spoke about extending her connections with the same competitive fire she brought to the pool. Right after our discussion, a meeting with a team executive resulted in the opening up of another group of contacts. However large and influential you think your network is, it isn't as big as you will need. Digital networking tools are helpful, but face-to-face interactions pay the greatest dividends in advancing a career.

Career Focus, Macro and Micro: Having an idea of what you want to do after college is something you may not think about until your junior or senior year. At that point, it is often too late. Later in the book we will explain why you should be thinking about this in your sophomore year. You should develop a macro career focus in the field of study you desire, and this will help you pick a major, and create a broad career path.

Within your macro focus, you also require a micro focus, a specific part of the industry or field that you want to drill down on. This may change as your experiences help shape this focus. An example of a micro focus would be wanting to work in financial planning within the business field. Another example would be wanting to work in event operations, but focusing on customer service.

If you can see the end at the beginning, you aren't going to get off to a very good start. This one is all about multitasking. The most valuable athletes are those who can play the most positions or at least know what everyone's responsibilities are. Same goes for the professional world. If you have a marketing focus, learn finance. If you are thinking about player personnel, gain experience in sales. If you have a desire to work in a particular career, it is always important not to develop tunnel vision. Never get so micro that you can't keep your eye on the big picture. The 360-degree view is the best.

SECRET: RIDE YOUR SUCCESS WHEEL

Your success wheel will be different than that of your teammates, and your wheel is always customizable to the success you desire. This is one of those occasions where it really is about you. Consider your wheel your guide and road map to live by while in college. Most of the aspects in your wheel will apply to life as well, which is why it is even more important to develop your wheel early, to update it often and—most important—to follow it closely.

Bill Shumard, a former Division I Athletic Director, and now President Emeritus of Special Olympics Southern California following a fifteen-year tenure (2005 to 2020) as CEO of the organization, provides a unique perspective on what parts of the success wheel he thinks are most important. He noted "having served as Director of Athletics at two NCAA Division I universities, I believe the student-athletes' 'success wheel' is indicative of the key components making up the life of a student-athlete." Shumard's perspective provided considerable input into the success wheel we present here. The following box provides his view on the three most important aspects (in his view) of the wheel of success.

BILL SHUMARD

(President Emeritus, Special Olympics Southern California)

MENTORS

As I look back upon my career that has spanned more than four decades in collegiate, professional, and amateur sports, my ability to select and emulate strong mentors has been a key ingredient to any success I may have enjoyed. Fred Miller was the Athletics Director at Long Beach State when I was an undergrad student working in the Sports Information Office. I admired Fred's leadership style and his ability to be the "face and voice" of the university's athletics program. He was clearly the one who first inspired me to pursue a career path to become an AD.

When I moved to the Los Angeles Dodgers, I was part of a front office team that was included among "America's Top 100 Companies" because of our strong ethics and impeccable business practices. I reported to Executive Vice-President Fred Claire, who was chiefly responsible for the Dodgers' uniquely successful organizational culture. I patterned many of the habits and disciplines I practice after Fred's leadership. When I moved to the collegiate level, I reported to Mike McGee, the AD at USC. Mike was a former football player and coach, with a doctoral degree in business and organizational leadership. Mike's sense of loyalty and unwavering financial acumen made a strong impression on me and patterned my own success as an AD.

When I became AD at my alma mater, Long Beach State, my president—Bob Maxson—had a strong background AND a keen interest in intercollegiate athletics and how it should be positioned/prioritized on a college campus. Dr. Maxson epitomized the power of encouragement, and brought a great sense of pride and tradition to a relatively young university. My leadership style is largely part-and-parcel of the leadership habits of Claire, McGee, and Maxson. I recognized each of them as a strong, admirable leader and would regularly pick their respective brains on a multitude of topics. I was fortunate that they took the time and thought enough of me to invest in my future. I will be eternally grateful.

NETWORKING

A student-athlete has an incredible opportunity to meet and connect with a multitude of diverse people—including university administrators and faculty; coaches and support staff; boosters and volunteers; other student-athletes; the campus; and the community at large. While the student-athlete has many competing priorities during their time in college, connecting and establishing relationships with like-minded people at various stages of life and career is invaluable.

The student-athlete must begin to establish a reputation of integrity, trustworthiness, and loyalty to everyone in their respective universe. This will set the student-athlete apart from others and will lead to initial opportunities in establishing a career while building life-long relationships. I would also note that the student-athlete should establish themselves as a "giver" and not a "taker." In other words, always be willing to help others in need instead of just asking for favors and advantages. This is an important part of character development.

TIME MANAGEMENT

It is a safe assumption that a student-athlete's weekly schedule, in the midst of a competitive season, is in the neighborhood of seventy to eighty hours a week. When you factor in class time, study hall, practice, physical training, training room, and travel, the student-athlete's time demands are incredible. When I was an AD, I would tell our student-athletes that, if they were successful in managing their collegiate career and obtained a degree, time management of their actual career would be relatively easy in comparison. Being a collegiate student-athlete prepares one for a successful personal and professional life that can be rich and full. As one matures and moves through life after college—establishing a career; perhaps getting married and starting a family; and becoming a productive member of society—having mastered time management as a student-athlete in college will be a key ingredient in that success.

The success wheel as developed and outlined above is a useful tool for student-athletes. So, where do you start? Let us provide a few straightforward steps to follow.

Step 1: Create Your Own Success Wheel

Review the ten aspects of the success wheel explained above and create your own "wheel" with each aspect defined specifically for your situation and reality.

Step 2: Follow Your Success Wheel and Revisit It Frequently

It is one thing to just create your success wheel, but another thing to follow it. Revisit your wheel at least once a month and track your progress against each aspect of your wheel. Importantly, while tracking your progress, make sure you hold yourself accountable. It is easy to get caught up in everything going on around you and forget your wheel. Don't be that slacker!

AUTHOR VIEWPOINT—JAKE HIRSHMAN

I graduated with my undergraduate degree in three years while also competing as a student-athlete, and I couldn't have done it without my success wheel. Of course there are other aspects outside of the wheel that are important, but we thought these were the most important and overlapping.

I prioritized my academics over athletics because I knew my chances of going pro were slim, especially given a mix of injuries. I was driven to reach my goals and succeed in baseball, but it was more important to get good grades and gain experiences to build up my resume.

My relationship-building started in my sophomore year as I started to have classes for my major. I created relationships with my professors, coaches, teammates, and other administrators around campus. Looking back, this helped open doors for opportunities during the following year of school.

At the University of Redlands, I took advantage of the career development office because I was able to receive help on interview preparation for graduate schools. I was able to get my resume reviewed and other key skills sharpened.

Obtaining multiple mentors while I was in college was one of the best things I could have done. Bill Shumard, Fred Claire, Tony Miller, and John Lombardo are just a few of many who served as mentors for me throughout my time as a student-athlete. Their help, advice, and ability to seek out opportunities for me was invaluable in my success. Without them, I don't know where I would be today.

Time management for me was most important as I aimed to graduate in three years. Due to an injury, I had to continue my rehab and practice while I was taking twenty-three credits in the fall semester, and working three different internships all at the same time. Without quality time management and efficiency, there would have been no way I could have done all of that. As a sophomore, I even interned at the Inland Empire 66ers (A-league ball for the Angels) while I was in season. This was extremely difficult with practice times, but was attainable through supreme time management and a flexible coach.

With everything that I had on a daily schedule, organization was a skill that I developed and improved upon very quickly. Organization skills helped me with my time management, and paid off in the classroom. I kept a very detailed schedule of every day of every week to help me stay on top of everything.

Motivation was never an issue for me because I was never the best. I was always motivated to get better every day in every aspect of my life. All my life, I was told I couldn't do things or I wasn't good enough, and that served as fuel for me to prove people wrong. I wasn't the best athlete on the field, and I wasn't the smartest in every class, but through motivation and dedication, I always worked the hardest of anyone.

Balancing well my academics and baseball was the single most important thing that helped me succeed in both. I was able to balance my time and put 100 percent effort into both responsibilities.

Networking has been my most valuable tool as I have started my career post–graduate school. My early objective from networking was to find out everything possible about what people did in their jobs to provide a perspective on whether I would potentially be interested in what they did in the future. From talking to hundreds of people, I was able to rule out certain industries or jobs in order to narrow my career focus.

Networking has opened doors for me that nothing else could have. Every internship or job I have had was because I knew someone and had developed a relationship with that person. The more people you know and can impress, the more you can help put yourself in a position to get lucky at the right time.

Step 3: Be Very Strategic with Your Success Wheel

Many struggle with the difference between strategy and tactics. Tactics are individual acts and capabilities that, when used in a coherent long-term plan, become a strategy. Tactics are usually short-term with immediate results; strategies create long-term systemic success. Be both strategic and tactical with each aspect of your success wheel.

To provide you with relevant advice on strategies and tactics around a success wheel, we sought the input of a successful student-athlete and interviewed Alexis Pinson, a collegiate volleyball player at Arizona State University and Ohio University. She graduated with her master's in sports administration degree during her last year of playing at Ohio and now works for the Los Angeles Rams as an Account Manager. This is the third NFL team Pinson has worked for (San Francisco 49ers, Kansas City Chiefs). She provides some great insight on how to ride your success wheel and succeed as a student-athlete.

ALEXIS PINSON

**(former volleyball student-athlete at ASU and Ohio University,
now Account Manager for the Los Angeles Rams)**

WHAT WERE YOUR TOP THREE PRIORITIES AS A STUDENT-ATHLETE?

My first priority as a student-athlete was school. That was drilled into me since I was a kid just starting to play sports and it always remained my main focus. My parents always preached to me that sports are great but your body will only hold up for so long. You could get injured at any time and lose your athleticism but you can never lose your education. In fact, it was my emphasis on education that allowed me to graduate early from ASU and enter the MSA program at OU.

My second priority was of course volleyball. Volleyball was (and still is) one of my passions in life. If I wasn't in class or doing homework, I was either practicing, training, watching film, or doing something else related to volleyball. My roommates at ASU were some of my teammates as well, so they shared the same passion for the sport as me. They also never complained when I would fill our entire DVR with volleyball matches. It's probably one of the many reasons we got along so well.

My third priority was making time for my family and friends. One of the reasons that I decided to attend an undergrad school so close to my hometown was to be make it easy to still see my family as often as I could. After each of my home matches at ASU, a big group of people including my family, friends, teammates, and their families would all go out to dinner—whether we won or lost. These are some of my most cherished memories because it always put the matches into perspective. I was extremely lucky because my parents were able to carry on the tradition when I played at OU as they never missed a home game in Athens either. I was happy to prioritize my family when they would travel across the country several times over the span of a few months just to support me.

DID YOU HAVE ANY RESOURCES THAT YOU USED
THAT HELPED YOU WITH YOUR ACADEMICS?

The one resource that I used the most when it came to my academics was the tutoring program we had at ASU. Our academic coaches would set us up with a tutor if we needed some extra help in a certain class. We could even just ask for help in studying for an exam. This was a resource that I found to be very valuable because not only were the tutors very knowledgeable in their respective fields, but many times they were familiar with a specific professor and provided you with special tips and pointers for those classes.

HOW IMPORTANT WAS NETWORKING FOR YOU, AND HOW DID YOU TAKE ADVANTAGE OF BEING A STUDENT-ATHLETE?

Networking was a crucial tool for me to get to where I'm at today, and being a student-athlete was the main channel that I networked through. I found that the easiest people to network with were former student-athletes themselves. There's a common understanding and respect between student-athletes that I discovered while networking. They know you can handle the challenges and stressors of that life and can translate that to being a successful employee. It's why employers always comment that student-athletes are great hires, and many of those employer-employee relationships are forged by networking with other current and former student-athletes.

WHAT WAS THE MOST IMPORTANT PART OF YOUR SUCCESS WHEEL AND WHY?

The part of the wheel that contributed the most to my success as a student-athlete was motivation. Something (besides my alarm) had to get me up for 6 a.m. workouts every day. That same thing had to encourage me to study my notes again and again when all I wanted to do was sleep. Without motivation to get my degree and to make it to the NCAA tournament each year, I would've failed. That motivation to be able to say "I did the best I could" is what kept me going and led to my achievements.

WHAT RELATIONSHIPS DID YOU BUILD AS A STUDENT-ATHLETE THAT WERE MOST IMPORTANT TO YOUR SUCCESS AS BOTH A STUDENT AND AN ATHLETE?

The relationship that was most important to me as an athlete was my strength coach. This is usually a relationship that is underrated or gets overlooked, but it can be so important. Your strength coach is the one that will actually push you to do things that you didn't know you physically could do. Achieving those physical goals can do wonders for your mental state as an athlete. I was also fortunate enough to feel close enough to my strength coaches that I could come to them with other issues I was having outside of the gym and they'd always seem to find a way to channel those struggles into my workouts. Not only would I get a great workout, but most times I'd feel better as a person after I left the gym.

Also a word of advice when it comes to strength coaches—*do not anger them*. They can be a great resource and help you in so many ways but if you upset them, they can make your life a special kind of hell. I promise that if you put in a great deal of hard work, you'll help your teammates, your coaches, and most importantly—yourself. And everyone lives in harmony.

The relationship that was most important to me as a student was my academic coach. You should really listen to them when they suggest what classes would be best for you to take with your schedule. They know what they're doing. They are also a great resource when you feel like you need some extra help in a class. Don't be embarrassed to go to them—even with just the slightest issue. They're there to help you succeed.

AT WHAT POINT DURING SCHOOL DID YOU START TO FOCUS ON YOUR CAREER AND THINKING ABOUT WHAT YOU WANTED TO DO IN THE FUTURE?

My future career was always on my mind since I started my collegiate education but it definitely became more focused probably a year or two before I graduated from ASU. I always knew that I wanted to work in sports but I just had to decide in which capacity. I had an idea that sports journalism and PR was something that interested me so I asked our team's SID if I could tag along and shadow them. I ended up really enjoying it but I didn't realize how much writing actually went into journalism and frankly, I don't enjoy writing enough to make it a focal point of my career. My advice would be to use those who are around you every day. If you think you may be interested in a position in the medical field, ask your athletic trainer if you can shadow them and learn from them. It will probably open your eyes and give you a firsthand look at what that job is really like. It can encourage and solidify your passions or, like me, make you realize that it's actually something that doesn't interest you that much.

LOOKING BACK AT YOUR TIME AS A STUDENT-ATHLETE, IS THERE ANYTHING YOU WOULD HAVE DONE DIFFERENTLY?

Looking back, I think the only thing that I would've done differently is to reach out and get to know more of my fellow student-athletes. They know exactly what you're going through living life as both a college student and athlete, so relating to them is a breeze. It's easy to get comfortable in your bubble and just hang out with your teammates, but I wish I would've taken the time to get to know more of my peers. Plus, they'll probably show up to your games and make you pretty cool posters.

Step 4: Prioritize within Your Success Wheel

In any strategic or tactical effort (and as emphasized in the Prioritize aspect of the success wheel), you have to make decisions about where to put your resources and focus your time. It is no different with the success wheel. In order to illustrate and provide an example, we interviewed Pim Thirati, a former student-athlete in golf from the University of Illinois, who is now Assistant Director of Marketing and Digital Strategy at Virginia Tech. The following is an excerpt in which she offers her advice on what the most important part of her success wheel was.

PIM THIRATI

(former golf student-athlete at the University of Illinois,
now Assistant Director of Marketing and Digital Strategy at Virginia Tech)

The most important parts of my success wheel would be Relationship Building, Time Management, and Motivation. Being a student-athlete has definitely taught me all the aspects of the success wheel to a certain extent, but I would say these three aspects continued to be the most impactful after I have graduated.

Working closely in a team with coaches as well as the athletics department, the media, fans, and competitors has taught me how to interact and build relationships with other people, which are very crucial skills in life after college. Balancing between golf and school has taught me how to prioritize my time wisely. Working in sports can be hectic and, depending on your responsibilities, you could be working with various projects at once. Being able to manage my time is one thing I found very helpful for my career. Putting a substantial amount of time and effort into a sport you are passionate about requires a high intrinsic motivation. I believe this is something that sets student-athletes apart. I have invested in one sport for over ten years and as a result, I tend to be very self-driven and *self-motivated* in other aspects of my life as well.

My advice for current and future student-athletes is to try to not lose sight of other intangible skills you are learning outside of your sport. It is easy to get caught up in the wins and losses. In the end, I really don't remember the putts I missed. I remember the friends I've made and the grind we went through. The wins and losses WERE a big deal but looking back, they didn't define me and I'm glad I didn't let it take over my life. The end result WAS a big deal but the process is what shaped me.

CHAPTER SUMMARY

This chapter provided a tool you can adopt and implement to help guide and focus your efforts over the course of your time as a student-athlete. Maybe you looked at the picture of the success wheel and skipped the words. But we hope you read this chapter and started to wonder whether now is the time to build your own success wheel.

Secret 5 Acquire the Life Skills You Need to Succeed

THE SECRET IN A FEW WORDS

We all want to succeed in life. No surprise there. But in order to achieve success and accomplish notable goals, certain skills are needed. Sport teaches an abundance of life lessons many people are unable to learn in a classroom or anywhere else in life. These life lessons can occur for many reasons, but the majority of us learn the most from failure (which sport easily provides). Getting things wrong or failing always clarifies the need to acquire certain new skills in order to prevent repeating the same outcome. So, learn from your failures, and the real secret is to gain the life skills you need to succeed.

As a student-athlete, you have the opportunity to develop many life skills through your sport. and as you mature as an athlete, learning those skills will become easier but also more important. There is no doubt you'll need various tools to succeed at whatever goal you pursue, but recognizing what to learn is one of life's vitally important secrets.

LIFE SKILLS YOU NEED TO SUCCEED

Sport can help a young person develop key skills such as time management, competitive response, a true work ethic, goal setting, resiliency, and value clarification. The earlier you are able to recognize what these skills are and how to develop them, the more you can improve those skills. These "assets" are important not only for success as a student-athlete but also for future success as an individual and working professional. Not all skills are part of your natural human makeup. Some need to be developed from the ground up, and it helps to have a little guidance in which skills to think about the most. To open this chapter, we noted that learning from losing was a secret. But we want to be clear that losing is not a habit you want to repeat. So minimize your losses . . . but learn from them when they happen.

Dawn Buth, a former professional tennis player and student-athlete at the University of Florida, featured below, talks about which life skills were most important for her as a student-athlete, as a professional athlete, and as a working professional. She is currently Assistant Director of Government Relations at the NCAA.

The first life skill Buth spoke about was a work ethic and how it was a key tool she learned as a student-athlete that has been foundational to her career development. We asked her to explain why a strong work ethic is so important. She offered the following explanation and supporting points.

> For me, work ethic has meant approaching everything I do with focus and commitment. It means having the self-awareness to understand my strengths and limitations, and the ability to maximize my capabilities within any given moment. It also means making short-term sacrifices and working through discomfort to accomplish long-term goals. When I retired from professional tennis, earning my graduate degree was an important priority for me.
>
> I accepted a position as the head coach at an institution that was my top academic choice and which had exceptional tuition benefits. The position, however, could only offer an annual salary of $15,000, so in addition to my full-time role and graduate studies I worked an additional twenty hours each week teaching private tennis lessons to support myself. During this time, I also had the opportunity to serve on the executive board of a nonprofit and participate in a once-in-a-lifetime internship opportunity. These experiences required making personal sacrifices and working long, physical hours, but they also opened doors of opportunity and provided some of the most incredible years of personal growth.

We also asked her to discuss the life skills that helped her the most in her professional life after a life in sport. First, she noted resiliency. For her, "resiliency is the most important life skill I learned as a student-athlete. We've all experienced setbacks, defeat or a lack of confidence and for me, resiliency meant experiencing these challenges and then finding a way to regroup, pick yourself up and try again."

She also highlighted time management as "the ability to manage multiple and competing priorities, [which] was always a part of my student-athlete experience and continues to be an important part of my professional experience. To this day, every morning when I get to work I take ten minutes to review my calendar and prioritize my workload for the day and week. Investing a small amount of time into planning on the front end goes a long way in efficiently and effectively managing time and priorities."

The ability to learn continually is another life skill Buth reported as being of high importance. Specifically, she noted "the skill that has been most important and most fulfilling for me is the ability to learn and recognize that you can learn from every opportunity, every person and every situation."

In developing all of these key life skills, she noted three factors she believes are crucial: goal setting, value clarification, and utilization of resources. She explained:

> Goal setting and value clarification have been valuable tools in my athletic and professional life. Goal setting often involves making the implicit, explicit. It invites an athlete to articulate what they want to accomplish from their athletic pursuits and identify a pathway to accomplish it. There is a lot of interesting research about the power that comes from scripting and verbalizing your goals and every great coach and teacher in my life has challenged me to not only set goals for myself, but also write them down and say them out loud.
>
> Values clarification includes taking time to identify and narrow down your core values. These tools are simple but are an impactful driver for self-reflection, effective prioritization and intentional decision making . . . be both resourceful and ask for help.
>
> The ability to independently problem solve on one hand, and on the other hand be courageous in asking for help, cannot be understated in its importance to one's personal and professional development.

TIME MANAGEMENT

Oliver Luck, former Executive Vice President of the NCAA, identified time management as the best life skill based upon his experiences. He described his view as follows:

> The best life skill that I was able to develop is time management and how to fit all of these different things into my day. Sometimes you can't because you run out of time. That's very helpful when you become an adult, when you're married, you've got kids, you've got a job. You have to squeeze a lot of things into a busy day. At work, you've got to look at a situation and figure out how you improve it.

RYAN SOLLAZZO

**(former Division I football student-athlete, now Senior Director,
Global Corporate Partnerships at Major League Baseball)**

From a time-management standpoint, map things out. I would write down my goals, and set deadlines. I would set midpoint deadlines, and then try to map out how many days it would take me to get to the midpoint deadline. By beating that deadline, I would ultimately bring the final deadline four or five days earlier. If I couldn't do it, then I knew I had four or five days extra to meet that deadline. Being able to map out a strategy, have a vision for the strategy, and then have a plan on how you want to execute it is extremely important.

TEAMWORK

Kristen Brown, a former basketball student-athlete at Northern Illinois University who is now Deputy Athletics Director at Texas A&M University, emphasizes teamwork as a key life skill. She noted "teamwork is crucial to learn as a student-athlete because you deal with so many different personalities on a team. Learning how to interact, and work well together with people from different walks of life, different ages, different backgrounds are certainly skills I use every day. Communication is very important in building relationships, and helps me out every day in my job."

MANAGING AND HANDLING PERSONALITIES

Nick Manno, a former student-athlete baseball player at Mount Union who went on to work for various teams in Major League Baseball and is now with the Toronto Blue Jays, provided a very interesting life skill which he called "learning how to manage personalities" and noted it was very important to him during his tenure as a student-athlete. He explained further that

> any team culture and atmosphere will have introverts, extroverts, and others who are outgoing and those who don't take criticism well. There will be those you deal with that you like and those you don't. The reality is whether you are on a team or working in an organization, you are going to have to deal with different personalities.
>
> You are going to have to manage those personalities accordingly. You are not going to get along with everyone you work with or play with, but understanding that not everyone is going to be like you, and not everyone is going to think like you is important. At the end of the day, you need a common goal and have to find out where you fit. My advice for managing

personalities is to be yourself, know where you fit, and know where you fall. Be your own person, and try not to fall into the traps of others. . . . Try to put yourself in their shoes and situation to better understand their perspective.

As a leader, you need to be able to manage any situation, and have the discipline to be able to still do the best you can even when you are not 100 percent. Athletes are the same as professionals. You don't always want to get up and go to work, but we have to be professionals.

DEALING WITH ADVERSITY

Manno recalled he believed the ability to deal with adversity is "the biggest life lesson that can be turned into a skill, whether it's a team concept or something you are not doing in your own job or own career, allow yourself to be reflective and figure out what you can do better in those situations. Self-evaluation is crucial; Learn how to be self-reflective and understand where you need to improve."

ACCOUNTABILITY

Former volleyball student-athlete at Arizona State University Alexis Pinson suggested that accountability was a key life skill. "Being a part of team in college really taught me the value of being reliable and knowing that my teammates could count on me as an athlete and as a person. This has certainly carried over to my professional life. I take great pride in knowing that my bosses and coworkers see me as an accountable person and I know that that is a skill that I honed as a student-athlete."

Nick Manno also touched on accountability, saying, "You have to be accountable to yourself, because you cannot get better without holding yourself accountable. Don't blame someone else for your shortcomings. You have to be able to learn from every situation, and understand that if I make a mistake, why did I make that mistake and can I learn from it?"

Ryan Sollazzo added that accountability for a student-athlete also means "being able to be coached and being able to take constructive criticisms is very important in being successful. A challenge for a lot of people is the ability to turn a negative into a positive opportunity."

Sollazzo tells a story showing how important it is to develop life skills outside of sport.

My redshirt sophomore year, I blew my knee out in spring practice. At that time, I thought it was the worst thing that could ever happen because as an athlete your whole life really revolved around sports. Looking back, it was probably the best thing that happened. While I was always very focused on academics, that actually gave me an opportunity to get experience and figure out what I wanted to do for a career.

Since I was still on scholarship, I still had to contribute in some sort of way. I was unable to do that on the field, so the new stadium plan presented an opportunity to be the spokesperson from the student-athlete standpoint. I got to travel with our head coach, our AD, our president of the school. I didn't get this experience because I was a star player, but more because I was available, with the team, and willing to help.

Sollazzo also suggested using summers wisely. He "always took summer classes" Impressively, Sollazzo followed his plan and graduated with a 4.0 GPA, went on to do graduate work, and is now well into a successful and rewarding professional career.

COMPETITIVENESS

Garrett Shinoskie, former football student-athlete at Capital University, listed a few more skills that we agree are important: "My advice is to apply the exact same skills that made you successful in sports: patience, hard work, pride, determination, being coachable, etc. Life is competitive and to be successful you must have the same mentality you had as an athlete."

Former Duke University wrestler Immanuel Kerr-Brown, who is now Associate Director of Development at Penn State University, warned against falling into the trap of "competing not to lose rather than to win." He explained that when you're in this state of mind, "you walk out into competition hoping not to embarrass yourself, and then you start to wonder what everyone else thinks about you because you just can't seem to win." Kerr-Brown suggested taking the same positive approach to your academic, professional, and other nonsport goals as well. He suggests identifying your "AOC's" (areas of concern) and addressing them as quickly as you can.

Kerr-Brown offered one additional and important skill for student-athletes. He suggested strongly that student-athletes view teammates and classmates as "motivation" and not competitors on and off the field. He describes the issue: "The problem with comparing yourself to your teammates without this critical approach leads to you thinking, 'They are just so much better than me,' which ultimately leads to 'I stink.' You do not want those thoughts to cross your mind. Anything you do that places you in a negative mindset is detrimental to your success. That applies to you athletically, personally, and professionally. Negativity gets you nowhere."

PATIENCE AND COACHABILITY

Patience and coachability go together in this section because you cannot be coachable without being patient. Many things in life are about the process.

In fact, almost everything is about a process. Patience is key during the process towards a goal. Not everything can happen at the snap of your fingers. As many say, good things come to those who wait. Whether your patience is tested in the classroom or on the field, you'll learn a lot by waiting for what's to come. For example, if you are a freshman that just walked into an extremely competitive program and you need to redshirt or ride the pine for the year, you must be patient. Many student-athletes would think about transferring once they don't get what they want, but wouldn't you want the challenge? Have the patience to keep getting better each day, knowing your time will come to shine. It may be the next year or your senior year, but when your time comes, you will look back and say it was all worth the wait.

And being coachable is a life skill that is one of the most important. Life is full of learning, and the ability to be coachable, on or off the field, enhances your ability to learn immensely. No one wants to coach someone who isn't coachable, and no one wants to help someone who isn't coachable. Being coachable is easier for some than others, but you have two eyes, two ears, and one mouth for a reason. Observe and listen more than you will talk. Soak up the information like a sponge and be flexible and open to learning new ways whatever the task may be. At the end of the day, being coachable will get you much farther than not, and people will be willing to help you if you are very coachable.

CHAPTER SUMMARY

This chapter presents a series of life skills, suggested by people who have "been there" and "done that." Prioritize your list of missing skills and address the most important or most needed ones first.

The highlighted traits in this chapter are:

1. Managing and handling personalities

2. Time management

3. Resiliency and grit

4. Work ethic

5. Dealing with adversity

6. Teamwork

7. Accountability

8. Competitiveness

9. Patience

10. Coachability and the ability to learn

It may sound hard. Some of these skills require personal reflection and then the discipline to change human behavior. Now go get it done. As Yoda told Luke Skywalker in a *Star Wars* movie, "Try not. Do. Or do not. There is no try."

Secret 6 Be Balanced in Everything

AUTHORS' VIEWPOINT

This may be the shortest "box" in the book. All of us strongly agree, and so did all the former student-athletes we asked, that Secret 6 (aka "the balance secret") is essential, really essential, to the future success of any student-athlete in the "other 99 percent" bucket. And by balance, we don't mean balancing academics with athletics, or balancing studying with training. We mean balance in all respects. Each aspect of your life, from sleep to partying, to relationships to a private meeting with your coaches, to television watching and video gaming, to your choices on commuting or how you spend your weekends . . . all of them require balance. Yes, we need you to dissect your entire existence and make it more efficient and more productive.

THE SECRET IN A FEW WORDS

Balance, balance, balance. Balance is a word you MUST put into your top-of-mind vocabulary. All the time, in all things. Given your two MASSIVE commitments to academics and athletics—and with the growing requirements around each from just the first four secrets—you need to really consider every activity and your use of time. Deciding to join a club to make friends, for instance, will remove a couple of hours a week from your other pursuits. You need to gauge the importance and value of each activity to your goals, your mental health, your academic success, and your athletic performance. Of course, we do understand

(and agree!) that you have to find enjoyment in life, but these decisions MUST be taken very seriously. As many athletes have learned, you can't always excel in all three areas of the student-athlete experience. Academics, athletics, and your social life are the three things you most need to balance. Our advice to you is that it is only possible to excel in two of the three, and academics is always one of them, so choose wisely and balance well.

BE BALANCED IN EVERYTHING

Secret 6 is about balance in all things. In everything. It is about reviewing all of your activities, pastimes, studies, and athletics, looking at them holistically, and determining the best way to use the most important resource a student-athlete has: time. Efficient time and effective time. In order to provide clear direction, we have organized this secret by the various activities of your student-athlete life and will provide you with direction in making these decisions.

Much of what you decide here may impact the plan you constructed after reading Secret 1. We encourage you to update your plan after reading this chapter and consider its direction.

To introduce our discussion of balance, we ask readers to imagine you're a gymnast on a balance beam. You can do many things on the beam, but lose your balance (and it can happen easily) and you fall off.

BALANCE IN ACADEMICS

Okay, so you've learned a lot about balancing academics in Secrets 1 and 2, but there is more here to consider:

1. *Focus on your most challenging class first.* Just as athletes always work on their weakness (for example, a decathlete who is amongst the best runners but a weak thrower puts the majority of his efforts into his throwing), so should you. That class you are worried about (perhaps statistics or accounting?) should be your priority and where you put any extra time. When you plan out your life each semester (see Secret 1) and allocate study time, review your courses closely and put extra time into those courses you are worried about or those courses you know you won't like (and will have a hard time studying for). Trust us, your GPA will thank you! And, if you ever apply for grad school many years down the road, you'll enhance your chances!

2. *Study often and early.* You are an athlete. Do you stay up all night practicing the night before the big game or key qualifying race? Never! So, why do that with your studying? Sure, you can push at the end, but work out a study plan that peaks as an exam approaches but allows you to go into that exam rested and ready,

and—very important for any student-athlete—does not negatively affect your physical training. Most athletes can think back to times where they had to stop training around a major exam. It's not good for mental health, not good for sport performance, and usually not good for grades.

3. *Access key academic resources before you need them.* This is very simple, very intuitive, and very logical, yet few do it. If you're graduating in May 2025, don't wait until April 2025 to talk to your advisor about a job or to set up a meeting with the career management office. Same for getting an internship or dealing with a class you might be failing. Get help (from a professor, an advisor, student services, or others) early. Universities are full of services and professionals to help student-athletes, but only if you seek them out.

BALANCE IN ATHLETICS

After academics, athletics is the second major part of your dual-focused life and a part that requires close attention to balance. A few suggestions from our collective experience:

1. *Train in the off-season.* Yes, this may seem like overkill, but many of the "other 99 percent" tend to slack off, just a little, in the off-season as they progress through college and find other interests, fall in love, get a great summer job, and so on. If you can focus on your fitness and the foundations in the off-season (regardless of your sport), you won't experience as much of a "shock" when you're back on campus. You'll also have less stress and anxiety about losing your spot or scholarship. Many student-athletes choose to stay on campus each summer to advance their academics, access awesome training facilities, work with their coaches, and enjoy their college towns. If this is an option for you, consider attending summer sessions. Having time to take a few classes and get ahead academically while also maintaining a training routine can be a tremendous benefit in moving you toward a great next season and lightening the academic load during the year.

2. *Choose a practicum or internship outside of your team.* It is both a waste of an opportunity to build your resume and experiences outside of your team and a potential drag on time if you work for your coach or manager for the team where your scholarship is linked. You'll end up working much more, losing balance and doing so for a position that will not advance your resume as much as an external one will.

3. *Take advantage of injury time or being red-shirted.* This may seem counterintuitive, as you are desperate not to lose your place on the team and want to show your loyalty and support even if you are not playing. Be strategic here. Be present and do your part but keep it to a minimum and use this time to get a practicum or internship done, join a club, connect with alumni, travel, work part-time, do an independent study with a leading professor, etc.

BALANCE IN FAMILY AND FRIENDS TIME

Balancing family and friends with all your other time commitments is especially challenging in your first year of college, and perhaps somewhat after that. Your family (parents, siblings, cousins, and all the rest) and friends (high school pals) have been a large part of your life, and now you've moved away. In the two semesters of school, you'll have precious few quiet nights and about twenty-six weekends to do "stuff." Those weekends are special for work, training, planning, volunteering, socializing, and studying. They are key. You'll want—especially at first—to head home often, to connect with friends, to go to events with them, and to uphold traditions you all had from high school. The same with your parents: you'll want to go home, they'll want you to come home, and there'll be various family events. As hard as it is, you need to make some tough decisions. Here are our top priority recommendations.

1. *Be picky.* You'll have so many opportunities and desires to go home. Many. Family events. Last-minute party invites from friends. And more. Before the semester starts, set your boundaries. One trip home per semester (even if you live close) plus Thanksgiving is a good rule. Or even less. Then pick the date and stick to it. You can make it up to your friends over holidays. But you must help your friends understand that because you are a student-athlete the demands on your time are way more than they ever were in high school.

2. *Have your parents (or grandparents or guardian) visit you or have them meet you at your competitions.* Your parents are the easiest to convince here. Your college likely has special weekends. Take advantage of these. Surprise them and book a hotel room for them and ask them to come to a game or event. They'll want to. That way you can balance their visit with school and practice. You can also have your family and friends meet you on a road trip. You'll end up with support from those you care about during the competition/match/game and they also will probably enjoy seeing you do what you love, play your sport.

3. *Put time in your schedule to call home.* This is a big one and an often unmeasured time crunch. Particularly if you are homesick. Instead of getting a great night's sleep, you stay up talking until 2 a.m. or later with old friends. So, before the year starts, set a time (say 9 to 10 p.m. on Sunday) for calls home. Try to keep them short (fifteen minutes?) so you can call three or four family members or friends each week. Mix it up. Then complement the calls with social media connections to keep in contact.

BALANCE IN SOCIAL TIME

This is a big one. Perhaps the biggest one. College life comes full of amazing opportunities to party, socialize, travel, play, chat, and more. Social life is a huge part of college and something you want to enjoy and take advantage of. But, it can also be the reason why you struggle academically, athletically, or both.

In fact, many students who are not student-athletes flunk out or struggle because they do too much socializing. This can be drinking, partying, playing too many video games, or just chatting nights away with friends. There is no parental supervision and life is easy and great. We have all struggled with this and have learned the hard way in many cases. So, our three priority recommendations here are:

1. *Figure out what you are addicted to and avoid it.* Maybe it's video games that you love or maybe it's binge-watching Netflix and snacking on junk food. Figure out your vice, acknowledge it, and either work it into your schedule in small chunks or avoid it altogether. For some people, it's an all-or-nothing proposition. If you find yourself doing anything that has a negative impact (sleeping through classes because you were up too late, gaining weight because you are drinking and eating too much pizza) on the priorities you have for yourself to achieve success, you need to get a handle on it immediately. Whatever your vice is, TV or partying, figure it out early and cut it out of your life.

2. *Put quotas on partying.* Partying not only takes away that particular night but also takes a lot out of you the next day. For a lot of student-athletes, 5 a.m. or 6 a.m. practice times put a damper on partying during the week, but with the demanding schedule you keep, you also need to put the brakes on for the weekends to catch up on sleep and rejuvenate yourself. Set a quota (once a month, once a week, etc.) for your partying and stick to it. Don't be persuaded otherwise.

3. *Choose a great living situation.* This is important. If you're in a residence hall, fine, but if you're not, choosing an appropriate

place to live is key. Live with teammates (who are serious students) or with classmates (who are serious students) and not with partiers, or in a place known as a party house, or even in an apartment building or on a street where late-night noise and partying are common. You will not last long as a student-athlete in such an environment.

BALANCE IN EMOTIONS

Emotions run high, and those who need to stay spiritually connected (whether through religion or not) to keep their emotions level must make time to do so. Not everyone needs this component in their life, but some may, and it may help others who don't currently have it.

Relationships are a big part of life. And, we're talking about romantic ones. Lovers. Sexual partners. Boyfriends. Girlfriends. One-night stands. There are many viewpoints on relationships, but the reality is that most college students engage in various relationships throughout their four years.

And unless you entered college with a supportive partner who understands your situation and gives you the time to focus on sport and school, we recommend thinking long and hard about whether a potential partner has your best interests in mind, and whether your student-athlete experience will benefit as a result of a relationship. There is plenty of time to find a partner after college. Don't think you need to be in a rush to find someone.

A few specifics from us here:

1. *Stay single, or date but do so sparingly.* A new partner typically will want a lot of your time—and you'll want to give it, too, which is hard to do while living the time-constrained life of a student-athlete. Then, if the relationship endures, stress will arise either from your declining performance (school and/or sport) or from your partner who feels like you don't want to spend enough time together.

    Dating can be great, and less of a time commitment. But, date sparingly and be clear that it is for fun and not for any long-term commitment. We know that is easier said than done, but just be aware of what you are or aren't getting yourself into along with everything else that is going on in your life. Check your priority list one more time, and act accordingly.

2. *If you have a long-term partner or meet a very supportive one, establish and communicate very clear ground rules to avoid problems.* If you stray from #1 on this list because you find someone you think is perfect or your high school sweetheart has moved to town, then consider using this simple tactic: Have a

very serious talk, explain what your goals are and that you need their support for the next few years. Let them know you want them in your life and expect the relationship to last but you only have a few hours each week to devote to it. This is a very hard discussion because no one likes being told they will be "fitted" into someone else's schedule. This talk may even end your relationship. But failing to have this discussion with someone you care about can lead to disastrous results.

3. *Connect spiritually if that is part of you.* Over the course of a semester, year, or years, a lot will happen, and a lot will be thrown your way. Keeping your emotions in balance is extremely important throughout your experience, and if staying connected spiritually or religiously helps ground you, then continue to do so and don't slack. Make it a routine for yourself if you know it is a big part of your life.

BALANCE IN DOWNTIME

Downtime is important for anyone's mental health. Chilling with friends. Lying on the couch watching your favorite team, movie, or concert. Playing your favorite video game. All are part of your downtime, and downtime is valuable. But you have to manage it. If you are practicing the time management strategies already provided in this book, you have this nailed already. Some simple steps.

1. *Set a maximum time for any activity.* If you love watching football on Sunday, pick one game (not three) and plan study and training and other commitments around that game. Even better, don't turn on the game until the paper that is due is complete, your assigned readings are done, you have gone out for a run or done whatever it is that is important to achieve that day.

2. *Cut out "useless" downtime.* Quite simply, things like aimless web surfing, staring at your Twitter feed, checking out the latest Snapchat features, television watching without a purpose, and other mindless activities need to go. These are not only unproductive but often leave you feeling stressed and more tired. This takes discipline.

3. *Try to double-dip downtime.* Use your downtime wisely—stretch during television or movie watching, play an online game with a friend from home, invite your mom and dad to a golf day, etc. By double-dipping, you achieve two or more things at once and save yourself time that you can use for other things later.

MATT VANSANDT

**(former track student-athlete, now Assistant Commissioner of Championships
at the Big South Conference)**

Make school your 9-to-5 job. Being efficient and focused during your day will allow you to enjoy a work-life balance. When I was at school, I made it my 9-to-5 job. While you could be napping, playing video games, or going out with friends, you can be working efficiently to prepare yourself for a routine you may have when you get that first job. In college, you have so much free time, that your transition to work is difficult because you are by yourself for the most part, and you have this bulk of time during the day to get work done, and if you don't get your work done, you won't be successful.

BALANCE IN ANNUAL PLANNING

When you plan your year, think balance. There is really one general strategy here: you need to have balance over the twelve months for each of the four years of your student-athlete career. Periods of push (academic and athletic), periods of downtime/friends/family, periods of push—academic only, periods of push—athletic only, periods of work experience and life experience, and be sure you don't develop periods you can't handle. Some suggested tactics.

1. *In peak competitive season, cut back on everything else except school.* Do not plan weekends or visits home, cut out extracurricular work, parties, etc. This is your time to shine athletically and keep everything rolling academically.

2. *At exam time, only staying fit matters.* Yes, for the period of exam week and before it, school is number one with just enough time set aside to stay in shape for sport. As in #1, remove everything else from your life. Be insanely focused!

3. *Use summers and winter breaks **very** strategically.* One of the great things about the academic calendar is that you receive periods of time out of school. This is when you can really catch up with friends and family, get work experience, do career planning, be social and more, while concurrently maintaining your fitness and sporting form and staying healthy via sleep and nutrition. Do NOT use these breaks as "benders" where you go on a party tour. Sure, you might kick back a bit more than during the tight academic year, but you have so much stuff to do when academic responsibilities are low and athletic competition is not happening.

BALANCE IN EXPERIENTIAL CHOICES VERSUS FINANCIAL CHOICES

Student-athletes sometimes make decisions based on very small amounts of money. We've seen some turn down an internship with a blue-chip organization so they could go home and work another year at their old (and non-career-forwarding) job. And the reason was mainly $'s. Which, in the long term, makes no sense. A career-forwarding internship (which may cost you a few thousand dollars as compared to your former job) has the ability to set you on your way to making hundreds of thousands of dollars more. Ask any professional in their thirties or forties if $5,000 more would change their lives and the answer will be "no." They wouldn't mind it, but it really is not a big factor. So, our tactics here.

1. *Make important life decisions based primarily on what moves you toward your goals instead of on cost.* As we noted above, a few thousand dollars now versus the opportunity to make much, much more later is something to remember. Think about your earning potential over time, not today's rate of pay.

2. *Prioritize experiential opportunities with career upside.* Yes, you know the term "opportunity cost." This is key to think about when you have options for practicums, internships, projects, summer jobs, work-study terms, and other work experience. Ask yourself, "Where will this lead me?" or "Could this organization hire me long term in a full-time role?" or "What are full-time salaries like in this industry and this job?" or "Which gets me to where I want to be (see Secret 1) faster?"

3. *Find a way to make things work financially in the short term.* This may sound obvious, but you don't need a fancy apartment for a summer internship or a cool car when you get your first job. Get a roommate. Stay in a cheap apartment on the subway line. Sell your car and bike to work. Do whatever it takes to get started and get the experiences you need. Money, mortgages, and stuff you "want" will come later.

MAKE A PLAN FOR RESILIENCE IN CHANGE

Michelle Pride, PhD (Embedded Psychologist, Ohio University Athletics)

After working with hundreds of college student-athletes as the embedded sport psychologist for the Ohio University Department of Athletics, I have learned that change and transition can be tough for student-athletes. Change is part of life, and in the immortal words of Sam Cooke, "change is gonna come." It's gonna come whether or not you want it to come. It's gonna come whether or not you've prepared for it to come. It's gonna come whether or not you feel like you can handle it. And change results in serious psychological consequences. At points of change and transition, people can experience increased feelings of anxiety, depression, grief, self-doubt, and worry. They can feel overwhelmed and out of control. In 1969, Elisabeth Kübler-Ross, a famous psychiatrist, identified emotional stages that people progress through when they experience change or loss: denial and isolation, anger, bargaining, depression, and acceptance.

Some people are more likely to use strategies that allow them to escape their feelings, like drinking, using drugs, or excessive video game playing. Others are more likely to use strategies that give them the illusion of control, like restricting calories or overexercising. There are some changes you can't predict, like a season- or career-ending injury. There are other changes you can predict, such as graduation or moving to a new location after college. Whether you have control over the change or not, you have some control over your response to it. Having a plan helps to respond to change with resilience and reduces the likelihood that you will rely on unhealthy coping strategies. Use the following steps to make a plan for resilience in transition:

1. *Assess your coping and self-care skills.* Review the information in the box in Secret 10 titled "Create a Mental Health Self-Care Plan" and take some time to actually create your self-care plan. Think about how you generally cope with challenge and change. Are you someone who tends to avoid/numb or confront/control? How can you use your resources to be proactive and healthy in your approach to inevitable challenge and change?

2. *Break it down.* Change often feels overwhelming and insurmountable, especially when you focus on the big picture or the end goal. However, if you break a situation down into its components and set smaller, more manageable goals, it allows for a greater sense of control and efficacy. For example, end-goal focus sounds like, "I need to get a job after graduation," while breaking it down sounds like, "I need to (1) contact the career center, (2) work on my resume and cover letter, (3) identify places I might like to apply to, and (4) reach out to contacts in the alumni network to get information on the industry." Breaking it down all of a sudden seems doable! If you are struggling with this step, reach out to someone, a friend, a teammate, a counselor, a trusted faculty member, or a coach, and ask them to help you break it down.

3. *Find your why.* Friedrich Nietzsche, a renowned philosopher, said, "He who has a why to live can bear almost any how." Figuring out why you are on a certain path can help you to stay grounded, focused, and motivated. What is your reason for following a certain path? What are your values? Priorities? Goals? What is really important to you? How is this change an opportunity to manifest your values, priorities, or goals in life? How can change help you become more skilled, knowledge-able, or experienced in a particular area? How does change help you

grow as a person? What parts of the change are interesting or exciting to you?

4. *Be mindful/present.* Anxiety occurs when you worry about things that have already happened, which you can't change, or about things that haven't yet happened that you can't do anything about. The antidote to anxiety is staying in the present. The present is where you can make change. When you start to feel yourself worrying about the things you can't change, bring yourself back to the present. Take a deep, slow breath and slowly release it. Ground yourself. Focus on five things you can see, four things you can feel, three things you can hear, two things you can smell, and one thing you can taste. Make a list of things you can do today (self-care should be on that list).

5. *Check your self-talk (if you don't, that voice in your head can be a jerk).* How do you sabotage yourself when you talk about change? Do you tell yourself that you don't do well with change? Do you tell yourself that you ALWAYS or NEVER do certain things in change situations? Do you procrastinate or engage in avoidance behaviors, hoping that the situation will just go away on its own?

   When you are stressed out, it's easy to fall into traps of all-or-nothing thinking, learned helplessness patterns, and negative self-talk. Oftentimes, you don't even realize you're doing these things until someone else points it out.

   Once you're aware of the negative thought patterns, what can you do? Try focusing on your strengths, your successes, your accomplishments. Reminding yourself that you have been successful in the past helps you feel more resilient and empowered in meeting the challenges of the future.

CHAPTER SUMMARY: ADVICE FROM TEN PEERS

We felt the best way to summarize this chapter would be to provide a Top Twelve list of advice on balance from ten peers—fellow student-athletes. We asked a large number for their input, reviewed the list closely, and selected these as the most helpful.

1. "You still have to balance your academics with your athletics because you do have obligations to your team. I get that, but ultimately, you have to stay focused on what's most important. Those three things: athletics, academics, social life. What is most important of the three is your academics. You either believe that or you don't. If you believe it, then you're going to act on it. If you don't believe it, you are going to have a really hard time getting through it. You probably won't get through it because you're not giving it the commitment that it deserves. What

happens with many young men and women is that they realize this, but not until they're maybe a Junior or Senior. At some point, the lightbulb is going to come on and it needs to come on as early as possible."—*Oliver Luck*

2.   "My first day in college, our head coach told us that there are three aspects to college when you're a student-athlete; baseball, school, and your social life, and you only really have time to be great at two of those. I tried my hardest to balance all three of those and it took dedication, time management, and a great work ethic that has transitioned well into my career. Any sustained success in life requires these traits, and seeing these things transition to success in college showed me that doing the same in my career would have similar results."—*Kevin Hurd*

3.   "It's important to figure out your daily schedule. Figure out when all of your things can take place during the week and don't procrastinate, don't push things off. Look day-by-day or look week-by-week to figure out when you have time to enjoy your friends and have fun, and know when you really need to buckle down."—*Oliver Luck*

4.   "You have to be very disciplined. That entails learning to say no. 'Sorry guys, I'd love to. Maybe I can catch up with you guys later or something. I've got three hours of studying I have to do. I got a test I have to prepare for. I got to write a paper.' The earlier that lesson can be learned, the better for a student-athlete because there are more time demands for a student-athlete than there ever were before."—*Oliver Luck*

5.   "If you can be disciplined in anything that you do—and I'll just define discipline as doing the right thing when no one is watching—when it's just you, if you can maintain that discipline and that routine, that will help serve you long term. For athletes, being disciplined, having a routine that's consistent, that will ensure a lot of success because your time management skills are going to be put into that routine. Your fitness, your training, it's going to be a part of your routine, it's a part of your schedule, it's a daily thing, it's a habit, it's a positive habit. It's a continual learning curve. For student-athletes, I would say, 'Hey, you can be disciplined and you can have a routine that includes these elements and if you're disciplined about maintaining that, you'll be successful, and you can apply that to every area of your life whether you're a player, a coach, or a professional, or whatever role you have.' The thing that is difficult is managing boundaries and managing other people's expectations, because you can't

manage their expectations. But, you can manage your own boundaries."—*Jeff Rodin*

6. "Redshirting isn't something that anyone really wants to do. Truly, it's a reality check for some and for some, it's a way to get better. It's basically a year of working out. Whether that's in the weight room, on the field, or whatever it may be; dieting; in the classroom, it's a year for you to get better. It helped me get a little stronger, get a little experience with our team and with our coaching staff and helped me fit in."—*JR Reynolds*

7. "If you are a player that gets redshirted, take advantage of it, don't shut yourself off. I've seen more kids that redshirt that waste the extra year than utilize that year. When you have a year that you can step aside from competition and focus on the process, it can sometimes be a blessing. I think you even see that with players who get injured. They are forced to focus on the process, and they come back a way better player because they are able to step back and see a different perspective on things. When you are always in competition mode, you can become very narrow minded, and you can lose sight of the process sometimes."—*Rob Smith*

8. "Social life, in my opinion, is very, very important. I don't necessarily mean like going to parties, socials, or the bars. I'm talking about getting to know your peers, whether that's on a team, in the classroom, or in your dorm. So many people come from a variety of backgrounds, different life experiences, different nationalities, everything. In college, learning about other people is vitally important for your growth, and understanding different points of views and perspectives. Being able to understand everyone's point of view, talk to people, and show a genuine interest in their background I think is extremely important particularly as it translates into sales, and interacting with people professionally. Without that experience, I would have a hard time getting into sales from the very beginning. In my opinion, having that social life is just as important as academics, as long as you can balance it, and get the grades you need to get to accomplish what you want to."—*Brooks Neal*

9. "Quite honestly, I still struggle with balance. It's easier at certain times of the year and at certain times of the season. There are certain times where that's all that you do, and you have to understand that, and the people close to you have to understand that. You'll end up spending more time with your team or with your job than you will with any other relationship. Understanding

that as a collegiate athlete, it's very different than high school sports. Being a student-athlete forces you to manage your time almost to the point where it's done for you. It can be difficult when someone transitions out of that lifestyle because you now have a lot of free time and it's not managed for you. Therefore, it's really important to have that understanding and application of time management, and when it's time to do certain things, whether it's training, studying, sleeping, you have to do it at that time. Otherwise, it's not going to get done."—*Jeff Rodin*

10.   "You have to manage your own life. There is no one to hold your hand anymore and schedule everything and map everything out for you. Understanding how to create balance in your life and recognizing that the balance amongst your various interests will change over time. A lot of athletes are very focused, driven, and goal-oriented, and that's good because they achieve their goals and they understand it takes steps to get there. There is a bigger picture sometimes that people miss out on, so how you figure out how to navigate that path is important."—*Chris Dawson*

11.   "You have to find a balance with friends. There are so many perspectives that you can gain from all the different people that you can meet on a college campus. If your career path isn't in sport, then you really have to branch out."—*Kelsey Cermak*

12.   "It is extremely important to have balance while you are in school as a student-athlete. There has to be some balance between the athletic side, preparation, getting ready for games, being successful, and being part of a team. There also has to be a balance with your academics. You've got to hit the books; you've got to make the time that you put into it count. You've got to have some level of social life too. Interactions with people are something that we all need. If they get out of balance, if any of those three things become dominant, I don't think that's going to lead you where you desire to go."—*Steve Cobb*

This chapter draws upon the experiences of the authors and the input of more than a dozen interviewees to provide some direction to student-athletes about balance and keeping your lives, objectives, and time in synch with your priorities and goals. However you read this chapter, we hope you take away from it the critical importance of balance in all you consider to how your four to five years will unfold. Seek balance. Find your balance. Be Balanced.

Secret 7 — Make Smart Decisions on the Other Stuff

THE SECRET IN A FEW WORDS

Secret 7 flows from Secret 6 but really puts the attention on the "other stuff" and not the academic and athletic elements. It is ONLY about the "stuff" outside of athletics and academics. It focuses on making smart decisions—the nonsport and nonacademic decisions that you have made or will make. This secret is straightforward and clear in its meaning: you must make smart decisions about nonsport and nonacademic matters because they will affect your success as a student and as an athlete. These decisions include anything and everything from how you use social media to how you pursue relationships, the time you spend with family or friends, your weekend behavior, your choice of transportation, and so much more.

MAKE SMART DECISIONS ON THE OTHER STUFF

The first five secrets were largely related to your athletic and academic lives: how to balance them, what to focus on, how to plan, how to develop life skills, support options, and resources. But, as was clearly described in Secret 6 (balance), these two pursuits, the primary foci of the average student-athlete, do not exist in a vacuum. Neither do you. As Secret 6 told us, your relationships, family life, friends, downtime, and so much more will all directly or indirectly influence your success as a student and as an athlete.

To shed some light on these other decisions, we reached out to Christa Mann, currently Senior Manager of Communications at Major League Soccer and a former collegiate and professional athlete, who outlined four particular areas of the "other stuff" that she would recommend any student-athlete consider.

First, she suggests seeking out a study abroad program to acquire international experience, to form a more global view of the world, to make new friends, and to facilitate nontraditional learning. She described her overseas experience as hugely important to her future career success and said this about her supportive coach: "If I could give anyone advice, it would be to find a coach who believes in you as an athlete but more so believes in what your dreams are away from the field."

Mann further emphasized how she was able to maintain her athletic fitness and readiness while taking advantage of her time abroad. "When I studied abroad, I went to Spain. I lived with a host family. After school I would run to the park and play pick up soccer and then run home. I still did my fitness every day, I still got a lot of touches on the ball."

In short, with a bit of effort, you can maintain your athletic preparedness while achieving some of the "other stuff" needed for success after college. "For me it was like striking that balance getting the study abroad experience traveling the world but also realizing that soccer was a major component in my life."

Second, Mann discussed the importance of building professional relationships. This advice builds on what we provided in Secret 6 about personal relationships. A key aspect of her advice to student-athletes was to take on leadership positions in college, such as joining a student club. She remembered: "I found myself in leadership roles during my junior year where I had to be the stand-up person, [so] I can't make mistakes or I can't be in the wrong places at the wrong time." She emphasized the importance of these leadership traits later in life.

So, find opportunities to build these skills and lead.

Third, she advised student-athletes to "make tons of friends. I think everyone should date, and understand the type of person they are and the type of person they'd like to be with." Mann told the story of a contact from a previous job who had "recommended two other women who were moving into the city who didn't know anyone either but were friends. The three of us live together now and we have a blast."

Finally, she discussed the tool of social media as a key "other stuff" component for student-athletes to consider. She suggested that "when it comes to social media, you should just be a part of the right conversation about social media. It's an opportunity to build your brand, to build who you are, to show your ambition, to show your preparation, and potentially get you where you want to go." When asked to explain, she noted that, in today's age, "your first impression to anyone is always going to be on social media . . . [which is an opportunity] to show you can be a student-athlete and this is what the life of a student-athlete is like."

Let's take a minute here and further discuss how you can use social media and how to be smart with it. We reached out to a few recent student-athletes to get some support for our points. Importantly, social media is not all positive. In fact, there is a high level of risk if you post inappropriate content or items that could be viewed negatively by your school, your coach, or your sponsor. Kelsey Cermak, a former student-athlete at Iowa University and now Assistant Director of Championships and Alliances at the NCAA, advised that "you have to be careful and not take any [compromising] pictures because you are under a microscope as a student-athlete."

We won't say don't post any photos or graphics but we would strongly suggest you think carefully about each photo before you click "send." Avoid overly intimate photos, avoid ones of you drinking or partying or looking out of control.

Hallie Olson, a former student-athlete and now Director of Notre Dame Global Partnerships, recommended, "You need to keep everything clean. You need to not have any beers, or anything incriminating on your feed or on Facebook. I would stay private on all of my social media channels like Instagram and Twitter."

Another key point with social media (like any communication efforts) is to consider who your specific target market is for each and every communication you send regardless of channel. Olson said she "would recommend that you know your audience, and know future employers are looking at your social media channels. Nobody wants to see you in front of a beer pyramid or saying anything controversial. Those things need to be private and it's really tough, but it needs to happen."

Matt Engleka, a former student-athlete at Ohio University and owner of LEJ Agency, provided this important advice:

> Now [today], as an athlete, you are living in such a fishbowl that people are looking to capture an athlete out of character and that's something extremely difficult to deal with when you're nineteen years of age. When Bryce Harper was growing up, the one thing he always did was carry a water bottle everywhere he went out in public. Why? Nobody can put anything else in your hand at that time. There's no question about what he was drinking. It's a bottle of water. The second you've got something else in your hand, someone is going to take a picture of it and then it's all over the place.

RYAN SOLLAZZO

(Senior Director, Global Corporate Partnerships at Major League Baseball)

I think people, nowadays, coming out of college need to be very careful and very sensitive with technology. I don't have any social media, but people in our world do look at that stuff and you need to be smart with what's out there. You have to understand that a lot can be taken out of context whether it is social media or emails, and sometimes it's best to just pick up the phone and actually talk to people.

Dan Butterly, Commissioner of the Big West Conference, pushed for a strong emphasis on "networking" as a key priority for student-athletes. He recommended that you identify whether networking is an area of weakness early on and if so, fix it. As an athlete and a student, you have social networks established around you by the university, and as people seek you out to support you (especially as an athlete) there is visibility benefit.

We asked Butterly to give some advice if you are in this situation. He said:

> If you're introverted, you have to associate with people who are, maybe, in your same career field or go to a speaker's series where you can learn more and meet people that are in your same wheelhouse. Challenge yourself to completely go out of your comfort level because that's the type of job that you're going to go into. That's the type of situation you are going to place yourself into.
>
> If you're introverted, you're not going to go into a development position or a sales position. It's going to be very difficult and very challenging for you in that career. There are other ways for you to network, though, with like-minded people who are going to be in your career field.
>
> Extroverts, obviously, have a lot easier time going to a mixer or going to a function that's not necessarily in their wheelhouse, but they just like meeting people. They like being out and about and having a drink and getting to know people. You just have to try and associate yourself with people that are going to be in your career path and get in a comfort zone and establish key relationships as best you can.

This is very important advice from a seasoned senior leader in collegiate sports in the United States. We recommend you follow it.

In addition to the four areas outlined by Mann and the point made by Butterly, you need to know about a few other decisions related to "other stuff" that a student-athlete needs to be ready for. We'll try to be very tactical here . . . to clearly illustrate how you need to consider each and every decision and how you need to really protect your time, as your primary resource.

1. *Work part-time or not?* This is often a very difficult decision but shouldn't be. Obviously, there may be cases where a student-athlete needs the money to make ends meet, but normally working part-time would be to earn extra cash for nonessential things. So, if possible, try to decline to work part-time. The answer is "no." Sure, it will cost you a few amenities, but as we outlined in Secret 6, the amount you would be likely to earn will have very little impact on your life down the road.

2. *Join a student club or not?* This decision is more difficult, as there are considerable potential upsides to joining the right student club at the right time. A key point is looking at the decision from a career perspective. Not all student clubs are created equal. Some are for fun and enjoyment, while others provide true networking, learning, and skill development for a career. For example, joining and spending time on the "analytics club" would make a great line on a math major's resume, provide beneficial learning opportunities, and probably catch a recruiter's attention.

3. *Do an extra concentration (major, minor, etc.)?* This is something to talk about with your advisor, but we highly recommend it . . . provided the major, minor, or concentration will really help your hoped-for career. So, if you're studying chemistry, a minor in religion may not add great value. Or, maybe it will. We suggest taking classes of high interest to you but be cognizant of your goals. Something that will help you get a job, advanced degree, or fellowship. From our experience, and you might find this surprising, when students take a set of more challenging courses within a specialization they are passionate about and plan to make their career in, they do better (in terms of both grades and enjoyment) than by taking a series of electives that they don't really care about but pick because they seem "easy." Yes, you are better off building your resume than cherry-picking easy electives.

4. *Go on a date?* Here's a very tactical decision that you should take seriously. Dating is often stressful, takes time, and costs money. Many student-athletes see it as part of their heightened visibility that people may want to date them just for being an athlete. Skip dating if you have no interest or feel it will place you in an awkward setting. Don't go because you think it is expected of you and especially if you have no interest in the person or in dating in general (see Secret 6). Dating is not all bad, but dating

someone on a regular basis creates obligations and brings a wide range of emotional highs and lows that you must manage.

5.   *Take a leadership role with a student organization or even with your sport team?* This is a very difficult decision and one where we would advise you to proceed with caution, serious caution. There is a significant career upside (including leadership experience to list on your resume and a chance to lead groups and test your own strategic approaches), but there is a huge risk of overcommitting your time, especially if you become captain of your own sport team where you are already highly implicated. One of the authors took the role as captain of the swim team in her final year of competition and had her most disappointing year athletically but gained the benefit of being a team captain, which helped multiple times later on. At least five times in job interviews, the topic of having been captain of a university swim team came up in a positive way from the interviewers.

6.   *Go to a party, event, luncheon, or meeting?* Much like going on that date, you need to critically review these decisions and opt out unless the benefit is clear and you want to attend and fully participate. Financial advisor Warren Buffet is famous for saying "when you're in the room, be in the room." What this means is that if you plan to go to a class, talk, or any event because you "should be there" but expect to sit at the back, not pay attention, not get involved, or play on your phone or check emails, then do NOT go. Either leverage the opportunity to the max or skip it. Simple.

7.   *Hang out in the lounge/living room and watch television?* Oh, it seems so appealing. Long day, tons of homework ahead, friends, and a comfy couch. But that couch will suck you in and you'll miss your studying, your workout, your important call home, or you'll delay them all and lose sleep, damage your health, and impair your performance the next day. The tactic here is quite simple but hard to do. Use the "lounge time" as a carrot. Once you finish your work, get your exercise in, and do your key personal stuff, reward yourself with some relaxing time.

8.   *Who should be my close friends?* As generally noted in Secret 6, this is a challenging decision as well. UNC Coach Anson Dorrance gave some great advice based on what he sees with his women's soccer team at North Carolina. He noted that "it is absolutely critical student-athletes develop close relationships with people around them and make sure the people they pick

are positive. The cliché we use and share with the girls we train is you are basically with the six people that you will hang out with the most. So choose wisely. Hopefully you have chosen people who have academic ambitions because if you have them in your circle of friends, you are ultimately going to have academic ambitions."

9. *Should I go to class?* The famous question, and the answer is very clear—Yes. Without exception. Not only will it help you pass, get a higher GPA, and improve learning, but it will show your professors and your classmates (all of whom become important allies in your career down the road) that you are trustworthy, focused, serious, and someone they may want to hire one day. Put class in your schedule and stick with it. No exceptions.

OLIVER LUCK

(Former Executive Vice President of Regulatory Affairs at the NCAA)

Go to class and take notes. If you go to class and if you take notes, you will pass. Think of class the way you think of practice. You wouldn't think of missing practice. Coach would be all over you, and you would probably get demoted. No athlete thinks of missing practice; so, take class the same way and when you're in class, take notes. Take down what the professor is talking about. You are spending the time in class, so you might as well be productive and benefit from it. The sooner you learn that, the better off you're going to be.

---

10. *Who should be the people I hang out with?* This piece of advice is similar to #8 above but different in certain respects. This is more about "association"—your choice of the people you associate with, and whose character or image might come to be associated with you. Are you known to hang out with fellow students in your program who are not athletes or do you avoid nonathletes? Are your friends on the team academically serious or are they partiers? Again, think it through. What clubs are you in? Think of the perceptual difference from being in the "analytics club" or the "accounting society" versus a "beer drinking club." People notice, and it affects your image. Serious athlete. Focused student. That's the brand you want. That is what you want people to think about when they think of you.

We could go on and on with this list but we're pretty certain you get the point. Every activity is a decision. Make each decision wisely and selfishly.

CHAPTER SUMMARY

Making smart decisions on the "other stuff" will not only help you during your student-athlete experience, it will create good decision-making skills and a sound foundation for later in life. We all make decisions every day on hundreds of things (whether you think about it or not), and by making smart decisions on a continual basis, we train ourselves to make prepared, quality decisions.

You won't make the right decision every time, but as long as you can make smart and prepared decisions, you will finish the journey well off.

Everyone makes mistakes in life (we are human, after all), but make the smart decisions at the right time by just taking an extra minute to think about "the other stuff."

Secret 8

Seek Support Everywhere

THE SECRET IN A FEW WORDS

There are a lot of examples in the world where one needs to find out how to do something hard and goes to a friend for advice. And in many instances, help and support can be just the start to a lifelong relationship. Life, of course, isn't always easy or simple, but there are many people around you who are actually paid to provide advice or facilitate solutions to challenges NCAA student-athletes face during their time in college. So here's the secret: Find those people and cultivate them as resources for the times when you aren't sure how to fix a difficult or stressful situation. Said another way: start building a network of "friends" (as soon as you can) who want to help you succeed.

SEEK SUPPORT EVERYWHERE

This secret draws particularly from a few of the specific aspects/tactics noted in Secret 4 about the success wheel (for example, time management, using resources, networking, mentors, etc.). Dr. Kevin Hall, a former student-athlete who is now a Doctor of Physical Therapy at the Mayo Clinic, outlines his experiences with this secret in the following passage.

KEVIN HALL

**(former student-athlete at Wichita State University,
now Doctor of Physical Therapy at the Mayo Clinic)**

The biggest lesson I learned in those five years [of college] was that people are your greatest resource. College sports programs are designed with an immense amount of personnel dedicated to helping the athlete succeed on and off the playing field. Coaches, trainers, academic advisors, teammates, even the people who check on class attendance—all played a role in my success.

I spent hours talking with advisors to create a class schedule that allowed me to finish the credits I needed for school while ensuring I made it to practice and games. I utilized study hall rooms for quiet places before tests and to print out study materials. And I sought out advice of coaches, teammates, and family when I struggled to find balance in my career.

Most importantly, what I did was create relationships. Relationships that helped me shape my game, opened up job opportunities, and made me appreciate the many resources I had. Letters of recommendation don't write themselves, and I was fortunate to have the endorsement of faculty and medical professionals because of relationships I forged years prior.

My former coach, Gene Stephenson, used to say: "You're only spoiled if you've been given a lot and you don't take care of it." While he was referring to our program's reputation, the same can be said for using the resources at hand.

To realize great dreams or goals, one must always have a solid support system and the intelligence to utilize the resources around them.

As high-performance, competitive athletes, the Hawaiian expression "Mo' bettah" makes a lot of sense. I want more of the good thing. Coaches and business leaders sometimes express the same sentiment by saying, "We need to get better faster than our competitors."

But what does that expression really mean? The two key words in the sentence seem to be racing toward a collision like a linebacker and a running back hitting the line of scrimmage at the same time. Or two field hockey players racing to control a ball in the midfield. We're destined to see a moment of "better" and "faster" beating "okay and slower."

The concept certainly fits the lines from the Bob Dylan song quoted above where you face a dilemma and we just want to say to someone, "Tell me quick 'cause I gotta run." But whom should you ask and what should you be asking them? More importantly, will they be "invested" in you enough to immediately start helping you get stronger, smarter, and more successful?

By this point, most of you who are NCAA student-athletes reading this book have settled into a routine of understanding the main players in your intercollegiate life. You have a head coach, a position coach, the head athletic trainer, a strength coach, teachers, and possibly the resident advisor on your dorm floor or the individual responsible for your housing (owner, landlord, property manager). These people are the primary folks issuing orders that you feel obligated to follow.

Coaches and trainers want certain physical achievements. Learn the playbook. Make this move here. Develop these muscles. Rehab this nagging injury. Work harder at your game.

Meanwhile, teachers want papers written or group projects finished. They hint about midterms, pop quizzes, and finals. Work harder at your books. Back at your "crib," there are rules about noise, trash, and parking. "Y'all better keep it down up there or we're going to call the cops."

In each of the above instances, someone is setting rules or establishing guidelines leaving little for interpretation. When Coach calls for a sixty-yard run, it doesn't do much good to think about negotiating the distance or the speed.

What this means is that many student-athletes get into the habit of expecting someone else to tell them what to do. There is always someone to set rules, create the culture, and dictate all of your actions.

For many, the number of people the student-athlete trusts for solving problems is a very small circle. In their sport it may be a veteran (or smarter) teammate. At school it may be a classmate or tutor.

This limits how a student-athlete thinks about problem solving (which is one of the most important traits that employers look for in hiring new employees). In fact, one interviewer we know is famous in job interviews for asking a hypothetical question for which there is no right answer. One of his questions runs along these lines: You are sitting in a rowboat in the middle of the Pacific Ocean right over the famous Marianas Trench. You drop a cannonball over the edge of the boat. How long will it take for the cannonball to reach the bottom?

For many of us, the question is just stupid and our first response is, "How the heck should I know?" But there are clues in the question that can allow someone used to solving problems to create an answer. Some of the ways in which someone might respond could include:

- Well, it would be good to know how much the cannonball weighs and whether the water temperature matters (wanting more facts)

- Well, if the trench is famous, it must be pretty deep, so I'll guess that it's at least five miles deep (showing some knowledge and a willingness to make some assumptions)

- Was there a reason I was dropping cannonballs in the middle of the ocean? (trying to determine what the interviewer is really seeking)

- I don't want to guess at something without the facts, so let me ask you if I can give that answer to you later today (buying time to find a solution)

- I can't give you that answer right now without more facts, but I can solve this problem by contacting one of my science professors (I'm a problem solver who gets things done)

What the interviewer is looking for is how a candidate starts to reason out a solution. What the student-athlete can do is create the perception (even without knowing anything about the Pacific Ocean or Newtonian physics influencing the laws of gravity in liquid) that they are up to the challenge and have resources available to them for problem solving.

But where would you start if you got asked that interview question? You'd be pretty certain none of your teammates know anything about dropping cannonballs in some faraway ocean. You certainly wouldn't want to ask your coach, English professor, or landlord. They'd give you that funny look and suggest you need to get your priorities straight.

Right. But this is where your support network comes in. This is when you know there are people who can help right away.

In many cases like this, there are a variety of stumbling blocks, depending on whom in your support network you ask. Some of your "network" resources might respond like this:

- I dunno, dude, that's a pretty stupid question (True meaning: I can't help)

- You should look that up on Google or Wikipedia (True meaning: Here's a clue but I can't give you more than that and you're on your own to solve the problem)

- Go ask _____, they're really good with weird stuff like that (True meaning: Let me deflect helping you and get you to work with someone else who may or may not have time for you)

- Go ask at the library. That's why they're there (True meaning: Let me deflect helping you but point you toward a support staff that doesn't know you)

- I'd like to help you but you need to come back during office hours (True meaning: I can't help you now and if I'm lucky you'll go to someone else to solve the problem)

Like the cannonball scenario above, there are other matters that might elicit the same responses.

- Who can help me create a good resume?

- Where do I go to try to get an internship during our out-of-season training window?

- Who can help me pick out the right interview outfit?

- I'm feeling really down about the amount of playing time I'm getting and my "significant other" seems mad at me.

- I wonder if I'm eating enough (or too much) or getting the right amount of sleep?

- I've had a death in the family and I feel really messed up about it

- I'm falling behind with my schoolwork and if it gets worse, it will affect my eligibility (or scholarship)
- How do I get my finances under control so I can afford stuff?
- How do I get a job I'll like when I graduate?
- How do I get a job in my field when I graduate?
- How do I make more time to get involved with nonathletics activities?
- Should I think about going to grad school right away or work for a few years?
- How do I get a job?

These are only a few of the questions a student-athlete might ask during four or five years at an NCAA institution, and the inability to get the right support can have crippling ramifications not only for enjoyment of one's sport but also for lifelong success. Additionally, small matters often become big ones or cause other small matters to multiply.

It reminds us of the legendary English proverb, possibly a reference to King Richard's defeat in battle in 1485:

> For want of a nail the shoe was lost.
> For want of a shoe the horse was lost.
> For want of a horse the rider was lost.
> For want of a rider the message was lost.
> For want of a message the battle was lost.
> For want of a battle the kingdom was lost.
> And all for the want of a horseshoe nail.

In the story above (which William Shakespeare alluded to a hundred years later in his play *Richard III*), the loss of the smallest item (the horseshoe nail that fitted the shoe to the horse's hoof) caused all kinds of mayhem including the loss of the rider, message, battle, and kingdom.

You may not think your postcollegiate career is as important as a kingdom, but the reality is that little losses (no bigger than a nail) can cause things to unravel and ultimately create situations far worse than you ever imagined. The kingdom you imagined for yourself when you were heavily recruited to play at your current university could possibly be slipping away as you realize you won't be starting this year and certainly won't be turning pro.

Said another way: getting advice about how to address the missing nail (or even larger matters) is really important—and a key skill set to develop on your own.

So what to do? In the movie *Ghostbusters* (and we're talking about the original one from 1984), the famous phrase was, "Who ya gonna call?" And the shouted response was "Ghostbusters!"

On the TV show *Who Wants to Be a Millionaire*, the contestants almost always reach a question for which they need help and can use one of their "lifelines," which have included "50/50" (the computer eliminates two of the three wrong answers), "Ask the Audience," or "Phone a Friend."

Brett Fischer, physical therapist for the Arizona Cardinals, suggested alumni are one of the options for that phone call.

> For student-athletes, there are so many alumni to take advantage of. Athletes have an opportunity to get to know them, and find out what made them successful. Some may have played sports when they were in school, some may have not. Regardless, they're successful. I think a lot of the athletes think their sport is never going to end. I don't care who these people are. They are just fans. They're just alumni.
>
> Well, they're successful alumni and they got there somehow. It's important for the college athlete to look at those people as positive resources for advice, for wisdom, for internships, everything. They're a great resource. It's something in college you've got to take advantage of.

In these examples above, there was a ready resource. Got a house with ghosts? Call these guys! Can't remember whether helium is heavier than oxygen? Call a friend. But which friend? And what is the college equivalent? Know of an alum who is really connected? Pick up the phone.

At most schools, the following people are probably a great place to start:

- An administrative mentor you've developed (possibly the associate athletic director for your sport) or a graduate assistant who played your sport and is spending one or two years assisting your team while getting an advanced degree

- The senior academic support staff individual (often connected to the Provost's office) who is responsible for selecting tutors for the Athletic Learning Community

- The Faculty Athletic Representative (FAR), who traditionally serves as the link between the university's faculty and all student-athletes and is also usually involved with your school's athletic conference and the NCAA

- The career counselor your athletic department may have established for helping student-athletes with matters involving post-collegiate careers; this individual often creates career fairs for athletes, brings in motivational or inspirational speakers, and sometimes is involved with the Student Athlete Advisory Committee (SAAC)

- The career counselor or internship coordinator in your specific college (not in the athletic department), if your university has different schools like business, education, music, etc.

- Your faculty advisor

- The leadership council for your SAAC (which generally requires one representative from each sport played at your school), consisting of fellow students recognized by their peers as leaders, who generally meet weekly or biweekly to discuss matters involving student-athletes like yourself—and like you, they are dealing with time demands placed on them by coaches and teachers

- Your Athletic Director

- The Chancellor or President of your university or college

At this point, having read the list above, many of you might be thinking, "As if I could just call up the university president or the athletic director and ask them a question. The people who wrote this book are so out of touch."

For us, this is the *gotcha* moment because we seriously believe you can reach out to people that you believe are *waaaay* beyond caring about your success. And we think you'll be surprised to find how many of those top executives or distant "adults" really do enjoy helping college students solve problems. In fact, one of the reasons they chose to work in higher education instead of on Wall Street or Main Street was because they truly enjoy the educational imperative of helping and serving others.

The secret here is finding people near you who really do care about your success . . . people who enjoy helping others.

Former student-athlete and now account manager at International Speed Corporation John Nowicki describes how he used relationships directly related to his status as a student-athlete to, first, gain internships and then to help him launch his career.

JOHN NOWICKI

(former lacrosse student-athlete, now Senior Manager, Partnerships at Oakland Athletics)

The one relationship that stands out to me was a university professor, who also served as a consultant for the University of Detroit Mercy (UDM) athletic department and the Miami University athletic department. Over the course of four years as a student-athlete at UDM, I developed a strong relationship with this professor by meeting with him regularly to discuss coursework, athletic performance, and post-college plans.

During the early part of my senior year, I received an offer to visit Miami University with him to interview for a summerlong internship within their athletic department. Over the course of my internship, I took advantage of every opportunity to meet with staff members from different departments, coaches, and administrators. Through this process, I developed two crucial relationships with staff members with the hockey program and on the university development staff, which led to my next two career moves—the Central Collegiate Hockey Association (CCHA) and Ohio University's Sports Administration Program.

The staff members with the hockey program assisted me with an introduction to administrators at the league office, the CCHA, which was based back in Michigan near my home. The staff members with the university development staff introduced me to the idea of getting my MBA and master's in sports administration at Ohio University, which has a strong reputation for launching the career of sports business professionals across a variety of disciplines in sales, marketing, communication, and management.

Through the process of completing the internship with the CCHA and attending Ohio University, I was able to apply similar relationship-based networking practices in the sports business, ultimately leading to my acceptance of a full-time role in the industry. The common theme through each of those roles was taking full advantage of the relationships that surrounded me while I was in each organization, which ultimately would lead to my next opportunity.

For all the student-athletes out there, my challenge to you is reflect upon the relationships currently surrounding you. Coaching staffs, athletic department members, university professors and staffs, and teammates' families, that may be able to provide the introduction that launches your career.

The questions for you are: Do you know who the right people to call are, and are you spending enough time thinking about what your full potential is? Student-athletes who hope to turn professional in their sport always know that "full potential" means getting drafted, signing a contract, and making a pro team (or making the cut on the pro tour). But for you, one of the other 99 percent who don't know what might happen after your college sports days are finished, "full potential" could mean almost anything.

Or think of it this way: Some people are good at sports or talking in public or answering questions in class. That's fine. You can be good at all of that, but you need to be one of those people who gets really good at asking for the right help at the right time.

HILLARY NELSON

**(former softball student-athlete at Arizona State University,
now Trainer at Positive Coaching Alliance)**

I think that your support network is crucial. The first day on campus, I introduced myself to my academic counselor and I let her know that I wanted to be an Academic All-American. That was number one, and number two was I needed a calculus tutor. Math was not my strong suit, but I knew I needed help and I knew I was going to have to take calculus in order to get my business degree. The best advice I ever got was to never be afraid to ask for help. There are so many opportunities out there, and we have to encourage those athletes to take advantage of the opportunities.

Don't forget to give yourself credit for the hard work you put in to get this far. There were late nights or early mornings that I missed school dances or I spent Friday nights at the ballpark instead of the movies with my friends. I had sunburns and scars, whatever it was in my career, I earned those. I have to remind myself that I earned this opportunity because it can be easy when you get to a big campus to be intimidated. You're not the big man on campus anymore. As a student-athlete, be grateful and enjoy it and understand that you're there for a reason. They recruited you there for a reason, and they need you to keep working hard and to sustain that excellence that you've shown up to this point. You can't just show up anymore. That's not what got you there. You got to keep running the same pace and keep fighting for your goals.

I really got involved in my college. For example, they had a writing center where you could meet with a writing tutor and they would give you corrections on your paper. All of that makes you work because you have to set your own deadlines before the actual deadline so you have time to get in there and make another revision and go back for a second revision. Secondly, team trainers were extremely important to utilize. Having an understanding that you're putting your body through a lot more than you're probably used to coming out of high school is important. Go the extra mile or get up the extra hour to stretch or do rehab or whatever you need to do to make sure your body is maintaining the optimal efficiency.

I think our boosters are underutilized by student-athletes. They're there because they want you to be successful. They're there because they care about your program. They care about you. They're cheering you on every game. They're following you. Talk to them. They're successful human beings. They all have a story. They all have a job. That was a great resource for me when I was a student-athlete.

Administrators on campus. Those people are there for your success. They really dedicated their professional careers to helping you live the best four years of your life.

Your professors are a big part of your support network, especially those teaching subjects that directly relate to your major. If they've been doing it for a while, hopefully they know a lot of successful people in the industry you're hoping to work for. Ask them for ideas. Ask them for contacts. Don't be afraid to walk up and introduce yourself on the first day of school because you want to have that first positive interaction before you have to go to them with a missed class letter or problem or a conflict down the road.

CHAPTER SUMMARY

You may not think "Seeking Support Everywhere" is much of a secret, but our collective years on college campuses have shown us that too few student-athletes actually ever master the system of solving problems and *getting better faster than their competitors* (which includes everyone around them who wants or needs to get a job when they graduate). No question, there are a lot of people on your campus and a lot of students with problems to solve.

So let's repeat that concept: Getting a job after graduation means that you are in competition with just about everyone on your campus who has the same challenge. Ending up with a successful outcome is a function, then, of the following:

- Knowing whom to ask for help (where to find them, how to get to them)
- Knowing what to ask and how to ask it
- Building a large network of "friends" and support staff who actually find great enjoyment in seeing you achieve long-term success
- Understanding that attention to the little details (the horseshoe nails) is really important to the big picture.
- Remembering that postcompetition career success is not a sudden thing. It is a developed thing

As management expert Malcolm Gladwell wrote in his book *Outliers,* no one makes it "big" on their own. Everyone needs help and those who learn whom to ask for guidance and assistance and how to ask for those things end up receiving advantages that lead to their individual success.

Start working now on getting "mo' bettah."

Secret 9 Your Major Really Matters

MATTIE WHITE

**(Deputy Director of Athletics and Senior Woman Administrator
at Indiana University Bloomington)**

You should major in something where you can develop a set of transferrable skills for taking into any career. Your career may not have to do with your major right away or five years down the road, but you want to develop transferrable skills that can apply to any career.

The three keys to picking your major are:

1. Determine what you are passionate about. If you do what you love, the money or fame will come. You will likely be more successful if you are passionate about your work.

2. Evaluate your skill set and know where your strengths really are. Know what you are good at and what you can improve at.

3. Trust the process. Picking the major is just the first step. There is a lot of hard work to follow, and you just have to stick with it.

Keep this in mind as you read this chapter: "High school prepares you for college and college prepares you for life."

THE SECRET IN A FEW WORDS

For many student-athletes who have never thought about anything more than playing their sport, the concept of getting a job when they "grow up" is pretty daunting. There's an inner voice that says adults have jobs but college students have fun. While we won't dispute that perception, the academic major that you pick plays a huge role in how you think about yourself and what you think you'll do after your playing days end. Pick the wrong major and you might not have very many choices for jobs. If you are indifferent about your future, you might end up lost for some period of time. So, like it or not, your major and your post-collegiate aspirations define you and will likely shape your future.

YOUR MAJOR REALLY MATTERS

Every university and college is different . . . just as every student-athlete is different. But strangely enough, there are a number of similarities with both groups. Every university or college is intent on providing its student-athletes with degrees (from any number of majors), and all student-athletes who imagine graduating see themselves strolling across a stage . . . and receiving a diploma stating they have developed some level of knowledge in a particular topic area.

For movie buffs, the most famous graduate in cinema history may be the Scarecrow in *The Wizard of Oz,* who, after the Wizard gives him a diploma, is suddenly "intelligent" and begins spouting a geometry equation. Before handing the Scarecrow his diploma, the Great Oz declaims that every living creature has a brain but people who graduate from college can actually think deep thoughts.

Perhaps the Wizard was right. Perhaps if student-athletes earn degrees and walk across various stages, they will be able to construct thoughts and utilize a highly developed sense of reason for solving complex problems. But . . . and this is a big but . . . will they be able to get a job they want?

So let's back up and talk to a career counselor who works with student-athletes every day.

Mark Trumbo is the Assistant Athletics Director for Student-Athlete Engagement at Syracuse University. He recently reflected that students have long been asked the question "What do you want to major in?"

He believes that might be the wrong question to ask those student-athletes, because now more than ever, students want to feel a part of something bigger than themselves. They want to connect more with an organization's mission, ideals, and culture.

"Identifying a major shouldn't be a mindless activity of comparing features and benefits," says Trumbo. "A student-athlete's passion and skills, put together, will provide a guide to answering the bigger question . . . which is . . . what problem do I want to solve?"

Trumbo's belief is grounded in the conviction that student-athletes' first class in college should be figuring out their career.

"For too long, students have been trained mentally to believe the point of college is to do well in college," says Trumbo. "This, frankly, is a detrimental mindset for any student. Changing or choosing a major that is the path of least resistance for your respective sport cheapens the value of an education. The process, to me, needs to work in reverse. What cause do I want to fight for? Where can I build a legacy that impacts human lives? Is there a problem where I can be part of the solution?"

How does Trumbo sum it up? He says student-athletes have to identify their passion and develop the necessary skills to work in that field. Then they need to find the educational platform that checks those boxes and leads them to like-minded employers.

Put another way, we think a student-athlete's selection of a major plays a huge role in how employers see a recently graduated student-athlete. And not only do employers study potential new hires but they bring certain perceptions with them.

All of us know there is bias in the world and it comes in many different forms. Some schools are thought to be better than other schools. Some revenue sports are thought of as more important than nonrevenue ones. Some cities are considered cooler than their country cousins. The list goes on.

You will be able to fill in hundreds of other ways that people create bias (both good and bad), but the one category you want to consider (and this is both hard to imagine as a freshman . . . and hard to handle as an abstract concept) is the perceptions of employers.

Think of it this way: for you to get a job, someone has to hire you. And that person doing the hiring is going to call on a number of considerations to calculate risk (in hiring you). Here are a few of the things employers and human resource personnel might review:

- The university or college you attended

- Your major (your primary area of study)

- Your GPA (if you provide it)

- The sport you played

- The success you had while playing (that is, did you go to a bowl game or Final Four, become an NCAA All-American, earn all-conference accolades, make the all-academic team?)

- Your region of the country you are from or country of origin

- Whether you know anyone at that company (particularly any senior executives)

- Your personality and how you dress (if they see you in person)

- Your social network habits (as available to them by way of casual or in-depth research of what you have revealed on social networks)

- Your references

For only a few of the above items . . . at this point . . . can you personally control the answer. Perhaps the most important one is your major and the second is your GPA . . . which does not have to be revealed.

The words you choose or the phrases your university uses to define your primary area of study—your degree and your major—are interesting. There are the "mythical" inscriptions that will be written on your diploma. For example, the diploma language, written in some fancy calligraphy, might indicate bachelor of science, public communications. But what you might say in a verbal interview is that you were a broadcast journalism major with a minor in finance. The parchment your parents get framed might simply say "Engineering," where you would fill in a bit more of the story by saying you majored in civil engineering with a focus on structural design.

You get the point. What you say about what you studied is important.

This handful of words, the expression of your accomplishment, the description of how you spent the majority of your academic time . . . are significant and will undoubtedly shape an interviewer's perceptions. And—BIAS ALERT—some majors or collections of words sound more impressive to certain employers than others.

When you start at your university or college, you might not think much about it because much of your youthful energy will go into impressing a coaching staff and earning the maximum amount of playing time possible. Those coaches study you (in one way or another) every day at practice and during games. Your "diploma" with them (think of it as your varsity letter) is shaped by a variety of optics and measurements:

- Are you punctual for meetings and practices?
- Are you committed to team and voluntary workouts?
- Are you respected by your teammates?
- Do you produce the expected competition results under pressure?
- Are you reliable and consistent?
- Do you cause headaches, issues, or problems?
- Are you a positive influence on others?
- Are you a winner?

Each day, those observations get made and often by the same people. In fact, most athletes get graded on a game-by-game basis and the results are often shared around well before the next game.

But on the academic side of the ledger, there is very limited daily grading because classes and faculty continually change, and even within a lecture hall, it is rare that a professor studies a student with the same intensity as a coach. Faculty members want all of their students to do well, but there is no scoreboard at the end of each class. In many cases, it's just meaningful material presented and notes taken. In some classes there will be discussion, but the professor may remain indifferent to whether you participate or beneficially influence others.

What this means is that after four or five years of careful scrutiny by your sport coaches, teammates, athletic trainers, strength coaches, and the local (or national) media, you may find that, beyond end-of-term grades, there was very little accounting done by your professors and instructors about you, the soon-to-be professional. Yes, they measured you with grades, but then they moved on to the next class. You were left with a GPA, some knowledge, and, for many, a gnawing sensation (maybe a growling) in your stomach that what you learned may not help you get the job you think you want.

Selecting a major or articulating your career aspirations is really important. And choosing a major that really interests you is far more important than grabbing an easy major.

Let's say that again: *choosing a major that really interests you is far more important than grabbing an easy major.* And you know that if we placed it in italics and then made it boldface, it must be important.

So let's make this chapter operational for you.

1. Make sure you have a target (your major) that might lead to a job you could want. For most athletes, sport is a passion, so don't rule out a career where sport is the business or a big part of the business. And don't rule out interests in music, movies, advertising, special events, marketing, video gaming, animals, and many other areas that can also lend themselves to a career. Work doesn't have to be a drag.

2. Make sure the major you pick is something that really interests you (not your parents, coach, or academic support staff). You are the one who will have to go to work after you graduate.

3. Make sure that if it's too late to change your major, you start aggressively determining if you can add a minor that you really like . . . or what the job opportunities are for people graduating with your major. Many people say it's never too late . . . but sometimes it is . . . for one thing. But not for another.

4. Go to every career fair your athletic department or university offers. Go meet with people who actually have jobs available and are looking for future employees. They can tell you what they are looking for. In addition, don't be afraid to talk to professionals in your athletic department and any of the sport organizations that support them (such as broadcasting companies, sports marketing agencies, legal firms, health care suppliers, equipment manufacturers).

5. While many people don't want to stay in school any longer than possible, understand that if you can achieve at least a 3.0 GPA as an undergraduate, you can keep the door open for going back to graduate school and majoring in a subject area you might really like.

6. Use the academic resources available to you before or after practice (your academic support staff and life skills coordinator) and within your college or current major to get known by the faculty and emerge as someone others want to help.

At the end of the day, your major and your grades will help you get into graduate school if that is part of your plan. We say this because a 2015 NCAA study (see the chart below) indicates that a high percentage of student-athletes think about going to graduate school after they are done competing. A 2020 Gallup NCAA[1] study reports that 39 percent of NCAA student-athletes pursue an advanced degree (as compared to 32 percent of all students). Stop and think, because although you may not consider this as an option right after college, you may reconsider a couple of years down the road. And let's face it, just being a student-athlete isn't going to get you into graduate school.

It is at least somewhat likely that I will go to graduate school at some point after college

Baseball	Men's Basketball	Football FBS|FCS		Men's Other	Women's Basketball	Women's Other
Division I						
54%	54%	61%	57%	59%	72%	73%
Division II						
55%	56%	62%		62%	70%	72%
Division III						
54%	63%	58%		65%	76%	75%

NCAA Research. (January 2016). *Results from the 2015 GOALS Study of the Student-Athlete Experience.* Retrieved on May 22, 2017.[2]

Based on the collective experiences of the authors, the last point in the list of six recommendations is—we believe—particularly important. Researchers have frequently commented that many of the most successful people were the ones who created meaningful relationships with a few key faculty members. Sometimes those experiences took place right after class and sometimes they happened during office hours or informally on a weekend or over a coffee. The mini-secret (now revealed for the first time in this chapter) is that getting a few faculty members to care about your personal success and the development of your postcollege life is key.

Best of all, you (the student) get to pick those faculty members you really like. Invest some energy in getting to know them, because they are an incredible resource for talking about your dreams, plans, crazy schemes, ideas, goals, and hopes.

If you've ever seen the movie *Back to the Future* (with Michael J. Fox), you'll know that high schooler Marty McFly (Fox) spends a lot of time with eccentric scientist Doc Brown . . . who has conveniently invented a device that allows time travel. Setting aside the quirky physics of the space-time continuum, what's interesting is seeing McFly engaging his curiosity and meeting with the equivalent of a professor outside of class. Marty gets a lot of advice/wisdom, and as the movie suggests, "hanging out" with Doc is life-changing.

You might not believe us, but the same thing could happen to you.

CHAPTER SUMMARY

We hear too often from students who don't like their major or, in some cases, don't even know how they got their major. People along the way told them what courses to take to stay eligible. That's a shame, because picking a major is one of the most sure-fire ways to influence how you see yourself and how you imagine the rest of your life unfolding.

Yes, we understand not all college graduates get jobs in the field of their majors. And we know that some majors don't lend themselves to exciting jobs. But failing to pick a major you are passionate about isn't the way to go.

As the late Stephen Covey (author of the seminal book *The 7 Habits of Highly Effective People*) advised, "Start with the End in Mind," which is to say, "start with a clear understanding of your destination." But then Covey added, you are your own creator. You get to design what you become. You create your own weather because "whether it rains or shines" you determine your own outcome.

You might not like "owning" your future, but start by identifying a major. That action will become a major strength (or foundation) and yes, we get that you might not yet know what you want for the future.

So ask for help and advice from professors, "Doc Browns," and life skills counselors early and often.

And keep in mind that you can't always get what you want!

Secret *10* Take Nothing for Granted

THE SECRET IN A FEW WORDS

Injuries can happen at any moment in your athletic career, and, in the worst cases, end it in a heartbeat. No amount of fitness and skill can guarantee you an injury-free athletic career. The only thing you can do to prepare for such an unfortunate outcome is put yourself in a good position on the off chance this does happen. In the meantime, you should prepare for anything and always have a plan just in case. Think positively about everything but remember life will throw you curveballs, and you don't want to get frozen at the plate and strike out looking. At least be able to foul off the pitch and give yourself another opportunity.

TAKE NOTHING FOR GRANTED

A lot of times we get carried away in the moment, and we never allow ourselves to take a step out of the figurative batter's box to realize how fortunate we are and appreciate what we get to do every day. As a student-athlete, you are fortunate to hang out with a small group of athletes who get to compete for their school in a sport they love. You get an opportunity many kids wish for. Our advice for you is simply this:

1. Take a step back to realize where you are and what you are doing.

2. Recognize how fortunate you are to play your sport collegiately.

3. Keep things in perspective . . . have you ever thought about the people who have career-ending injuries and what their lives are like?

4.   Appreciate the little things, because you won't realize you'll miss them until they are gone.

5.   Finally, play every day like it's your last. We know this is clichéd, but it is really true. You never know when something will be taken away from you in the blink of an eye.

Believe it or not, a minor injury, or even a career-ending injury, can teach you more than you could ever imagine. We wouldn't wish this on anyone, but if it does happen, you need to have a positive perspective and mindset.

The stories presented here illustrate how student-athletes who experienced physical injuries learned the importance of developing perspective on their situations. We hope their stories about confronting and overcoming unexpected setbacks will provide you with models worth learning from. The key lesson from these stories is that things change, stuff happens, and plans go out the window. You must be able to adapt all of the secrets we've shared in the first part of the book to whatever comes.

Pat O'Conner, who—after twenty-eight years in Minor League Baseball—retired as President and CEO of Minor League Baseball at the end of 2020, gives some valuable advice here: "One of humanity's greatest flaws is the willingness to settle for too little. Do what makes you happy and chase your dreams in the process. Do not expect anyone to believe in you, or your dreams, if you do not believe in yourself and those dreams. Never look to someone else to accomplish something you should do. As the saying goes, 'Don't let good get in the way of great' and never shy away from an honest day of hard work. People will notice hard work."

In a nutshell, O'Connor is telling you not to take anything for granted. He further advises you to "stay in the present. Commit to the task at hand, give it all you have, and the next opportunity will present itself at the appropriate time. Work with all your heart and might in the position you have and you will learn a skill, build a good reputation, and become an attractive candidate for the next big opportunity."

Shauna Happel, a former soccer player at the University of Northern Iowa, also dealt with injuries in her career, and her experiences define this secret.

SHAUNA HAPPEL

(former soccer student-athlete at the University of Northern Iowa, now Assistant Women's Soccer Coach at Mount Mercy University)

As athletes, injuries are simply part of the sport that we love. Our passion, commitment, and dedication are what drive us to give everything that we have in order to compete. Day in and day out we continually work to achieve success. There isn't a day that goes by that we don't think about our sport and reminisce about the moments that we spend with our teammates.

Oftentimes athletes take all of this for granted. We live in the moment and take each day as it comes.

The scary thing is we never know what practice tomorrow may bring. Some days we can't wait to get out on the field and then there are other days where we dread the mere idea of what physically exhausting tasks we may encounter. Whether it be negative or positive our thoughts and our heart are always with the sport and we couldn't imagine life without it. However, with the blink of an eye all of this can change and leave us in a blur of confusion and emptiness. Our sport can be taken away from us at any moment and the culprit can be described in one word: injury.

I can't remember hardly ever having to sit out of a practice or game. I could probably count on one hand the number of times that happened in fifteen years of competitive sports. However, as my final season of high school soccer was coming to a close my athletic career would take a turn for the worse and be greatly altered. I was diagnosed with a stress fracture in my right shin. I worked through the injury as I headed to Northern Iowa University on a soccer scholarship. Fast forward to my freshman year, and I acquired another injury.

I suffered a spiral fracture to my fibula (on the same leg that I had the stress fracture). To make matters even worse, the doctor said I was going to need surgery to repair it. I could not believe what I was hearing. Here I am on my first day of the spring soccer season and I find out I am going to be out for the entire season. I went into my sophomore year dragging my shin pain with me. I kept playing throughout the season as the pain continued to get stronger and more frequent. It got to the point where I was wearing a boot during the day and took it off to play and practice. Fast forward to the next season, and I found out that during the first week of preseason I tore the labrum in my left hip. It turned out I needed surgery to repair it, and an even longer rehab process than anything else I had done before.

Being sidelined with a season-ending injury meant that I was going to be watching my team play and practice from behind the confines of the sideline. I never could have imagined how hard this task would be and the toll that it would take on me mentally and emotionally. I already knew the physical toll that this injury had taken on me, but I could have never predicted the effects that this injury would have on me in other aspects of my life.

I felt like I had been on a mental and emotional roller coaster for the previous few months. Even though it has been really tough to get through this, my driving force has been positivity and to be grateful for everything that I have and have been able to experience. One of the hardest things to come to grips with was that I was not going to be able to play soccer for an entire season with my teammates.

When people think of an injured athlete they don't really think about much more than the fact that they are injured. Most people don't even consider what the athlete is going through mentally and emotionally. The biggest part of getting over an injury isn't the physical aspect like most people would assume. How an athlete deals with the injury mentally plays a huge role in the athlete's recovery process.

My advice to athletes who are sidelined for the season is to keep a positive mindset and be grateful for the opportunities that they have had. Instead of dwelling on their current situation they should focus their thoughts on getting better and what they can look forward to when they make a full recovery and are back playing. Don't let the sideline be a barrier that separates you from your team; instead view it as a motivator. The sideline is like a finish line that, once crossed, indicates the completion of the rehab process. Each day work hard to make strides in your recovery and make your way closer to crossing the finish line. There is no greater feeling than accomplishing your goal and crossing back onto the playing field with your teammates.

Scott White, a former NCAA Division I baseball player at Ohio University and now ER Paramedic at the Mayo Clinic, also experienced injuries in his career that quickly taught him to never take anything for granted.

SCOTT WHITE

(former baseball student-athlete at Ohio University, now ER Paramedic at the Mayo Clinic)

I tore my labrum, rehabbed it, played through it, and played with a lot of pain. I only had one year left, which made me realize my playing career wasn't going past college with my injuries because I then had a torn UCL [ulnar collateral ligament] at the same time I found out. My whole right arm was basically useless. It made me realize that baseball wasn't in my future and I wasn't even in a major that I wanted to be in.

There had been some days I was playing as a sophomore and I would think, "I've got two more years and possibly more . . . ," and the possibility of being injured in a split second can happen at any time. The thought of not being able to play again doesn't really cross your mind. It really hit me the day after my Tommy John surgery when I woke up in the hospital in my sling. I had a huge scar and my elbow was the size of a balloon, all swollen and everything. I was in so much pain and I thought, this could be it, the last time I play.

There is a mindset you acquire. Being injured helped me acquire that mindset to not take everything for granted. It is hard to put yourself in that mindset if you haven't been through an injury or some kind of big setback. I would suggest taking an extended period of time away from the game to make yourself realize how much you miss it, or stop doing something you love to do and see what that feeling is like.

So, based on what we've learned from these comments, what should you do if an injury or an unexpected absence forces you away from the game? We've come up with a list of three key and simple suggestions.

1. Play every day like it's your last.

SCOTT WHITE

(former student-athlete at Ohio University, now ER Paramedic at Mayo Clinic)

I always tell current players now to soak up everything. Enjoy practice, enjoy training, and enjoy the little things, because you don't appreciate them while you are doing them, but when you look back at it, you will. Make the most of your opportunities because you never know when your last time will be; sports are unpredictable.

---

2. Be prepared for the worst and always have a Plan B.

SCOTT WHITE

(former student-athlete at Ohio University, now ER Paramedic at Mayo Clinic)

Never look too far into your successes and never focus too hard on your failures. Let them motivate you a little, but don't dwell on them too much. Find a support system, whether it is your coaches, teammates, or other support staff, to help you deal with those failures. It is also much sweeter when you can share those successes with your support system too; they aren't just there for you when you fail.

---

3. Always have an alternative image of yourself that does not depend on sport.

Even if you are one of the top prospects in the world, you still need to have a game plan for yourself outside of playing your sport, because you just never know what the next chapter of your book involves. There are literally thousands of examples of athletes at every level who had a brilliant career full of potential (and probably wealth) stopped because of injury, personal challenges, or other setbacks.

CREATE A MENTAL HEALTH SELF-CARE PLAN

Michelle Pride, PhD (Embedded Psychologist, Ohio University Athletics)

One of my primary goals as the Ohio University embedded sport psychologist is to help student-athletes become aware of how they can help themselves during their time as student-athletes as well as throughout their lifetime. It's important to understand that about a third of college student-athletes experience significant mental health concerns, but only about 10 percent will seek help.[1]

Taking care of your mental health can feel like one more thing on your task list each day. However, it's important to do because mental health concerns, which can include depression, anxiety, eating disorders, trauma, or grief, can affect sleep, motivation, attention and concentration, and even physical health. Self-care is essential to mental health; it builds resilience and increases your capacity to effectively engage in your responsibilities (including schoolwork, practices, and competition). Depending on what is going on in your life or what your current stressors are, you may need to do different things to care for your mental health. And just like your physical health, you need to take care of your mental health every day.

Creating a self-care plan can help you stay on track and accountable for caring for your mental health. The good news is that it's not very hard to create the plan, but it does take some thought. The following mental health self-care planning process can put you on the right track toward a lifetime of awareness about mental health wellness. There is no one-size-fits-all approach, so as you will see in step 4, it will take some time and effort for you to identify strategies that work for you, and those strategies might change depending on your life circumstances at the time. If you need help developing your plan, turn to a trusted family member, friend, teammate, coach, faculty member, or mental health professional to help.

FOUR-STEP PROCESS FOR MENTAL HEALTH SELF-CARE PLANNING

1. *Know your burnout signs.* For example: withdrawing/isolating, procrastinating, giving up, feeling overwhelmed, angry, or helpless.

2. *Identify what your stressors are.* For example: injury, loss, relationship stress, academic challenges, performance anxiety.

3. *Identify how the stress is affecting you.* For example: headaches/stomachaches, trouble sleeping, irritability, shutting down, avoidance.

4. *Find strategies for addressing the stressors.*

   • Connection
      a. Call/text/message a friend, family member, or teammate.
      b. Smile at a stranger or give someone a compliment.
      c. Kick it old school and send a letter or a postcard to someone.
      d. Tell a friend why you are grateful for their friendship.
      e. Attend church services or participate in other group activities.
   • Reflection
      a. Journal (use Pinterest to find journal prompts).
      b. Meditate or pray.

    c.   Think of three things you are grateful for.

    d.   Take three to five slow, deep breaths and ground yourself.

    e.   Create a vision board (again, see Pinterest).

- Emotional expression

    a.   Have a good cry.

    b.   Have a good laugh.

    c.   Mindfully listen to music.

    d.   Create something: color, paint, write, sing, knit, etc.

    e.   Talk to a therapist.

- Movement/physical health (not because you have to, but for the joy of the movement)

    a.   Stretch/do yoga.

    b.   Go for a walk or a hike.

    c.   Dance.

    d.   Get good sleep/rest.

    e.   Eat nutritiously.

CHAPTER SUMMARY

Our favorite quote from one of our former coaches is "Yesterday is in the past, tomorrow is not promised, so control the only thing you can, today." This applies not only to sports, but to life. You never know what is going to happen tomorrow, so treat each day like it's your last. It sounds clichéd, but it's true. As many athletes who were injured during their careers will tell you, "You don't know what you have till it's gone." Or as Boy Scouts might advise: Be Prepared.

Secret 11 Manage Your Highs and Lows

This secret is about managing your success and/or nonsuccess on the field and in the classroom. Both pursuits—academic and athletic—will produce good days and bad days, great results and disappointing results. It is important that you manage both.

As an athlete, you are used to having a coach explain expectations, demonstrate desired behaviors, and then provide feedback on your performance, based on which you make adjustments. Unfortunately, your coach can't always be by your side as you navigate your athletic, academic, and personal life in college. There will be support staff in place to explain expectations such as the grades needed for academic success and to retain eligibility, but rarely will there be someone around who educates you about the highs and lows you could face as a student-athlete.

Without knowing what might be coming your way, you can find both the triumphs and the disappointments overwhelming. This secret shares with you many of the possible highs and lows you could face as a student-athlete and coaches you through some approaches for managing them. Not only will this information help you breeze through whatever comes your way as a student-athlete, but the strategies will also prepare you for your professional and personal life after college.

MANAGE YOUR HIGHS AND LOWS

Highs and lows are part of life. Maximizing the benefit of the highs and avoiding or rebounding from the lows are key to a balanced life. Big wins and small losses. You've heard the sayings and the slogans. Kelsey Cermak, a former student-athlete and now an Assistant Director with the NCAA, notes that "you always have to be prepared for success and failure. You can never get too high off of a win, and you can never get too low after a loss."

Rob Smith, NCAA Division I baseball coach, has the following advice for first-year students:

> My biggest advice for freshmen is to understand and be open minded to learning how to handle failure and adversity. It's not that you aren't good enough, it's that you may get swallowed up by the process, physically and mentally. It's a shock for many freshmen to have to balance all that you have to, especially at the Division I level.
>
> I think the ones that handle it all the best are the ones that come in with the least amount of expectations. When freshmen come in with too high a level of expectations, failure can really set them back too much. When the walk-on guy is just excited to have the opportunity, he rapidly adapts and that is because of the lack of expectations. Have realistic expectations so that you can exceed and succeed.

Smith emphasizes the need to manage your expectations. Be realistic in your goals, plan for the long term, and do not get derailed by one bad result or test score.

"THAT LOW": WHEN YOU REALIZE YOU MAY NOT BE GOING PRO OR THAT YOU'RE LOSING YOUR SPOT

A potentially life-altering "low" can be realizing (perhaps gradually, when reality finally sinks in; or perhaps suddenly, when reality hits for the first time) that you are not going to go pro.

Eddie Gill, a former NBA player and student-athlete and now a successful Financial Advisor and an Analyst for FOX Sports, told us about a "low" like this he went through.

> For me, coming out of college as a senior and going into the draft was one of my down moments. I kind of built some steam up going into my senior year, and throughout my senior year, there were some projections of middle first round and middle second round. I fell completely out of the draft and was not drafted at all.
>
> That was a harsh reality for me that I had to come to grips with and realize that it's going to be a harder path, and that I could only control what I could control. That's the game of life, some things aren't fair. You can do everything "right" and it doesn't happen for you, which is okay.

You have to continue to pick yourself up and get back after it. Throughout my professional playing career, I had a variety of ups and downs where I thought I was at a place and was like "I'm here. I'll be good for X amount of years." Then boom, something else happens and you're somewhere else playing again. It happened a lot, but I've always tried to remain self-confident and sure of myself and continued to keep pressing on.

Another former student-athlete and now Trainer at the Positive Coaching Alliance, Hillary Nelson, described her reactions when her playing time was drastically cut and her role on the team lessened.

The toughest year of my life was my junior year. I was a pitcher, had a new pitching coach, and my playing time was cut by 80 percent. I was in a rough roommate situation. I was having a hard time at home, and then my mom passed away. It was the sudden death of my mom in April that really just put me over the edge.

For me, that year really put things in perspective. It helped me take my internal focus, where I had been so focused on Hillary Nelson and how I was going to be successful. It helped me see life through an external focus on how I was going to make the world better, how I was going to make my team better, and how I was going to make the game of softball better.

In response to the "toughest year of her life," Nelson said there were three keys to her getting through this mental minefield. First, she set high goals (academically and professionally) to challenge herself off the field of play.

Second, she said she really relied on the resources provided to her and the people around her. "Surround yourself with winners," she advises, and she also stresses "never being afraid to ask for help if you need it."

Third, she tried to work harder that she thought possible and test the limits of her work ethic. "If you want to succeed more than you want to sleep, you'll find a way to make it happen."

Nelson also noted the importance of learning from failures (on the field, in the classroom, or in your personal life). She noted: "If you don't have failure, you don't learn to appreciate success. Specifically, my failures, in those bad times, those hard times, made the best times seem so much greater."

WHAT ARE THE HIGHS AND LOWS TO EXPECT?

The life of a student-athlete is already a whirlwind as you balance your academic, athletic, and personal lives. As a student-athlete, however, you will experience highs and lows athletically, beyond the successes and failures that all students face.

A first element of this "secret" is to know where these highs and lows might come from so you can be prepared to maximize the highs and mitigate (reduce) the impact of the lows.

As a student-athlete in college, you can expect that your coaches, professors, fellow students, and maybe even the media will take notice of your victories and losses on the field (or on the court, in the gym, on the ice, in the pool, etc.). Your successes and failures outside your sport will get less attention but are no less significant for your overall success. It is important to be aware of potential challenges that could come your way. In some cases, you can work to avoid pitfalls such as academic problems, but in other cases there is absolutely nothing you could have done differently to avoid a troublesome situation.

- *Academic Highs:* Achievements such as scoring an A on a challenging statistics exam, receiving an acceptance letter to graduate school or medical school, completing all the requirements for your degree, and making the Dean's List or honor roll should not be filed away or kept quiet. Embrace the success. Call your parents. Celebrate with your friends. Have a wall in your room where you post the results. Share the good news on social media.

- *Academic Lows:* Depending on your goals and plan, you'll know when you've failed. If your goal is to get your computer engineering degree, then a C+ in a challenging math course may not count as a "low"; but if you're hoping to go to law school one day, then a C+ could affect that goal if your overall GPA is borderline. Failing a test, scoring well below your needed level of achievement, falling off the Dean's List or honor roll are all examples. Your response to these "lows" needs to be VERY proactive. Assess the situation, figure out what went wrong, and come up with a solution. Do you need a tutor? Do you need more study time? Do you need more sleep to be alert in class? Ask the hard questions and make changes to solve the problems you identify.

- *Athletic Highs:* These are big, and given your spot in the "other 99 percent" for whom this will be the highest level of sports achievement, you should cherish these accomplishments. They can be as "small" as a terrific workout, making all morning practices one week (or month), hitting your nutrition goals, or getting positive feedback from your coach. Or they can be major, like a victory over a key opponent, a conference championship, or qualifying for a bowl game. These are moments you will never forget and are ones to treasure and celebrate, as that will help as you transition to life postgraduation and without high-performance sport.

- *Athletic Lows:* Again, like the academic highs and lows, these can be minor (for example, sleeping through practice, loss of playing time, a minor injury, making a bad play at a key moment) or major (for example, getting cut from the team, a major loss, not qualifying for postseason, losing your scholarship, a major injury). The same response as to an academic low is necessary here: conduct a deep analysis of the situation, identify the problem(s)/issue(s), and fix them (right away and with a clear plan).

- *Personal/Social Highs and Lows:* These have been discussed previously, but we're noting this area again as these personal and social accomplishments and challenges need to be addressed and celebrated (or mourned) along with academic and athletic extremes.

WHAT IS THE SECRET TO MANAGING YOUR ATHLETIC SUCCESS HIGHS?

Athletic success is defined differently by each individual. For some student-athletes, success is winning national or conference championships, while for others personal skill improvement, personal bests, or even a spot on the team might be the measure of success. Whatever the definition of success is, managing it requires diligent attention. The following list provides you with a sample of approaches that you can adopt to help you manage your athletic success (that is, the "highs"!):

- *Enjoy your success:* It is okay to be proud of yourself and share your accomplishments. You have worked hard for what you have achieved.

- *Be respectful of teammates:* Teammates may be struggling to hit their own athletic goals, so be respectful when celebrating your individual achievements. This is especially true if you are "passing" teammates with a throw, lift, or point total, or by earning a starter role or breaking their record.

- *Understand your school's media protocol:* Many institutions have a protocol in place for student-athletes interacting with media (that is, all media inquiries must go through the media relations staff member for your sport). If your achievement results in media attention, be sure you're aware of the procedure for how media should be contacting you and follow established expectations.

- *Know how to handle media:* Talking with media and sharing on your own social media affect how you and the institution are perceived. Be humble, be appreciative to those who support you, and consider how what you say or write could be perceived by both teammates and competitors.

- *Move forward:* Accomplishing goals and achieving success are awesome, but then what? Athletes can flounder and lose focus if other goals are not in the pipeline. After recognizing success, it's time to attack the next goal! This also goes for continuing to celebrate an achievement for too long. After a day or two, your teammates will get tired of hearing about what you did, so move on for everyone's sake, including your own.

SEEK OUT THOSE ACADEMIC "HIGHS"!

You may feel like an athlete-student, but remember that you are a student-athlete. That means that academics deserve at least as much attention as your sport. The "highs" for either need to feel equally important for you. We get that the media doesn't really care about your B+ on the scary accounting exam or the all-nighter you and your group did to get that major project done on time—but you do, your groupmates do, your family does, and so you need to call out those "highs" as well. The "Enjoy It" and "Move Forward" tactics above should be adopted for the academic highs as well as the athletic ones.

Many student-athletes encounter academic problems that often have nothing to do with intellectual ability. Typically, your academic problems occur because you have not committed to academics the way you have to your sport. A lot of time goes into athletic goal setting, but how much time do you spend on academic goal setting? You need to balance this.

Where do you find the motivation to achieve academic highs? Well, of course, we all know that staying eligible to play is the bare minimum in academic achievement, but for many, achieving that goal is a high that deserves to be celebrated. If you aim for more than staying eligible and earning passing grades, then you need to commit to academics just like athletics. The benefits of making the Dean's List or receiving an academic award will be noticed later when it's time for a job interview, grad school application, or scholarship consideration.

A very simple and useful plan is to take the same approach to academic goals as you do to your athletic goals. For example, think of the approach you use for your strength and conditioning workouts: you attack them. You probably have goals related to increasing your speed, strength, and stamina and know that unless you show up to strength and conditioning sessions ready to give 100 percent, you will not reach your goals.

You probably have a detailed plan of exercise, times, and goals to follow for each workout. Those goals translate into improved athletic performance in your sport or else you probably would not have them. Take exactly the same approach to your academic goals. Think about mandatory study hall. If you approached studying the way you do your strength and conditioning workouts, you would be setting goals for yourself related to what you need to accomplish in your study sessions each week and overall for the term. Additionally, you would recognize the direct link between achieving these study goals and your improved academic performance. It really is that simple: a change in your perspective almost guarantees improved performance in the classroom.

Approaching academics the same way as athletics will also help you deal with academic problems or frustrations. College is challenging for most, and not every class is going to be one that you are in love with. Just like when your coach makes a change you are not very excited about and you suck it up and keep on moving along, you can do the same thing academically.

Another idea that worked for some of the authors in their time as student-athletes is to approach any academic concept or class that you are struggling in just as you would attack a challenge in your sport: get the help you need, buckle down, and throw yourself into figuring out how to overcome the obstacle. If you are having trouble with a blocking technique on the field, you spend extra time practicing it. The same principle applies to academics: if you are having trouble with something, it will require extra practice. But you can get through it!

It is true that academic success is unlikely to catch the attention of local media, but think about how good you feel when you put in the work to study for an exam and then have that pay off with a high grade. What about all the people who care about you? I suspect many of them would be as excited to hear you earned an A on a test as they would be to hear you scored a goal.

AUTHOR VIEWPOINT—DR. HEATHER LAWRENCE

As a student-athlete diver at the University of Florida, I experienced my share of both highs and lows. In my four years I accomplished a variety of academic and athletic goals such as winning an individual Southeastern Conference title, setting school records, being recognized as an Academic and Athletic All-American, and even being inducted into the Student Hall of Fame for my academic college. Reading this list, you may think that college was smooth as can be for me, but the reality is that it was not.

I also had my share of struggles while at Florida. The biggest challenge was during my junior year when all of a sudden, right before the championship season, I became unable to get myself to do even the simplest of dives. These were movements that my body had been doing since I was ten years old and there seemed to be no explanation as to why it was happening. Mental blocks are not new in the world of athletics, but I was not ready for it to happen to me and I clearly was not prepared for how to handle it when it did. The level of frustration directed toward me by teammates and coaches about my inability to perform escalated as time went on and I didn't just snap out of it. At one diving meet, I even just had to jump off the diving board and take "0's" from the judges. Understandably, that was not received well by anyone, including me.

Initially, I tried working with mental health professionals on campus, submitted myself to hypnosis, and also talked with medical staff, but nothing seemed to be helping me.

Along with the head diving coach, I finally did my own research into sport psychologists who might have expertise in working with athletes with similar issues. As a result, we identified a sport psychologist in Miami, Florida, who had experience with divers and thankfully he was willing to work with me. With the support of the Director of Athletics and medical staff, I packed up the car and headed to Miami to work on myself. This took me out of school, conditioning, and practice (or at least the minimal practice I was getting) for a week.

The experience in Miami was worth the sacrifice as I was able to overcome the mental block by working with the expertise of the sport psychologist. Some days he was even up on the ten-meter platform with me helping me work through all that was causing the performance problems for me.

At other times, it was more about helping me realize that diving was not the only part of my identity and that the pressure I was putting on myself was disproportionate to the real amount of me that was a "diver." Basically, I was way out of balance. I was training too much, putting too much pressure on myself to excel, and had my self-worth entirely wrapped up into how I competed and practiced.

Although it took some time, I did completely overcome the mental block I experienced and went on to an undefeated senior year of dual meets serving as team captain, became an SEC champion, was an NCAA All-American in two events, and most importantly, had fun again being a diver. Looking back at this tough time in my life, I know that putting in the work and being willing to sacrifice to get better taught me how to handle other types of adversity. Whether it was having a fussy newborn at home and going into severe sleep deprivation, being incredibly overworked professionally, or just feeling out of control with all life has thrown at me—I know that all of the various roles I fill as a person do not define who I am. So, the perspective I learned through having a mental block as a diver continues to be a valuable experience for me in my personal and professional life.

DEALING WITH THE HIGHS AND LOWS

Next, we'd like to share some general principles that apply to dealing with the various highs and lows we've outlined.

1. *Keep a Level Head*. Take a moment to pause and think before you react to whatever is happening. As you know, everything you

do could be blasted out on social media immediately. Perception is reality, so whether the situation is good or bad, work hard to ensure your reaction reflects how you want others to see you. This goes for in-person interactions with friends as well as more formal media interactions.

2. *Know, and Use, Your Resources.* The good news is that you are surrounded by coaches and administrators who care a lot about you. The bad news is that everyone is busy and it is up to you to reach out and get the help you need to navigate the circumstances you find yourself in. Focus on asking the appropriate person for assistance and the sooner the better. Rarely do bad situations get better on their own, so reaching out as soon as you have a feeling about something not going your way could save you a lot of headaches down the road.

3. *Keep Perspective.* A college campus can make any situation seem better or worse and definitely bigger than it really is. Remember that the situation will pass and you will get through it, so making a conscious decision on how you will handle it is important. Whether it is a success or a failure, one situation does not define who you are as a person, as an athlete, or as a student.

EXAMPLES OF USING THE STRATEGIES

Here are examples of a triumph and a disappointment to illustrate how to activate these strategies.

Example: Dealing with a Triumph

As your final semester of college begins, you are nominated for both conference and NCAA postgraduate scholarships. In your four years, you have not been an individual champion athlete beyond some dual meets, and your team has qualified for NCAAs but never placed in the top ten nationally. However, you have dedicated yourself to being a team leader and supporting your teammates, being engaged in community service on and off campus, and achieving a GPA of 3.8 in a rigorous major. Additionally, you have already been admitted to grad school and plan on starting after a summer of traveling abroad.

Shortly after the nominations, you learn you have been awarded $20,000 in postgraduate scholarship money from the NCAA. How do you handle this success?

1. *Keep a Level Head.* You are the same person before this award as you are after this award. It could be tempting to feel superior to teammates as they struggle to decide what to do after college and you already have a plan in place as well as no financial stress now

because of the scholarships. Continue to be the team leader you always have been, and now even more student-athletes may start to look up to you as they learn of your awards. Mentor and guide those younger than you to help them achieve just as you have.

2.   *Know, and Use, Your Resources.* What could you possibly need help with after winning a postgraduate scholarship? The answer is, a lot. After being on an athletics scholarship, you may know very little about how to access the award money via your institution or how it affects other financial aid or even taxes. There are probably expectations for academic performance to retain your scholarships, so find the individuals in the athletics department who can point you in the right direction to begin to understand graduate school and how scholarships are awarded.

3.   *Keep Perspective.* Find out who put together the nominations that led to your being awarded the scholarship and thank them by writing a handwritten thank-you note and stopping by their office. Other handwritten thank-you notes should go to your parents or guardians, your coaches, the athletic director, and any other people on campus who supported your success. Then, realize that you have a long road ahead in a challenging graduate program. Enjoy your summer and return to campus ready to give back to the athletic program (that is, volunteer) that has provided you this amazing opportunity.

Example: Dealing with a Disappointment

Despite your best physical preparation, you suffered a season-ending ACL injury only halfway through your sophomore year as a field hockey player. It is a big blow to the team overall since you have been the conference player of the week twice already as well as being the team-leading scorer for the season thus far.

1.   *Keep a Level Head.* You are the same person before this injury and after this injury. It could be tempting to feel sorry for yourself (and you can for a few days before it's time to get back to work), but that does not move you any closer to recovery. During your rehab, you have an opportunity to take on a new role supporting your teammates and a chance to lead by example by how you approach your rehab. Since your teammates are likely feeling a bit bummed about your injury too, you can help the coaching staff get them back on track by understanding how good other players are and spending time individually with some key players, encouraging them to really step up their playing to fill the void.

2.   *Know, and Use, Your Resources.* You will be spending a lot of time with athletic trainers and the sports medicine staff. Recognize how hard they are working on your behalf to help you heal. Head into every early-morning rehab session with a great attitude and ready to do whatever they ask of you. They know how to get you playing again as quickly as possible, so it only ends up hurting you if you don't use them as your resources.

3.   *Keep Perspective.* Although you end up missing the rest of one season, you still have two more seasons to play and will come back stronger than ever. Plus, you hopefully have at least seventy more years of living to do after college and you want that knee to be as strong as it can be for all of the life adventures that await you. Your recovery period is also a great time to excel academically. If you end up with a little extra time because you aren't traveling with the team, put it to good use and work to earn the highest possible grades you can that term.

Sometimes life hits you from all sides (athletic, academic, personal) at the same time. You might even be in the middle of an athletic success and an academic challenge at the same time. There is no playbook to get you through every possible scenario you might face, but you can get through anything that is thrown at you and come out on the other side of the situation feeling proud of how you handled it and knowing you were strong enough to tackle the challenge and beat it.

As a student-athlete, there will be times you feel like you are on top of the world, and there will be times you feel like nothing more could go wrong. How did you handle the highs and lows, along with stress? What advice would you give to a student-athlete on how to deal with stress? How much do the "highs and lows" relate to life, and have you pulled from past experiences as an athlete to help you in the work world?

DEALING WITH FAILURE

Drew Saylor (former student-athlete, now Hitting Coordinator with the Kansas City Royals)

Learning how to deal with failure and how it motivates you, and how it should inherently inspire you to work harder, is one of the most important lessons you can learn. I think, for a multitude of reasons, having failure is vital to the improvement process because when you fail, you get a chance to rework the equation, then you test it again. If you're truly a lifelong learner, you're always going to be finding ways to push yourself to the extreme. You're going to fail. Once you fail, it's an opportunity to go back and re-work the equation and try again. At the end of the day, it is imperative that student-athletes find a way to maintain that process because that's what makes them valid.

As a student-athlete, wins, losses, and personal statistics, that's kind of what you live and die by. Inherently, we're all committed as people. We don't like to lose. I think that, being able to look at it from a scientific standpoint, going, "Okay, well this is my process, this caused failure. How can I fix it?" I think that understanding similarly, Urban Meyer talks about, "the outcome is the event plus your response." When you look at that equation, your event, you really don't get a chance to choose your event—the event basically chooses you. The outcome, you don't really have much say in that because you go out and you compete and the outcome is really a product of your process. The only thing that you can control is your response. How do you deal with what goes on? Is your response to shut down and say screw it and drop your wrench and walk off the worksite? Is your response to sit there and have an uncontrolled rage outburst that actually hurts your teammates and the environment that you're in? Or is your response to press onward? Is your response to continue to work harder to find a different process to change the outcome?

In addition to Saylor's lessons on dealing with failure, Nick Manno had a piece of wisdom to add as well.

NICK MANNO

**(former NCAA baseball student-athlete,
now Player Personnel Coordinator with the Toronto Blue Jays)**

When you play baseball, failure is a big part of it. You can't have a fear of failure. I think that applies to scouting. Scouting is not unlike playing. You are going to be wrong a lot. Learning to deal with failure and adversity is something you definitely take with you as you go on any other walk of life. You have to understand that process is really important. In the professional world, if you have a process, a plan, and you stick with those, you will be successful more times than not. If you don't have a plan or process and you fail, you have nowhere to turn.

CHAPTER SUMMARY

Life isn't easy, life isn't fair, and when life kicks you down, you have to get back up. You may be on top of the world one day and on the bottom of the ocean floor the next, but you have to learn how to manage your successes and failures.

As the great Johnny Cash once said, "You build on failure. You use it as a stepping-stone. Close the door on the past. You don't try to forget the mistakes, but you don't dwell on them. You don't let it have any of your energy, or any of your time."

When you fail in life, just get right back up and try again. And when you succeed in life, cherish it, and keep wanting more. Stay humble, don't forget who you are, and keep things in perspective.

We now turn from secrets focused on succeeding as a student-athlete and preparing yourself for the end of your playing career to a set of nine secrets that will guide you as you transition out of sport and into the next chapter of your life. The worst part about this transition is that it happens to everyone, whether you go pro or not. It's only a matter of time; you have to move on.

Secret *12* Face Reality in Sports and Life

THE SECRET IN A FEW WORDS

Most young people between the ages of seventeen and twenty-four want to live life to its fullest. To get busy living. To live like an immortal. In fact, many twenty-year-olds behave as if they are immortal. They believe they will be young forever. But there is risk in not facing reality. We all age and even the greatest athletes eventually slow down. They lose a step.

So think about these truths. A college degree may suggest you are educated. Playing a sport in college confirms you are physically talented. Wearing a team uniform or team-supplied apparel implies you are privileged.

But those perceptions are often misleading. If you skipped classes or cheated, or if you ended up in a major you didn't care about, you may not be as educated as you'll soon wish you were. If you think you're unlikely to turn pro in sports, you'll soon know for certain if you weren't talented enough to go pro. If you are relying on a varsity jacket for recognition and special treatment around campus, you will soon learn the emperor's new clothing doesn't mean much a month after graduation.

Those are realities and they come to all of us at different times as we get a handle on how the larger world works. This chapter is for the realists. This chapter makes sure you are looking at the truth about your skills as an athlete and the life rushing toward you.

FACE REALITY IN SPORTS AND LIFE

It's one thing to seek reality or know it when you see it . . . but it's another thing to face reality when you are uncertain. Many people hope that even though the truth (or the reality of a situation) may be unwelcome, a little luck or self-persuasion will still produce an outcome that isn't all bad. That innocence, naïveté, or positive thinking is okay up to a point, but there comes a time for all of us when the truth can't be denied or ignored.

To provide you with some perspective on facing the reality of sports and life, we interviewed four former professional athletes and a professional basketball coach who have all been successful. We asked all five to give us their views of the reality facing a student-athlete postgraduation.

Eddie Gill, former NBA player and student-athlete at Weber State, and now a successful Financial Planner and a TV Analyst for the Indiana Pacers on Fox, said:

> Let's just say you do play professionally, and now you are a part
> of the 1 percent that do go and play professionally. Let's say
> you're one of the very few that get to play for ten years, because
> in most sports, the average careers are three to four years long.
> By the time you get out of the game, you're around thirty-two
> years old, and you may have fifty more years of life. What are
> you doing with it? I think being a freshman student-athlete, you
> should start developing the thought of, "What do I want to do
> with my life?" If you're able to utilize those four years to really
> train yourself for what you would like to do, or any passion you
> might have developed, that's going to turn into success.

Dawn Buth, Assistant Director of Government Relations at the NCAA, noted:

> I feel it's essential that college athletes approach their academic
> experience with the expectation that professional athletics will
> likely not be a part of their long-term career development. Even
> if an athlete finds they are in that 1 percent, injuries, performance,
> and sustainability can be unpredictable variables—investing in
> your collegiate career can maximize your opportunities and pay
> long-term professional dividends. I encourage student-athletes
> to take ownership of their career development, exposing them-
> selves to a variety of academic and life experiences during their
> collegiate careers. Be a sponge, explore the world around you,
> learn about yourself, and discover the classes, topics, and career
> paths that resonate with you and will help inform your academic
> choices.

Seth Etherton, former MLB pitcher and student-athlete at USC who is now a minor league Pitching Coach with the Cincinnati Reds, responded:

> Education is first. There aren't many who can make a good salary
> in minor league baseball, let alone making it to the pros. Having

an understanding for the grind that minor leaguers have to go through is important. People are unrealistic on what the professional baseball life is like. I would advise student-athletes to understand your talents. Each organization drafts new guys at your position each year. Guys who were done with the game struggled the most with not having a plan for when they were done playing. Just like student-athletes, you need to be aware of when the end is coming and having your plan in place.

Matt Engleka, former student-athlete at Ohio University and owner of LEJ Agency, said:

You're going to know fairly early if going pro is a potential reality. It's not about the people within your inner circle that are telling you that. It's when you get the confirmation from outside that you're good enough, that you're recognized at that next level. I think there is a lot of false sense of possibility of going professional from today's athletes simply because everybody is "the big fish in a small pond." You have to ask yourself, "How long do I think I can pursue a professional career?" Every year, there are thousands of you out there doing the exact same thing. What makes you stand out that's going to make you that much better than the others? I think that it's hard to accept, but if the question was posed to prospective college athletes, "What if your athletic career ends in your freshman year?" would you be okay with where you're going?

Rod Baker, Assistant Coach and Scout for the Philadelphia 76ers, comments:

The sooner you realize that the game cannot become a job, the better off you will be. The smart ones realize that it may not continue for long. In the pro's, there is someone that is after your job every year, just like there are freshmen after your roster spot or starting position every year. You have to continue to prove yourself every day. Student-athletes have to be realistic. There are some who will go pro and some who won't. As a coach, I never wanted to steal anyone's dream, but I would tell my guys that they needed to have something else to do. Have some other skills, and get your degree, because even if you do go pro, it isn't going to last forever. Most won't be able to live off the money made as a pro, so you are still going to have to go get another job. I would always tell my players that you need to create as many marketable skills for yourself as possible once the basketball goes away.

Some student-athletes ignore a variety of slowly accumulating or fast-moving warning signals and never master nonsport skills like facing the facts and owning the truth. Let's look at warning signs that are pretty common:

Language	Outcome
I can function on four hours of sleep.	Illness, injury, depression
I don't read the assignments. I just skim them.	Poor grades on tests, low GPA
Burgers and pizza. The diet of champions!	Overweight, less playing time
My prof doesn't take attendance so I skip a lot.	Poor grades, no benefit of the doubt
My natural skills have always been good enough.	Outworked and outplayed
I'll play pro for a few years and be set for life.	For real?

Granted, college is a place to make mistakes and learn from them, but college also ends rather abruptly . . . from flunking out, dropping out, or graduating. We want every reader of this book to graduate and find a successful pathway through the rest of life. But like the board games *Monopoly*, *Life*, or *Chutes and Ladders*, there are days when negative realities take place. It's when you land on the wrong square and slide backwards. You suddenly face a brand-new reality. I was ahead . . . or I was making progress and . . . BANG . . . now I'm behind.

The same probably holds for video games like *Halo*, *League of Legends*, *Grand Theft Auto*, *World of Warcraft*, *Super Smash Bros.*, *Fortnite*, *Valorant*, *Overwatch*, *Diablo*, *Call of Duty: Black Ops*, *Super Mario*, and even *Tetris*. Some days you level up quickly and some days the computer or the other online players are just that much better.

Many of us learn early on to make excuses to explain our bad luck. Or failure. If we can shift the blame for our failing reality onto someone else, then the reality isn't really our own fault. It begins with someone else. If my parents had only been smarter . . . If my family had only been wealthier . . . If I'd only been given a second chance . . . If I'd only gone to a better school . . .

The "If only" game works for a while but, like many other escape vehicles, it runs out of gas quickly. At some point we have to "own up" to the present reality. We have to face facts and then make new decisions on how to survive and thrive.

We caught up, again, with Drew Saylor, who played baseball at Kent State and briefly played in baseball's minor leagues. He is now Hitting Coordinator with the Kansas City Royals. Saylor is a great example of that NCAA student-athlete who put most of his energy into making it as a pro and then had to learn about the reality of jumping from good college player to an athlete trying to make it as a full-time professional player.

"The biggest challenge for me was understanding the difference between the college game and the pro game," said Saylor when we caught up with him.

I didn't know who I was. On the baseball field, I was just kind of told, arbitrarily, to do these things and I was just physically better than most of my peers and that's how I got drafted.

As you get into professional baseball, the ability for you to be able to comprehend, apply, filter, delete and add information is imperative and I look at that, in the same context, as if you're getting an actual, real job. You do all of this studying. You do all this other stuff. You think you are ahead.

What the studying should do for you in college is it should make you think. It should make you sit there and challenge the things that go on. In a workplace environment, your thinking should make you sit there and become serious.

I think from a student-athlete perspective; my main goal was to be drafted. I knew that was one of my biggest challenges. That was my goal. Once I was drafted, I found the first few months I'd suddenly lost my drive. I lost my motivation, I lost my "Why?"

Once you achieve that goal and that's the only thing you ever thought about, you eat, breathe, and sleep that same sentiment, there are tons of points where once you get it, you say "Okay, well that's it. I'm done. What am I going to do now?"

I see the same thing in a lot of players that go into the minor leagues, but also in the major leagues where it's all about just getting that first contract. Let me get paid. Let me make my first $10 million and then all of the sudden, you start to see the lack of production.

You see their lack of effort. You see their lack of preparation. I really do think it's because they've finally achieved that goal, and they lost their direction, they lost their rudder. They are kind of just drifting wherever the wind takes them.

In your journey, it's all about finding that "Why?" Finding that direction. Finding that ability to be motivated on a day-in and day-out basis. We need to be journey-focused, not destination-focused. I think, at least for me, it is imperative that student-athletes are nimble [and thinking about the long haul].

I think having a backup plan is imperative. I always thought that I was going to teach in some way, shape or form. I really enjoyed the interpersonal relationships, and I loved my interaction with people. I think it's also because I grew up in a household where my father taught and coached for forty years.

It's something that I've always been drawn to, something I just innately learned as my life has continued to evolve. I think a lot of times people just have this one goal in mind, and then if they don't get it, their lives are completely in ruins.

More than anything else, find out what you are passionate about. Whatever it is. Continue to understand that whatever you do in life, you're going to have to work for it, you're going to have to press for it. The same stuff that you do in school, you are going to have to do that 100-fold to be successful in life.

I think that a lot of student-athletes get into this notion that, "I'm going to go play and nothing else." Players have to have the mentality going into college that they're going to have to work extremely hard. The amount of time they put into your weightlifting, study tables, etc. That's how life is, and I think a lot of student-athletes think, "Well, I'm working so hard to try to achieve this goal, and then once I'm done with this goal, then it's going to get easier."

Life doesn't happen that way.

I kind of relate it a little bit to having kids. You have a baby and you have to carry out all this stuff for the baby. Then you're like, "Oh, I can't wait for him to be a toddler because when they're a toddler, I'm not going to have to live around all of this stuff." Then all of the sudden they become a toddler and you say, "Okay, well at least I'm not lugging around all these different blankets and stuff, now I just sit there and I have to carry toys."

Then they have all of this stuff, toys. "I can't wait until they become older, then they'll be able to able to move and do things on their own," you know so on and so forth. They get a license and a car. At the end of the day, you're trading in things. You're not eliminating things. There's going to be different phases you go through that are going to require the same amount of effort out of you regardless of whatever it may be. It's just the responsibilities kind of modify.

Effort and responsibility are two great words Drew Saylor used to finish his interview. Facing reality in sports and life is largely about keeping your effort levels up when a situation gets tough but it's also about taking responsibility for the outcome you still want.

Most student-athletes dream of pro sports careers because of the perceived lifestyle advantages that will come with playing at the elite level. They'll enjoy big contracts throwing off loads of money. Big houses. Big hotel rooms on the road. Limos. Private yachts. Servants. Agents. Accountants. Mad parties. Attractive fans. They covet the lifestyle they've seen in *Entourage*. They will be Vincent Chase (or the female equivalent) and life will be filled with people telling them how good looking they are.

Well, to quote Cher in the old movie *Moonstruck* (where she slaps Nicolas Cage in the face), we need to tell you to "snap out of it." The *Entourage* lifestyle exists for maybe a few thousand people in the world, and odds are great you will not be one of them.

One of our favorite stories (and part urban legend), is told by super-agent David Falk about a young rookie joining the Chicago Bulls when Michael Jordan was the star of the team. On the first day of practice, the rookie showed up early to make a good first impression. Jordan was already there with a full sweat going.

So the next day, the rookie arrives an hour early convinced he will get there ahead of Jordan and show famous No. 23 his commitment. To his surprise, Jordan is already there. So the next day, the rookie gets up in the dark and leaves for the gym before the sun is even up. He gets to the gym as the janitor is opening the doors. He knows he's beaten Jordan because he was the first one there when the building got opened.

You know, of course, how the story ends. The ultracompetitive Jordan is already inside the building shooting around. It is at this point the rookie realizes how bad he will have to want it if he wants to run with the best.

BRIAN SANDERS

(former baseball student-athlete, now Senior Vice President of Stadium Operations for the Los Angeles Angels of Anaheim)

You have to have the passion and drive to keep going in your sport. At some point you have to be realistic that it can't last forever. As a student-athlete you have to know you put in all of the effort, know you've put in hard work and effort when is right time for you to say it's over and take the needed time to refocus. Having a good perspective and outlook on what it is you're going to do after the fact. Taking those experiences from sport and whatever drove you as a student-athlete you've got to use in the next phase.

To reiterate this idea:

DREW SAYLOR

(Hitting Coordinator with the Kansas City Royals)

We need to be journey focused, not destination focused.

Facing reality takes many shapes, but here are a few key thoughts:

- Own your own reality. Don't live someone else's.

- Don't put off owning the facts. They'll only get worse. Said another way: Things may look bad (at times), but addressing problems sooner rather than later almost always limits the damage. Putting off confronting reality usually makes things worse.

- Generally speaking, you will know your own reality better than anyone else. Yes, there are things beyond your control (for example, whether you will start or play; how someone else feels about you), but you are generally the only one really paying attention (all the time) to you. Know yourself.

- Denying the truth and putting blame on others will not protect you forever. Eventually, the harsh truth comes out. Translation: Lying, denying, and crying (on command to get out of trouble) are troublesome habits and the sooner you get beyond those traits, the better off you will be.

- Being a student-athlete can be as good or as bad as you make it. But one major reality is that if you are a student-athlete, others will hold you to higher standards, possibly cut you less slack, and believe that you are more fortunate than they are. Accept that reality and understand that your reality is shaped by the perceptions others have of you.

- Make sure that you know that many people on your campus are prepared to help you face your realities, be they mental health, career development, personal development, physical health, academic, or aspirational (such as going to grad school, getting internships, or studying abroad). One of your best realities is that many people want to help you.

Lastly, to provide you with some perspective from those student-athletes who didn't go pro, one former student-athlete who is now an associate athletic director summarized her story for you.

KRISTEN BROWN

(former basketball student-athlete, now Deputy Athletics Director at Texas A&M University)

I was a basketball student-athlete at Northern Illinois University. Where my story actually starts is my senior year in high school when I tore my ACL. That was an injury I never really 100 percent recovered from. It was an injury that probably led to other injuries. I ended up having a really injury-prone career at NIU. After having three surgeries in three years on the same knee, I ultimately decided to call it a career. I interned with my coaching staff my entire senior year as a part of my scholarship to stay in the game and be around my team.

You always want to go out on your own terms knowing you had that four or five-year career and reached your full potential as a player. It's something everyone wants for their ego and pride. I didn't get to go out on my own terms but for those who have a serious injury, you have to ask yourself if you really want to still push yourself and play? At some point, you have to think of the long term and the one sentence my doctor said that got to me was "Kristen, I know you are an active kid, you're competitive, but I know there's going to be a time you want to do things with your kids that you are not going to be able to do if you have another knee surgery." You have to live another fifty to sixty years after you are done playing.

CHAPTER SUMMARY

We have all heard friends or family talking about someone who lives in a fantasy world. They generally are writing that person off because he or she can't see what everyone else sees.

As a student-athlete you have to deal with a lot of challenges and juggle a lot of balls simultaneously. Schoolwork, playing time, practices, weight training, eating properly, preparing for life after college—the list is practically endless. You also have to manage expectations (your own and those of others) and draw certain conclusions. In short, you have to see yourself as you really are.

Learning to be honest with yourself may sound like a TV cliché, but there is significant power in developing the ability to call "bull crap" on yourself. When you look in the mirror, the truth will always be evident in your eyes.

So get comfortable facing the facts and get busy with living. It's okay to have doubts and to not be sure about which way to go. But face reality. If you've hit an iceberg, you have to give the orders to evacuate quickly.

If you've broken a rule, don't assume you can hide that truth forever. It may not be pleasant in the short term, but dealing with the truth early on is more beneficial to who you really want to become. Put in the effort but also take responsibility for your own outcome. Don't blame others for your life's trajectory. You get to create your story and how it progresses.

AND . . . If you still don't believe in the reality of going pro, take a look at Appendix A, where we have provided data from the NCAA studies to put the pro "thing" into perspective. Notably, Appendix A makes clear that the NCAA is the best pathway to going pro in North America but that student-athletes vastly overestimate their chances of "making it," with great variability across sports. Interestingly, the reports also note that making the jump from high school to the NCAA is comparable in difficulty to going from the NCAA to major pro.

Secret *13*

Mentally Move On as a Senior

THE SECRET IN A FEW WORDS

One of the hardest parts about your transition into postcollege life is mentally moving on from your sport. In today's world of sport specialization at a young age, many of you have played your sport since you were five years old. At the latest, you probably started by age twelve.

Regardless of when you started, you have devoted a lot of years, time, and dedicated effort to becoming the best athlete you can be. The amount of time you put into being a student-athlete might even trump the amount of time you have put into anything else in your life up to this point. You have put hours into your training every day, hours into the gym, and hours into all the other aspects of getting recruited and chosen to play at your institution. As you play and compete, you try not to think about the day it will be all over. Unfortunately, that day comes for everyone, and how you deal with it mentally is important in your transition.

Our secret is that you have to mentally move on as a senior. Many student-athletes hold on to their dream until the last possible second and struggle with being mentally prepared for when that time expires. Chase your dreams to the fullest, but be mentally prepared for when the time comes that you won't be going pro.

MENTALLY MOVE ON AS A SENIOR

Wally Ritchie is a former Major League Baseball player who had a thirteen-year career in the pros and spent time with us reflecting on his ability to mentally move on from his career as a professional athlete. Imagine how much harder it would be to separate from your sport if you played pro after college. Ritchie provides some advice on how to mentally prepare for that transition.

WALLY RITCHIE

(former Major League Baseball pitcher)

When you're playing, you don't think about the end of your career.

Athletes are not one dimensional. The transition from after your playing career affects many facets of your life, including education and career, mental well-being, relationships, finances, health and wellness. These areas are all important parts of life outside of sports, but you need to manage your education and careers along with your mental well-being to successfully navigate this transition in all spheres of life.

Whenever an athlete's playing days come to an end, transitioning to the next phase of life can be a difficult process. Whether you're a senior in college, or, in my case, a thirteen-year veteran of professional baseball, it's difficult to leave behind a sport in which you've invested so much time and effort/heart and soul and it's been such a big part of your life. Very few athletes choose to walk away from their sport. The choice is often made for them, which makes it much more difficult to separate and leaves many ill-prepared for what lies ahead.

Education and career decisions are one piece an athlete can put in place before their playing career ends. Prepare an educational and career plan with help from academic and career advisors while you're still playing. Find something that you enjoy and provides a challenge. I didn't have a plan in place when my career ended, so not only did I have to figure out what to do with my life, but I also faced the mental and emotional challenges that come with not competing anymore. No one prepared me for the realization that what I'd worked for my whole life was now gone. One day I was a professional athlete, someone that others looked up to, and the next, I was done. The mental transition remains the toughest part because it's hard to explain to others if they haven't been through it and it's not tangible. Finding a way to stay involved in the game and fill the void made it a somewhat smoother transition for me. But, don't expect it to be easy.

One of the things that many athletes deal with when they look back at their playing career is regret. Regret can cost you unnecessary time and energy and it gets you nowhere. I know from experience that running through scenarios of how you could have done things differently and how that would have changed the outcome of your career is fruitless and frustrating.

The solution? Do everything you can to succeed in your sport while you're playing. Prepare yourself mentally and physically for your sport. Practice to improve each day and be ready to excel during the games. Push yourself and leave it all on the field during every single game, so when you are done, you can look at yourself in the mirror and your teammates and say "I did everything I could."

Life after being a student-athlete is a difficult shift, but with a realization (usually early in the senior year) that it will happen, early preparation, an awareness of the challenges, and a willingness to reach out for help, student-athletes can more easily navigate the transition.[1]

James Biddick, a former athlete and career management expert, provides similar insight.

JAMES BIDDICK

(former field hockey athlete in New Zealand and Student-Athlete Career Development Program Manager at the University of Notre Dame)

There is a scene in the movie Moneyball where a baseball scout cautions a teenage Billy Beane (played by Brad Pitt) that "we're all told at some point in time that we can no longer play the children's game. We . . . don't know when that's gonna be. Some of us are told at eighteen, some of us are told at forty, but we're all told." This is true for every athlete, but particularly pertinent for the student-athlete.

How does one simply "move on"? How does a student-athlete begin to mentally move on from something that has occupied such a large part of their life—not only in terms of time through early-morning trainings and long travel; but for many student-athletes, their sport is also a huge part of their identify and social grouping.

Having been a former student-athlete and played to a high level in multiple sports, particularly field hockey, I know the mental adjustment from playing to no longer competing can be a challenging one. There are a number of different ways to help with the mental transition and it is hoped that the following paragraphs provide some understanding, as well as guidance, when faced with the inevitable task of moving on mentally from the "children's game."

There are those student-athletes who, as a result of the high demands placed on their time, body, and mind during college, are thankful to see the end of their college sporting career and are more than ready to embark upon the next chapter in their life. This specific group of student-athletes will never again feel the desire to pick up a bat, lace up a cleat, or put on a helmet. For them it is a welcomed transition, and from a psychological standpoint, they may experience greater happiness the day after their final game.

But what about those student-athletes less eager to leave the sporting spotlight upon graduation? One obvious and very common way to help with the adjustment is to remain involved with the sport through coaching. Although no longer on the field, there are many mental benefits gained from coaching that are similar to those felt by the student-athlete, such as being part of a team, as well as being around like-minded people who speak the same lingo and who inherently understand one another. Coaching also provides the former student-athlete with the satisfaction of "giving back" to the game they still care so much about, and the opportunity to act as a mentor for younger athletes (similar to the role played by seniors toward freshmen).

Another option that is less formal than coaching is social sporting leagues and general forms of physical fitness. Athletes who particularly enjoyed the training aspect of their sport, and still feel a desire to compete, continue with their fitness endeavors, through such communities as CrossFit. Social sporting leagues or CrossFit-type activities mimic many of the mental benefits experienced by student-athletes—comradery, physical enhancement, and perhaps the most important of them all—the challenge of competition.

Whichever path a student-athlete decides to take postgraduation, it is important to consider how no longer playing the game will impact their psyche, as well as what practical steps can be taken to support the mental transition.

Biddick's advice above is specifically for those who play four or five years and graduate with a degree. However, as we know well, there are different ways for a student-athlete's career to end:

1. End of eligibility/graduation (the aforementioned "traditional" path where the student completes four years of eligibility and earns a degree)

2. Injury (as described in numerous chapters so far, a major injury can quickly, if not instantly, end the athletic career of the student-athlete)

3. Being cut or released from team

4. Voluntarily choosing to stop

5. Not getting drafted or picked up as a free agent, or missing an Olympic team spot

All five career-end scenarios require different ways for the retiring student-athlete to mentally move on from her or his sport. One can be much better prepared for graduation than for either a career-ending injury or being cut. These two unexpected and sudden routes are much harder to move on from because there are a lot of "what if's" or "if only's" that many athletes think about and endlessly assess. If you voluntarily choose to stop competing, it is more likely you have already moved on, and it's easier to make your transition mentally on your terms. If you don't get selected in the draft or picked up as a free agent, you just have to accept the reality of the situation. If you miss the Olympic roster spot, maybe it just wasn't meant to be, but perhaps waiting another four years isn't going to work either. Is it time to move on?

Previous "secrets" in this book have covered the reality of your career finishing at the end of your eligibility. We have also shared the secret that preparation for this transition needs to start in your sophomore year. You've also been advised to be prepared for an injury to end your career at any moment in time, and how difficult that can be.

Getting cut or released from a team happens to student-athletes who don't improve or whose place is taken by a more talented younger player or who don't fit into their coach's plan anymore. In these cases, their scholarship is often revoked, and other decisions about staying at the university result.

In other cases, a coaching change or an institution's decision to cut a program for various reasons can affect your athletic career. These cases are out of your control, but nothing says they can't happen.

There are many ways you can deal with the end of your athletic career, and each is affected—as noted above—by the way in which your career ends. We summarize three approaches here.

1.   Going cold turkey (that is, hard stop, full change to your new life, move on from your sport completely). This is the most challenging and possibly the most depressing.

2.   Ongoing involvement as a nonathlete (for example, fan, volunteer).

3.   Continuing to work in your sport in a professional capacity (for example, professional employment in ticket sales, sponsorship, analytics, officiating, administration, coaching, training).

Most student-athletes are able to move on successfully if they have other passions to pursue. A career focus or other interests and activities can occupy the time the sport previously took up. This draws on a number of our secrets.

Kevin Brice, a former Division III baseball player at Pomona College, works for the Los Angeles Angels as a quantitative analyst. He reflects on his transition period and how he had to move on from playing the sport he loves. He was fortunate to find a job quickly, but the transition period for him was sudden and rapid. His experience provides valuable insight on the challenges that graduating student-athletes "changing status" encounter.

KEVIN BRICE

**(former student-athlete in baseball at Pomona College,
now Quantitative Analyst for the Los Angeles Angels)**

I found out I got a job two days before graduation, just after the season had ended, and I started the next week. The quick transition didn't allow me to think about it all that much, and I didn't have time to contemplate anything. The transition from playing to working got smoothed over by the fact that I am working for the Angels, and I am around my sport of baseball. Having that job set up after graduation is key in smoothing that transition out. . . . I would advise any athletes to try and stay around their sport to help with that transition.

Coming from a school like Pomona College, where academics are the priority, most of the guys have the reality that they are done playing after school. I think I realized I wasn't going pro after my first summer ball season after my freshman year of college. I was a good college baseball player, but didn't have the tools for the next level.

When I realized that, I decompressed a little bit and just tried to have as much fun as possible playing the game. Once I accepted that, and it is hard for a lot of guys to accept it before it's too late, I just wanted to enjoy playing the game, and enjoy being around my teammates. I wanted to make sure I had a plan B, and was prepared for the end of my collegiate career.

Elizabeth Woerle is a former Division I soccer player who had a successful collegiate athletic career and played professionally overseas after graduation. She attended graduate school at Ohio University and is now Assistant Athletic Director for Development at the University of North Texas. Like Kevin Brice, she had a successful transition from her senior year, heading to Europe to play soccer professionally for two years before returning to the United States for graduate school and to begin her career. She has this advice for senior student-athletes:

ELIZABETH WOERLE

**(former collegiate and professional soccer player,
now Assistant Athletic Director for Development at the University of North Texas)**

I think the best thing you can do is to continue to play if you have the chance. You can get a "real job" the rest of your life, but you can't always play sports [at a high performance level]. If you have the opportunity, your body allows it, do it. Second, enjoy every bit of your college career and invest as much as you can of yourself into it. If it hurts when your career ends and you have to hang the boots up, that means you truly invested yourself and you were committed.

If you can walk away and brush your hands off, then I would question your commitment and passion for the sport you were playing. Anything in life that we love and invest in, whether that be a sport, job, or relationship, if we lose it, it stings and it causes a bit of heartbreak. It's not bad that it meant a lot to you. It is important to grieve and recognize these emotions.

Sport can always be a part of your life one way or another. Lastly, my biggest piece of advice would be to not wish it away. Put your everything into every time you step on the field because that way you won't look back and think I wish I would have, could have, should have.

CHAPTER SUMMARY

No student-athlete wants to think about that last practice, meet, game, tournament, or competition, nor do you want to think about the day after your playing career ends. When it's accompanied by being told that you aren't going to make it pro, it stings even more.

But now you know that you should think about "the end" and plan for it (starting in the sophomore year)! That kind of thinking will go a long way toward preparing you for your senior year and life after.

Secret 14 Identify Who You Are

THE SECRET IN A FEW WORDS

Having an "identity crisis" is to be expected at some point during the transition out of sport and into the next chapter of your life. All those hours you have put into sport from the time you were a child now need to be focused on something else. As a student-athlete, you are always told to be in the present, enjoy the moment, soak it all in. Yes, you should do that. However, when you have been identified as a tennis player, football player, swimmer, or any other elite athlete for over a decade, you can feel lost when you no longer have that identity to those around you and to yourself. Right or wrong, it's common for your purpose in life to be associated with your identity. But you are not your sport. You are so much more than what you have done on the court or field the past few years. As you transition from your athlete identity to the next chapter of your life, it is time to reorganize your identity and adjust your goals to serve your new purpose.

IDENTIFY WHO YOU ARE

When we interviewed Jeff Rodin, Director of Community Outreach and Development for the Arizona Diamondbacks, he talked about the identity aspect of your transition, drawing from his experience as an athlete and a coach. Rodin stated,

> You must also ask yourself, "What's my purpose? Did I already fulfill my purpose? What's the point?" Knowing that your identity is not a student-athlete, or coach, it's much broader than that and that's why I think the things outside of the game—the people you

surround yourself with, the things you do, the things you believe, the things that you spend time doing—perspective is huge. If people don't have that perspective and you don't have someone help remind you where you came from and to not forget who you are, what is your identity? If your identity is the game, or your identity is your job, at some point that is going to stop.

Everyone has a different identity and a different experience after transitioning from sport to life. Because of this, we interviewed six former student-athletes to provide guidance on how to find your identity.

JONI LOCKRIDGE

(former softball student-athlete, former Director of Digital Strategy at the PGA, now Vice President of Strategy and Operations at iX.co)

HOW DID YOU HANDLE THE TRANSITION FROM SPORTS INTO LIFE, AND HOW DID YOUR IDENTITY CHANGE?

My graduation from college sports into life required that I shift from a physically driven team structure where I had developed and polished my skills over fifteen years, to a knowledge-driven organization . . . where I didn't know anything.

Looking back, I'm not sure I realized that I was facing a transition until I had to force myself up the steep side of the learning curve. But just like running hills, we all learn that it becomes easier once you embrace the burn. I recognized that the same skill sets that helped me achieve my athletic goals can also help me achieve my professional ambitions. It was not, however, a clean process:

I felt an overwhelming sense of *disappointment*. This isn't why I spent the last twenty years of my life in school. I *questioned* everything. It wasn't until I began taking control in answering some of the questions about myself that I started seeing breakthroughs.

I recognized that the more uncomfortable I was in the task, the more I learned, and the more satisfied I felt in the end. The logical next step was to find more responsibilities that made me uncomfortable and challenged me. From there, I found a sense of quiet confidence in my own skin and really started to get to know myself.

WHAT ADVICE WOULD YOU HAVE FOR FUTURE STUDENT-ATHLETES ON HOW TO HANDLE THEIR CHANGE IN IDENTITY?

The shift from athletics to work forces former student-athletes into a new social category—one that humbles us, but that spans our adult lives. My advice:

be open to new perspectives and be ready to modify your approach, but do not abandon what makes up your core identity. Your fundamental values and your culture should remain true. Your moral compass should not shift from North to South. You may find that your identity becomes more layered and more complex, but it's an evolution over time, not a revolution overnight.

Athletes come with a set of guiding principles that give us an advantage. We know how to work with people through wins and losses. Follow your instincts, and work as hard on yourself as you work on those TPS Reports (Oh, and watch *Office Space* if you didn't catch that reference).

WHAT WERE THE TWO HARDEST ASPECTS OF YOUR IDENTITY SHIFT, AND DID YOU SEE THE SAME THINGS HAPPEN TO YOUR FRIENDS AND TEAMMATES AS THEY WENT THROUGH IT TOO?

The hardest aspect of the transition was defining the strange, foreign ecosystem around me.

If you think about a traditional sports team structure, each competitor has a clear idea of other roles, personalities, strengths and weaknesses. A traditional work structure is more fluid. There is rarely a scoreboard or a shot clock. Positions aren't as clearly defined, and there are often three to four competitions going on at the same time. Training is loose, and more resembles that time your friend showed you how to drive a stick shift, than the hundreds of times your coach broke down your swing in painstaking detail.

My former teammates and I all dealt with this in our own ways. Most of us became a chameleon of sorts, changing colors to blend in or stand out . . . then returning to our natural state as soon as we were able to catch up with one another. A few changed their identity overnight in order to fit in quickly. I believe these individuals struggled the most.

Which brings up the second aspect: don't give up. Carry forward your athletic goal of developing the best version of yourself. Every. Single. Day.

Brooks Neal, Director of Corporate Partnerships at the New York Jets and former lacrosse student-athlete at Syracuse University, also talked about his identity upon graduation.

> For me, losing my identity was very, very challenging from the sense that you spend your whole life kind of working towards one thing. I grew up wanting to play football and lacrosse at Syracuse because I grew up outside of Syracuse, New York, and lacrosse is huge in the region. Ever since I can remember, it's all I really wanted to do. I made it. I got there and accomplished my goals . . . and it was exciting. Then it's all over in the blink of an eye. Lacrosse is a spring sport and I had everything going for

me heading into the NCAA tournament with graduation right around the corner. But, we lost in the first round of the NCAA Tournament and my athletic career came to a screeching halt. It felt like the world came crashing down on me and it was hard to cope with.

Dawn Buth, Assistant Director of Government Relations at the NCAA, talked about her experience as she had the opportunity to play professionally as well. She provided her perspective on values during her transition.

My transition from athlete to working professional was one of the most difficult identity challenges I have faced. I devoted hundreds and thousands of hours to the sport that I loved, then suddenly, skills that once seemed critical to my success no longer seemed useful or to have the same type of value. Early in my administrative career, one of my supervisors offered an important insight, "I don't care how hard you work, I care about results." As an athlete whose upbringing and athletic philosophy revolved heavily around the concept of process and work ethic, this statement generated a profound paradigm-shift. While it did not change my approach to work ethic or the degree to which I valued it, this statement taught me an important lesson about perspective: Not everyone values the same things, and to have the most impact, I needed to be proactive in understanding and considering the values of others. This began an important period of self-discovery in which the skills I developed as an athlete grew and evolved to help serve me in a new way.

Christa Mann, Senior Manager of Communications at the MLS, highlighted self-evaluation during her transition after playing overseas in Iceland.

It was definitely a situation where you are going through a lot of self-evaluation and you're trying to assess who you are and what you are. The hardest thing is seeing yourself as more than an athlete. Prior to going to Iceland, I saw myself as someone with a multitude of skills who just happens to play soccer and be pretty good at it. After Iceland it was like I was only a soccer player. When I stopped playing, I didn't know what I was supposed to be and was questioning if I had I prepared myself.

Hillary Nelson, former softball student-athlete at Arizona State University and now Trainer at the Positive Coaching Alliance, spoke about what she saw with her teammates and other student-athletes in relation to their identities. "The biggest mistake I see in athletes and all sports is when they fall for that mischaracterization that their identity is in their sport, meaning that they are only as valuable as their abilities as an athlete, and I had a friend tell me once 'I don't know what I would do without softball. I'll never do anything as well as I hit that ball.'"

Nelson's transition may have been easier than most after playing professionally, because she states, "My transition was much easier because I used sports to launch my career. I leveraged the contacts I made during my playing career into references for my first job. The world doesn't care about how much you know, but who you know and how hard you're willing to work." One could assume that getting a job right away and working hard toward different goals can provide you an identity instead of searching for one.

Hallie Olson, a former student-athlete at Ohio University and now Director of Notre Dame Global Partnerships, tells her story of how her identity changed once she started working for the Chicago Bulls, her first position out of school.

> I was a swimmer my whole life, and that was something that I identified with. I was never the most talented by any means, but my work ethic was there enough to where I could try and set myself apart from folks. Come college, as much as people say they're a student before an athlete, it's really hard. I would say that I was probably an athlete over a student. I definitely put a lot more focus on athletics. That's what was always driving me and running through my mind. I certainly cared about what was going to be happening with my career down the road, but that just seemed so far off that it seemed more important for me to focus on sports. From an identity standpoint, it was a challenge to transition into life because once I was done with school, I thought, "Okay, well who am I now?" I don't really have any sort of identity anymore. You're identified sometimes when you have your job, like when you introduce yourself at a networking event it's, "I'm Hallie, I work for the Chicago Bulls." It used to be, "I'm Hallie, I'm on the swim team," when I was hanging out with people at school. There was certainly a void that I felt, and I did feel a little bit lost because you lose all of that time that you spent doing things involved in your athletics. The year after I graduated, I didn't know what do I do with all this time? That whole year was just funky. I think back, I feel like I didn't have a direction. I feel like I wanted to work in sports but I didn't really know what capacity, I was really trying to find myself.
>
> It's just fine-tuning how you're describing yourself and also thinking of yourself. You are a brand. At the peak of what your brand used to be, your entire brand used to be athletics, and now it's not anymore. It will always be a part of you, but it's just not

something that is at the forefront anymore. Now it's just developing what's the next chapter? What is the next chapter of your life? What are you looking to achieve? Once I started feeling successful somewhere else, when I got a job, or when I was doing things in Ohio where I felt like I was making an impact, that's when I started feeling like I don't have this crisis, I'm not going through this brand-identity crisis anymore.

Hopefully you can relate to some of these stories, and realize that you aren't alone in this. Most student-athletes, and many non-student-athletes, go through this stage of trying to find their identity as they transition out of college. Knowing that your identity is always evolving and changing, you have to understand it isn't a quick fix. You can't just snap your fingers and make one appear. You can't go to McDonald's and order a new identity, either.

Now that you have read about finding your identity and have received advice from those who have gone through that process already, it is important to know that many student-athletes are easily depressed during this search for an identity.

It is common for any human to deal with depression and anxiety when making a major change in life. In the case of making a big decision, for example, such as getting married or buying a house, many people go through a period of "cognitive dissonance" or regret about making that momentous decision. It is normal and common.

This is no different, if not more profound, in the case of the graduating senior student-athlete. In fact, "about 30 percent of the 195,000 respondents to a recent American College Health Association (ACHA) survey reported having felt depressed in the last 12 months and 50 percent reported feeling overwhelming anxiety during the same period."

Often athletes claim it takes at least three years after their playing career is over before they play their sport again for fun, especially after competing at a high level. Most sports played at the intercollegiate pace cannot be repeated in a different recreational setting. Therefore, the competitive drive athletes love is hard to find in their specific sport again.

To illustrate that depression after college is very real, comments from three interviewees are included here.

Jamilah Ali, a former gymnastics student-athlete at Bowling Green State University and now Director of Compliance at Fordham University, recalled:

> When I graduated from college, everything changed. I was instantly depressed not knowing what would come next. Everyone my whole life knew me as the gymnast and when people would ask how my gymnastics was going, my heart broke more and more. Gymnastics was the one thing I always prided myself on,

since I had worked so hard to be successful in my sport. The depression just seemed to get worse and worse as the summer went on and life did not go the way I wanted.

I ended up becoming a club gymnastics coach and some days would tear up during coaching just thinking about how that was never going to be me again. I was so depressed because I never mentally prepared for life after gymnastics and felt I would never be as good at anything else. I ended up seeing a psychologist for about a month to really help me realize that I was so much more than just an amazing athlete.

So my advice to the younger athletes is for them to find another passion besides their sport while still playing. And not to be scared about opening up about how hard it is no longer being a college athlete, and to start talking about life after athletics before it happens.

Kristen Brown, a former basketball student-athlete at Northern Illinois University and now Deputy Athletics Director at Texas A&M University, added the following from the perspective of an administrator:

Some student-athletes can be depressed during that transition phase if they can't see the big picture or don't have any long-term plans. I could see the big picture and the long term because basketball wasn't everything for me, it didn't define me. I loved the game. I'm passionate about it. But if I didn't have it in my life, I was okay.

I had a good perspective on it. I think I was aided by the fact that I was still involved in my program and I was still around my team. When it is a clean break and they are not involved, not traveling, not interacting with their team, depression can occur because you they go from all those things to nothing.

As you can see, sport provides emotions and confidence that few other activities can when performance goals are achieved and awards are won. Thus, when a career ends via the student-athlete choosing to stop playing, being cut, getting injured, or running out of eligibility, the act itself can easily lead to depression. One way or another, "sport career termination induces dramatic changes in athletes' personal, social and occupational lives. This can, in turn, potentially affect individuals cognitively, emotionally and behaviorally."[1]

In some of these scenarios, depression arrives as student-athletes lose a core part of their identity and must redefine themselves. As we have stated, depression is something that 30 percent of graduating student-athletes deal with. You aren't alone. But don't ignore it—address it, and learn how to avoid it or deal with it.

If you have any symptoms of depression or concerns about mental health, get professional help immediately. Your institution will have mental health services available to you, just like any other student, in an anonymous, confidential manner. Additionally, some athletic departments offer further support to student-athletes. Be sure to become aware of the resources you have available to you.

Here's what we advise:

1.   Include time in your plan/schedule for friends (old or new) who are not your teammates.

2.   Find at least one interest/passion outside of your career choices and your sport (music, language, gaming group, etc.) that you can manage.

3.   Book at least two weeks a year in which you are free from sport and academics to focus your thoughts and expand your view of the world. Travel. Spend time with your family or friends.

4.   Talk to a sports psychologist or talk to your mentor(s) about any issues you may be having. Talking it out helps more than anything else.

5.   Spend more time involved in activities outside and with other people.

6.   Make sure you have a diet plan that works for you, and eat healthy as it pertains to your lifestyle.

7.   Continue to exercise regularly, as it will keep up your confidence and health.

8.   Develop a plan for stress management, as unexpected events will occur throughout life and create stress.

9.   Assess your strengths, build upon them, and then use them to your advantage.

10. Remind yourself about the positives that lie ahead and leverage your positive attitude about your future.

DIVERSITY, EQUITY, AND INCLUSION INTERVIEW WITH KERRY MCCOY

Kerry McCoy is one of the most decorated US wrestlers in history, having been a two-time NCAA champion, three-time NCAA All-American, and two-time Olympian. In addition to his athletic success, Kerry has become a national leader in the sport of wrestling through coaching and service to USA Wrestling, serving as the Secretary of the Board of Directors and the Chair of the Diversity Committee. He is the Executive Director and Head Coach of the California Olympic Regional Training Center. Recently, we spent some time with Kerry asking him about his experience as a Black student-athlete, coach, and national leader.

HOW DO YOU THINK ISSUES OF DIVERSITY, EQUITY, AND INCLUSION HAVE CHANGED IN COLLEGE SPORT SINCE YOU COMPETED AT PENN STATE FROM 1993 TO 1997?

My buzzword is "awareness." More people are aware of the differences that exist. The old saying is "In the locker room, we are all athletes." While this is still true, there is now an awareness of ethnic, racial, socioeconomic, and geographic diversity. You are all still athletes working toward that common goal of team success, but there is a recognition of the differences in a more meaningful way.

There is also more of a willingness to be open and be wrong. Making mistakes is okay, especially on college campuses. For example, you might be talking in a group and someone says something that stops conversation. Twenty years ago, someone might get punched in the mouth! Today, on college campuses, there is a willingness to have those conversations about why something is inappropriate or not understood and then you can bounce back and move forward from the situation. This is really important for you because it will make you a better leader after college.

ARE THERE ANY INSTANCES THAT STAND OUT TO YOU ABOUT BEING A BLACK ATHLETE?

The majority of my interactions have been implicit bias, and fortunately I have been able to rise above them. It's mostly the stereotypical "Oh, you aren't Black, you are Kerry." But I am Black, so when well-meaning people say they don't see me as Black but as a great wrestler or leader, it strips away part of my identity. Even if it's not said outright, it can be implied. For example, I might be in a conversation and someone says something about another person that is Black or makes a general statement and I have to stop the conversation to help them understand why it's not appropriate.

There have also been a handful of times athletically and professionally when I felt like I was judged differently because of the color of my skin. Even when I was being recruited at Penn State, it was common knowledge that there was a lack of diversity in the wrestling program. When I won NCAAs, I became Penn State's first Black NCAA wrestling champion. I understand there always has to be a "first," but even twenty years later, there have not been that many diverse wrestling champions [in the NCAA]. It's a reminder about where we still are as a society, because we are still having a lot of "firsts." From a leadership perspective, there were not a lot of Black and brown faces in wrestling leadership until recently. Instead of dwelling on it, I have focused on empowering the next generation while the diversity on the USA Wrestling board and committees continues to grow.

WHAT DO YOU WANT WHITE STUDENT-ATHLETES TO KNOW ABOUT HOW TO BE AN ALLY TO THEIR BIPOC TEAMMATES?

The best thing you can do is just be there as an ally all the time. I compare it to the motto that we see often when traveling, "If you see something, say something." It also works for being an ally. Even if someone from a diverse population is not around, if you hear something, you have to put a stop to it. That is the biggest thing: it's great to be supportive when somebody is around, but you have to be supportive all the time. You have to stop the conversation or action and stand up for the person or people not there.

Also, don't be afraid to make mistakes. But make them with an openness to say, "I'm sorry, I didn't understand," or, "Teach me how I can be better in this situation." I still make mistakes, but I am very open to learning from mine so I understand why and can choose my words better in the future. We all have blind spots, need to recognize that we do, and work together to be better.

WHAT IS ONE PIECE OF ADVICE FOR COLLEGE STUDENT-ATHLETES AS A KEY TO SUCCESS FOR LIFE?

Be open to learning. It's one of those concepts that I learned when I was very young. As an elite athlete, I was being coached by one of the national-team coaches, who had me working on a specific technique for two years, with me thinking, "It's not for me," "I can't do it," "I am wasting my time." But I never stopping trying. Finally, after two years, it clicked, and it became one of my highest-scoring techniques and helped me make my first Olympic team. So, even though I did not want to work on it, I trusted the coach and kept working, and it paid off.

To this day, I spend a lot of time deliberately learning from expert coaches from all sports. If you are open to learn, the likelihood of your success will increase exponentially.

CHAPTER SUMMARY

As you transition out of being an athlete and into the next chapter of your life, you must consider these four major actions:

1. Self-reflection and think more about who you really are

2. Look in the mirror and ask yourself what you want your identity to be

3. Figure out what your next move is and identify with that

4. You be you. Don't try to be someone you aren't

Your identity is always changing and adapting to life. Remember who you were as an athlete because it will always be a part of you, but find that next thing to take the place of being an athlete.

As simplistic as it sounds, if you get depressed for feeling lost, just talk to someone. The more you talk to people and try to figure out who you are, the more you will learn about yourself. With that said, it takes many former athletes a long time to move on from their sport, so patience is the key. In a world where everyone wants instant gratification, you may have to wait just a little bit to truly find yourself and your new identity.

Secret 15

Find Your Other Passions in Life as You Prepare to Be a Sophomore

THE SECRET IN A FEW WORDS

The majority of student-athletes don't participate in their sport after they transition to life after college. Either the competition just isn't the same or they are burnt out or it's impractical (for example, who goes out just to throw around a javelin for fun with friends?). Finding new passions will help you enjoy life moving forward. And this is something you must start to do in your sophomore year. You've survived your freshman year, so now is the key time to prepare for your transition to postgraduation life and find those other passions. Sure, we get that it is three years away, but that also means you have only three years to prepare for your career launch or grad school. Just imagine you are walking into a job interview for a position that you'd love to have. Early in the process, the interviewers ask you to describe the relevant experiences you've had for the job. You haven't had many but explain that you were a student-athlete. You then hear another candidate has a double degree and completed two internships, three international learning experiences, and two practicums with industry-leading blue-chip organizations. How can you possibly compete? This secret is to "find your other passions in life" in your sophomore year, because if you aren't passionate about what you are doing, you aren't likely to succeed at it since you won't want to.

DANNY WHITE

(Senior Associate Athletic Director, Student-Athlete Services and University Affairs, Virginia Tech)

It is really hard to learn about yourself when you aren't experiencing things. Different experiences will help you determine what you do and don't like.

FIND YOUR OTHER PASSIONS IN LIFE
AS YOU PREPARE TO BE A SOPHOMORE

Every student-athlete comes from a different background, plays a different sport, and has different success in athletics and academics. However, to remain balanced (Secret 6) in the postgraduation years, it is important to have other passions—at least one—beyond sport and school. Your sophomore year is the time to begin this discovery journey. Try new things, develop different interests, and then figure out what you care about.

This is a pretty open-ended secret. We get that. But it is not to be underestimated nor delayed to your junior year. A passion for something is rare. Don't misconstrue watching something on television regularly (your favorite TV show) as a passion. A passion should be something you can do forever, that you can get better at, and that can draw you to other social groups. It could be history, playing the guitar, or woodworking.

And this does not need to wait for graduation. Some quick tactics you can start anytime. In fact, start today. These are randomly presented, and some are vague while others are specific. Just some ideas to draw from, in no particular order!

- Take an interesting elective on a topic you might really like.
- Join a student club that is unrelated to your major or your sport (and that you might be interested in).
- Develop a new social network around a topic you find interesting.
- Join a club or some other social competitive group.
- Attend a guest lecture on campus.
- Join a local community group.
- Learn a trade.
- Be curious.
- Learn to play golf, pick up tennis. Or an instrument. Or to speak a new language.
- Run a marathon, do a triathlon, try CrossFit, or take a yoga class.
- Share a hobby with a parent or grandparent (for example, hunting, travel, etc.).
- Volunteer at an event, a gallery, or a charity.

After graduation is also a time to find another passion or two. Here are four things to consider when finding other passions in life postgraduation:

1.   Revisit prior passions. Before sport was all-consuming to you, what else did you enjoy? Now that you will have time to explore other interests, an old passion may resurface.

2.   To play an intercollegiate sport, you have to have passion for your sport. Your sport may be your ultimate passion, and that is okay, but figure out how to pursue that passion in another way after your athletic career: as a coach, fan, professional, volunteer, and so on.

3.   When your sport is your identity for much of your life, a new passion will bring about new identity and excitement.

4.   Trial and error will be required to find your passion. You might not hit it on the first attempt and you may not even be sure what precisely you are looking for. Try new things and see what keeps your interest.

Former student-athletes had a lot to say on the topic of passion.

Brooks Neal, former lacrosse student-athlete at Syracuse University and now Director of Corporate Partnerships at the New York Jets, told us, "For me, it sounds dorky, but I became an avid reader of books. I never read a book in my life for pleasure, honestly, unless I was forced by my parents or my school. I became an avid reader because I didn't know how to settle my mind or my body. It was a good way for me to calm down at night rather than being exhausted from athletics."

Neal also would "encourage you to take up triathlon training as it keeps that competitive fire going, or find something intellectually stimulating. I have teammates who have become elite-level CrossFitters or elite-level tri-athletes who realize that their athletic ability can be used in other ways outside of the sport they played. For athletes, it is filling that void in their life, and when you graduate, I think just going wide and going deep with experiences and interests can really help."

Hallie Olson, former student-athlete at Ohio University and now Director of Notre Dame Global Partnerships, said that volunteering was her passion, as it was a way for her to give back. "Your priorities change, and you realize there's more you can do outside of yourself. I was very selfish in school. I cared where I was supposed to be and it was always me, me, me. Now, it's me and my husband, and . . . and giving back to other people and really making an impact on my community here in Chicago."

Eddie Gill, former NBA player and now successful Financial Planner and a TV Analyst for the Indiana Pacers on Fox, agreed that "volunteering in the community is one way to get outside of your comfort zone and do something different, while being a productive member of society. Throughout my career, I did a number of camps and things like that with kids so I knew that that was one of my passions. Being able to provide a service is a passion for me. The service component has translated to where I'm at now in the financial service industry. By being proactive during my career, I was able to find a passion to carry out a different career when basketball was over for me."

Drew Saylor, now Hitting Coordinator with the Kansas City Royals, mentioned curiosity, saying "curiosity is one thing that college should do for people from an athletics and from an education standpoint, and even just from a human being standpoint, you should always be curious. You should always sit there and find the "Why's?" You should always sit there and find ways to improve yourself on a day-to-day basis. Curiosity may lead to those newfound passions you can improve on."

Kristen Brown, former student-athlete at Northern Illinois University and now Deputy Athletics Director at Texas A&M University, expressed that her "two passions in life are young people and mentoring," which led her to a career in college athletics following graduation.

So, what should you do to pick this right passion? How do you find yours?

Garrett Shinoskie was the former Director of Athletic Performance at Zone Athletic Performance in Scottsdale, Arizona. He was a Division III football player and is a believer in student-athletes finding additional passion(s) outside of sports and academics.

> Keeping an open mind is critical in all aspects of life! When you're exploring other interests, especially new interests, you have to walk into it with the mentality that you know nothing and are starting at the bottom. Putting unrealistic expectations on yourself will only lead to unnecessary pressure and disappointment. I would advise student-athletes to immediately explore new passions or potential passions with your newfound time [post-graduation].
>
> Being able to check out multiple avenues of interests will be the key to separating passions that could lead to careers or are better left as hobbies. The best recommendation I can give for making a career out of a passion, is to get experience in the industry and ask questions.
>
> Whether it's interning, part-time employment, shadowing an expert in the field, check out the industry and ask the right questions. What are the requirements of the job, will you need more education, does the industry standard of income work for you, etc. If you think you have any interest in something, do your research and found out how to become involved and learn more. If you never try you'll never know.

Steve Watson, Athletic Director at Loyola University Chicago, talked about how he found the passion of working in college athletics. In our interview with him, he stated, "I had such a great experience as an athlete. I knew that as I was wrapping up the professional career that college athletics was where I wanted to be. I enjoyed my time as a professional. Watching the freshmen become seniors and coming back to campus as professionals out in the workforce, that is the best. To be able to experience that, it doesn't get much better than that."

Pat O'Conner, who retired as President and CEO of Minor League Baseball at the end of 2020, stresses that student-athletes need to be ready for other pursuits in life. He gives the following warning: "Transitioning from athlete to former athlete involves more than having your uniform taken away from you. The very nature of your life will be altered at some level. It is an exciting new beginning in your life and nothing more detrimental than a rite of passage to maturity as a person. With a couple of caveats, successful transition is incumbent on you making smart decisions and committing to this new path with the same zeal and intensity with which you competed as an athlete."

For those who want to work in college athletics after being a student-athlete, Terri Steeb-Gronau, Vice President of Division II at the NCAA, has some advice: "College athletics is still a part of higher education. If you are a person who wants to be involved in college athletics and you don't like teaching or coaching or mentoring, then college athletics is not the place for you. I tell people if you want to be involved in college athletics, there is a teaching component regardless of what you are doing. If you don't like working with young adults, it isn't the place for you."

Steeb-Gronau also mentioned that, "ultimately, you have to look inside yourself, and find what you are passionate about, outside of sport whether that is teaching, finances, environment, or working in the community. Is there something you look back on your life and say this is something that I enjoy, other than your sport? What energizes you? What gets you up in the morning? These are questions you have to ask yourself to determine what you're passionate about."

THE IMPORTANCE OF THE SOPHOMORE YEAR

In doing the research for this book, the authors thought back to our collective experiences as student-athletes and found everything pointed to the importance of the beginning of our sophomore (second) year. We were settled in the routine of college, had found our place on the team, had acquired a supportive social circle, and were comfortable with our choice of academic majors. It was the point to start focusing extra activities on finding a career (or obtaining entry to a graduate or professional degree) postgraduation. A key to this was finding our "other" passions.

If you're early in your sophomore year, now is the time to plan. This book can certainly help, as can your academic advisors, mentors, coach, parents, and classmates.

THE TRANSITION

When student-athletes graduate, they need to find a career or continue to progress toward one. In today's world, a college degree is a requirement for many careers and the number of people who hold one is very high. In the United States in the fall of 2021, according to the National Center for Education Statistics,[1] approximately 19.7 million students will attend US colleges and universities. About 3 million of these students graduate each year.

Importantly, for you, the next competition (for a career) is against the entire market of job seekers, not just other student-athletes. In this world, there are only "starters." Everyone else gets cut. As previously noted, in many careers (for example, accounting, electrical engineering), being a student-athlete has no impact on your "hireability." In fact, the time and effort put into practicing for your sport might represent an "opportunity cost" that detracts from your ability to win a job competition. Of course, you have the inside track on how to capitalize on your student-athlete experience to make sure you won't be in the situation of "only" having been a student-athlete.

THE CAREER

A career is not easy to find or stay in. Industries change, jobs disappear. For example, in the 1960s, there were thousands of jobs in the printing industry partly because companies like Kodak made a lot of film for cameras. Those jobs no longer exist. Other fields, full of opportunity in the future, may not even exist yet.

You may choose one career path and decide shortly thereafter that you want to follow a different track. The Bureau of Labor Statistics reports that the average US working woman changes jobs every 4.5 years, followed closely by the average US working man, who alters his employment every 4.7 years.[2]

Matt Vansandt, a former track and field student-athlete and now Assistant Commissioner of Championships at the Big South Conference, recalled his path: "I worked in real estate lending for the first three years out of college. I figured out I hated it and it wasn't what I wanted to do. I went back to grad school to pursue college athletics. Track taught me how to fail and keep getting back up again and again. That helped me with my career path in the sense that I failed at my first career path and had to get up and try something different."

There is no grand plan for a career, but it should be taken in steps. Some steps go forward, backward, or sideways, and sometimes you may feel like you are walking in circles. You don't have to decide what your whole life path is going to be, because you simply can't. Many aspects of life are unpredictable, and therefore you need to be equipped with more than one plan.

A career requires diligent planning and preparation and the ability—like sport—to beat other competitors seeking the same thing. Many coaches will say, "When you aren't getting better, you are getting worse because someone else is getting better." Make sure you prepare and plan for a career just like you do for your sport, because if you aren't getting better every day, you will fall behind others. Make it a goal to become better at one thing, even a little thing, every day.

SO, WHAT SHOULD YOU DO?

Step 1: Create a plan before your sophomore year to find other passions

To ready yourself for success in life, figure out your passions, make a plan, and follow it. Truly activate your sophomore (second) year.

Here are the significant elements of your plan:

1.   Get a career coach—if one is not provided by the university, find one.

2.   Finalize your major, and study what you want to study, not what's easiest.

3.   Schedule your classes so you have more freedom to gain experience in your junior and senior year.

4.   Make a list of at least five postgraduation goals (for example, go to law school, start my own business, get a job with a pro sports team).

5.   Identify and build a relationship with a mentor/advisor in each of the areas noted in your answer to element #4.

6.   For each answer to element #4, research and list the experiences, skills and aptitudes required for success in that pursuit.

7.   Prioritize what is most important to you when making decisions about a job/career and its fit (things like salary, benefits, geography, proximity to friends or family, etc.).

8.   Keep up on industry trends and career trends that will help you in your research as you develop a career plan and path. One way to do this is by getting involved on campus with an organization or club (if you cannot get an internship).

9.   Gain as much knowledge as you can so you will make informed and educated decisions about career options.

10.   Realize that finding a job or getting into a professional program (like medical school) is highly competitive, difficult, and requires

years of preparation. Apply the same type of planning and preparation as you do in athletics toward your efforts to achieve the goals from element #4.

Step 2: Keep a realistic perspective on things

Many of the former student-athletes we interviewed highlighted having a realistic perspective. It is vital to have an open mind and be realistic about your upcoming decisions. Two interviewees below specifically help describe this step.

Kristen Brown said during her interview that "you have to look at it as one door shuts, another one opens. You have to change your perspective and your mentality, and look for an opportunity to make something happen."

HILLARY NELSON

(former softball student-athlete at Arizona State University, now Trainer at the Positive Coaching Alliance)

Focus on controlling the controllables. For me, that was always attitude and effort. Looking back, I was most successful when I controlled my attitude and efforts toward practice, training, studies, and everything else. All I ever wanted was a national championship. I wanted to go to school. I told my coach when getting recruited. "I want to graduate in three years. I want to get my MBA and I want to win a national championship."

Coach Clint Meyers gave me all those things. At the end of the day, we were holding the national championship trophy above our heads. We went to bed that night and woke up the next day and then we started all over again. The next year, we just wanted to win a national championship all over again. Understanding that you'll never be fulfilled by that [big win] is important. Keeping things in perspective, happiness is the ultimate prize and it is not going to be a trophy or a piece of paper. It's going to be the relationships and the experiences you build with the people around you while you're a student-athlete.

CHAPTER SUMMARY

Eddie Gill summarized the search for new passions perfectly with his favorite saying: "Get comfortable being uncomfortable."

Everyone has different passions, and some may have only one. Passions may come and go or completely change. No matter how many different passions you have, it is always good to find a new one. However, passions can't be forced; it's all natural, as they say. Now that you are transitioning from being an athlete to the rest of your life, you need to find some other passions in your life, because life has a lot to offer.

At this point, you should also be very aware of the realities of going professional (or making an Olympic team) and you should have started your preparations for life after sports. These include identifying your other passions. The reason we suggest the sophomore year for this passion identification and career planning is that, for many of you, the freshman year is for growing up and figuring out who you are. However, many wait too long to think about their future until it hits them square in the face at graduation. So, sophomore year is the time. We're not trying to scare you or be your therapist, just encouraging you to plan.

Secret *16* Invest in Yourself, Your Health, and Your Future

THE SECRET IN A FEW WORDS

One of the hardest aspects of transitioning from being an athlete to being a working professional is the change in lifestyle and habits. Retired athletes do not train as they used to when they were competing. When you, the student-athlete, are done competing, other responsibilities will take priority. Jobs, family, and many other endeavors will take priority over working out. Each individual has his or her own priorities, and there is no specific magical order that one must follow.

Throughout life, priorities change all the time, and your change in priorities as you first transition into life as a nonathlete is only the start. Nutrition not only becomes more difficult, but the eating habits you developed as an athlete most likely won't work for too much longer. During college, you could sleep in some days based on your class schedule, but when you have a job, your sleep schedule will likely change and you may find you need more and higher-quality sleep.

This secret is simple: It's necessary for you to invest in yourself, your health, and your future. All these changes in your lifestyle are just a few of the adjustments you will have to make as you start your career. At the end of the day, it is a lifestyle you create and you live by. Why not strive to make it a healthy lifestyle in hopes of healthy results?

INVEST IN YOURSELF, YOUR HEALTH, AND YOUR FUTURE

While you are competing and training, eating habits become a little abnormal due to the amount and type of food that you need to consume. In college, because of events and classes, you may eat at odd hours, creating bad habits for when you are not training (or training less).

Your daily student-athlete schedule is quite rigorous and can be a grind for those who take their academics seriously or who are enrolled in challenging or high-volume programs or majors. After you have finished your athletic career, many won't change their eating and nutrition habits. This can cause issues over the years because of potential changes in your training levels and your metabolism as you get older.

Yes, the transition from being a student-athlete to being a working professional isn't easy. No one said it would be. Having more money is a positive (and a prospect you are likely excited about!), but there are also downsides, such as the many aspects of our lifestyle that we may have to put on the back burner (or let slip from time to time) in order to maintain employment, family, parenting, home ownership, and other adult responsibilities.

Brett Fischer is a Licensed Physical Therapist, Certified Athletic Trainer, and Certified Strength and Conditioning Specialist. He has worked with the University of Florida, New York Jets, PGA and Senior PGA TOUR, and the Chicago Cubs. He currently provides sports performance training and rehab to MLB, NFL, NBA, NHL, and world-ranked tennis players. Fischer is also currently the staff Physical Therapist with the NFL's Arizona Cardinals. Over the years, he has dealt with many athletes and professionals, providing him with the experience to offer the following.

BRETT FISCHER

Student-athletes are usually given a program by a strength coach or some medical professional. All of the sudden, now it's over and there's no one there to tell them what to do and when to do it. They have to rely on what they were taught in high school or college then all of the sudden, they're on their own. From a principle standpoint, that's probably the biggest adjustment that student-athletes have to make during their transition into life.

From a nutrition standpoint, a lot of student-athletes face problems when transitioning because they were probably provided some kind of stipend, food plan, or prepared food. . . . All of a sudden now your workouts aren't as long, you're not training as hard as you used to, and now eating the same way you used to eat back in college doesn't work. It's an adjustment because even in the NFL, I'll see guys post-career that are heavier a couple years later. I've seen some guys who were defensive backs who weighed 190 pounds, and they're 265 now, and you can't recognize them.

Athletes have been training so long and hard that it's something they use to get away from things. It's so much a part of their whole life. UCLA did research on Brain Mapping, and it showed whether you were in college or pro, when you no longer have a team to go to, the brain perceived that as being rejected. It's the same mechanisms that the brain detects as an injury. They lose their purpose of life. It's always been make it to the pros or be in the pros, and then one day it's over, now what? They don't have a team to go to. There's no schedule for them anymore. It's like you get divorced.

Mentally preparing and physically preparing for that transition is important, but so is emotionally preparing. College is different because they're not making money yet, but they'll still have that same soul-search as professional athletes do when they retire. I've seen that too where players didn't make the NFL and they put all of their dreams into playing a sport, and now they're no longer a part of a team and the locker room with all the guys and they're all alone. That's a big change emotionally as well as physically.

Your emotional health is going to affect your physical health, and you really can't separate the two from each other. The emotional struggle is the biggest part of transition struggles. They have no place to go. They feel like they're not a part of the team. They miss the locker room atmosphere. They miss their friends.

For many student-athletes, they've been told where to go, when to go and, in real life, that's not really the case. You're now in a situation where you have to make your own choices. What time do you eat? What time do you work out? What time do you go to work? Are you late? No one's going to be knocking on your door, making sure you wake up or giving you wake up calls. There's a transition of being responsible.

Louie Iglesias, a former Division I tennis player at the University of Toledo who went on to a successful career in sport business, offers his perspective as a former student-athlete.

LOUIE IGLESIAS

(former tennis student-athlete, now Relationship Banker at JPMorgan Chase)

When I was competing, I didn't really watch what I ate because of the amount of hours that I'd be on the court. At least three to five hours a day. I just ate and I was probably putting down about five thousand calories a day. After my career was over and I stopped playing, the eating never stopped. I never trained myself to portion control or count calories or control carbs. At age twenty-two, I gained fifteen pounds in the first year that I had stopped playing. I wasn't burning the same amount of calories that I was burning previously, and I never conditioned my body to eat at a certain time of the day or be disciplined about my diet, which didn't help me when I stopped playing. When you start working, you don't have as much downtime as you did when you were an athlete, or certainly a student. When you're working, especially in your twenties, a lot of those first jobs out of college are where you're putting in sixty to seventy hours a week.

For a lot of those jobs, you're young, you're expected to put in a lot of hours and it's not uncommon to have a job where you only get thirty minutes for lunch. Then it becomes a matter of convenience. The average American between the ages of twenty-two and twenty-nine will change jobs seven times. So, why is that relevant? It suggests that between the ages of twenty-two and twenty-nine your schedule is going to be all over the place and at the very least, less stable.

When someone's schedule gets thrown upside down, the first thing impacted is always the diet. For an athlete, it's all about the routine. You want to get into your comfort zone and your routine because we are all "Creatures of Habit." It's almost like saving money, either you make it a priority or you don't.

When you enter that phase in your life where there's instability in terms of your schedule, what you need to do is plan the day around your meals. If you know that you only have thirty minutes for lunch, then pack a lunch. Everybody's a little bit different, but the main point is to create good habits and create a routine for yourself.

The biggest lifestyle change for me [following retirement as an athlete] was adjusting to the fact that I wasn't preparing for a tournament. I was a creature of habit. Every month of the year, I was always preparing for something. Tennis really didn't have an offseason, and there was always a tournament coming up.

Essentially when I graduated, it was like all of that stopped suddenly. All I knew how to do was to be a student and an athlete. I never worked at an internship in college. I never did any of that. I was just a student-athlete, and that's all I knew until I was no longer doing it. I found myself really behind the eight-ball, and really behind many people I went to school with. For me, I felt like a huge part of me died and there was a new Louie emerging that I didn't really know what to make of because I had no previous bearings to make any sense of it.

I got so much fulfillment in playing my sport, practicing for my sport, and working on my craft, that I didn't know where I was going to find my fulfillment now. Now I ask myself all the time, what do I want to aim for?

CHRISTINA WRIGHT

(former student-athlete at American University, now Assistant Professor of Instruction and Multicultural Faculty-in-Residence at Ohio University)

Christina Wright is a former Division I indoor and outdoor track-and-field student-athlete at American University (AU) in Washington, DC. She currently holds the indoor and outdoor shot-put records, and is number 2 on the AU All-Time Top Ten List for discus. She formerly worked at the NCAA in various roles. We asked her some pointed questions related to health following retirement as an athlete.

HOW DID YOUR DIET AND EATING HABITS CHANGE FOR YOU AS A NONATHLETE?

My diet and eating habits as a student-athlete did not change when I completed my eligibility in May 2007. Like many student-athletes, it was a bittersweet moment. For me it was no more lugging my throwing equipment on and off campus for practice, van rides with the men's team because my events always started early and ended late, scheduling everything and anything around my practice, class or competition schedule, it was freedom. But with this newfound freedom, I was still chained to bad habits. I had spent the past six years "bulking up" because throws are about physics.

I wasn't growing taller and getting longer limbs, so naturally, we focused on power and force. I went from two meals a day to five meals a day and mega carb-loading. I mean who doesn't eat a big bowl of pasta at least two days before a track meet, right? I kept eating at the same pace and portions as a student-athlete, but aside from a few club volleyball and softball games, I ceased all physical activity. I didn't handle the transition well—mostly because I love to cook and bake—and after living in the residence halls for four years, I finally had the freedom to cook and eat what I wanted, whenever I wanted.

I didn't drink much alcohol or soda during those years, but adding those items to already unbalanced eating habits didn't help. Instead of the freshman fifteen, I gained the retired student-athlete thirty, and maybe even more.

WHAT ADVICE DO YOU HAVE FOR FUTURE STUDENT-ATHLETES ON LEARNING TO MANAGE THEIR DIET WHILE THEY ARE COMPETING?

Almost a decade after the end of my student-athlete career, I was diagnosed with type 1 diabetes. Now I have to keep food and activity logs, just like I did in college, to help me manage my condition. If I could do it all over, I would have continued keeping a log because then I would have a visible accountability log showing me the caloric intake was way off-balance from my physical activity.

I am more conscious now of how my body reacts to certain foods—foods that make my glucose levels soar, foods that give me energy, etc. The other piece that would have helped me with the diet transition is the trendy concept of meal prep. This would have reduced eating out all the time and controlled my caloric intake with portioned meals appropriate for my age, health, and physical activity levels.

WHAT WAS THE BIGGEST PART OF YOUR LIFESTYLE CHANGE WHEN YOU FINISHED COMPETING?

Believe it or not, sleep. I finally was sleeping at least eight hours a night. In college I would average four to five hours at night and a two-hour nap, which I commonly referred to as siesta time. I look back and have no idea how I survived college without sleep. And then I think how much better a student and student-athlete I would have been if I had slept more regularly.

WHAT ADVICE DO YOU HAVE FOR FUTURE STUDENT-ATHLETES ON CONTINUING TO EXERCISE AFTER YOU ARE DONE COMPETING?

I tried many different programs, even hired a personal trainer at one point. I found if I could blend exercise with some sort of social activity, that was the best motivation for me. I let myself fall into the trap of focusing on weight loss goals, and don't get me wrong, that's important; but when I was a student-athlete, setting realistic goals was key.

If I focused on weight, I didn't weigh myself every week. I focused on percentage lost and not number of pounds. My sport isn't one where I randomly pick up a discus and go into a backyard and throw. Post student-athlete days, my best workouts were thirty-minute intervals on an inclined treadmill, two to three times a week. Like anything else, you have to make it a priority for yourself. I was so eager to finally take a break that I lost the health benefits associated with playing sports.

WHAT ADVICE DO YOU HAVE FOR FUTURE STUDENT-ATHLETES ON MAKING THEIR EXERCISE FUN?

Friends, or at least an accountability partner or group. As much as we love our respective sports, our teams were our social support web. Why wouldn't we want to create a similar team post–competition days? There are so many great options now: hot yoga, Zumba, CrossFit, etc. And when did 5K's, half-marathons, and marathons become so popular?

I hated running, probably because I associated it more with punishment than conditioning, but still, some people find running fills that competitive hole. Find something you enjoy and attach goals to it and that's the winning combination, as simple as that.

PREPARING FOR A HEALTHY TRANSITION

As your student-athlete days start to wind down, what should you do to prepare for a healthy life after competitive sport? We have a few suggestions based on our research and experiences.

1. Create a Structure Built around Physical Activity

As you've read, structure is a must as an athlete. Everything is scheduled, every day. Class, practice, training, competitions, tutoring, and all other aspects of your life are scheduled. After having been accustomed to so much structure, the majority of athletes struggle when there is no longer structure to their days and there are no longer professionals structuring their days for them. Having to create your own schedule based on your priorities is tough, especially when large stretches of time are now free, and scheduling is not a task you are used to doing.

For example, twenty-four to thirty-five hours a week of structured training and physical activity are all of a sudden gone. Having thirty hours a week to do whatever you want is quite the overload for athletes who don't know what to do with the time that was once part of a routine built around training.

Most athletes' motivation to maintain and continue training disappears after their athletic career is over. Thus, you need to build a structure that includes physical activity, social time, nutrition (based on current output), and sleep (expecting to move to a lifestyle based on a forty-hour work week or a variation thereof, depending on your professional aspirations).

Then within that structure, replace the former training (thirty hours is certainly not necessary, but daily activity that burns calories is).

Brett Fischer suggested that you try to figure out what you enjoy doing:

> Try different things. It could be rowing. It could be hiking. It could be something of a fitness nature to keep yourself going because you have to create endorphins.
>
> Athletes hate to work out because they've worked out their whole life and they had to run sprints. We encourage former student-athletes to find those things they enjoy to do (and not running sprints anymore is just fine), but just find something else to do. There is just something about breaking a sweat that makes you feel good. Secondly, find something that's not going to hurt your body. Some student-athletes who may have had some injuries over the years playing college sports may not be able to run as much as they'd want to. Find yourself something to do just to keep yourself active.

2. Institute Portion Control in Your Diet and Be Aware of Nutrition

Brett Fischer advises that "with nutrition, you always want to continue with the proper proteins, carbohydrates, and fats along with portion control.

It's easier to eat healthier in today's world . . . so there are no excuses because there are so many more options."

The keys as you transition from a calorie-burning athletic machine into a regular person are to reduce your portions, balance intake of food with calories expended, and remove or limit alcohol, desserts, and other sugary foods. Ensure that you get enough fruit and vegetables daily (some guidelines suggest five a day is a good rule). Most important is portion control, which is the key for maintaining moderation. There are a number of methods to make sure this happens. Ask a nutritionist or do some online research to find out.

Mike Doehla, Founder and CEO of Stronger U, and NASM Certified Fitness Nutrition Specialist, gave us his take on nutrition for former student-athletes.

MIKE DOEHLA

(Founder and CEO of Stronger U)

The transition from student-athlete to postgraduation life can be quite a shock in some areas of life. However, in other areas, it is more like a slow, gradual evolution. In the case of nutrition and body composition, it is a mix. Immediately, your activity likely reduces, training changes, and external motivation may wane. Even though these changes are immediate, the impact on your body may not be evident for months or even a year or more. Because of these changes, former student-athletes often experience weight gain, muscle loss, and a deterioration of overall health.

In my time as CEO of Stronger U working with hundreds of clients, many of whom are former athletes, I have developed a list of suggestions that will help you avoid the pitfall of losing the muscle you have worked so hard for, gaining body fat, and starting down the road to poor overall health.

TEN NUTRITION TIPS FOR FORMER STUDENT-ATHLETES

1. *Be aware of overall caloric intake.* With reduced activity, there is less energy expenditure. Eating the same amount with less activity results in fat accumulation.

2. *Watch your fat intake.* Fat has the most calories at nine per gram, and it's everywhere! Keeping your fat intake in check will automatically reduce your calories.

3. *Eat a lot of protein.* Protein will keep you full and help you preserve and build muscle.

4. *Eat your veggies.* Vegetables can be very filling, low on calories, and packed with nutrients.

5. *Eat out less.* If you keep meals out to a minimum, you can save a lot of calories (and money). Restaurants love fat and carbs. These foods are easy to overeat and quickly add up in overall calorie consumption.

6. *Learn to cook.* Learning to cook will help you choose foods that align with the food-related tips listed here. You control the ingredients and portions, and it's easy to cook a little extra and pack it up for lunch the next day.

7. *Step on the scale.* What can be measured can be managed (just like your sport performance), and having an eye on weight fluctuations can keep you on track.

8. *Go for walks.* Walking accounts for a large portion of the calories you burn, so make sure you're moving. A general rule of thumb is to figure out how many steps you are getting now and increase that by two to three thousand per day. For most, the sweet spot is between eight and ten thousand per day.

9. *Prioritize sleep.* You've known this for years and it still holds true. Getting adequate sleep is not just for recovery but also decision-making. A well-rested version of you is a better decision maker.

10. *Reduce alcohol consumption.* Not only does alcohol have a lot of extra calories, but it also impairs sleep, fat loss, muscle building, and decision-making.

Fischer provides some good guidance:

> Sleep is a big part of a healthy lifestyle. There's a lot of things with sleep that are important. It's important to get six to eight hours every night and that's just to refuel the body. You want to find a place that's dark, and a place that's cool. Video games and cell phones really stimulate you before bed, so try to make sure you are in rest mode before you go to sleep. It's just stimulating your brain and your nervous system where it gets to the point where it's hard to turn it off. With professional sports teams, they research how much time guys are getting their sleep in and it's important that these guys get at least that six to eight hours. The good thing about sleep is you can make it up. If you had a short night, you can take a nap, and your body will make up for it. But if you keep doing that over and over, it puts a toll on your physical system as well as your mental system.

Here are five tips to help improve your sleep habits:

1. Don't eat too close to bedtime.

2. Limit exposure to light and electronics.

3. Wind down with reading, meditation, or prayer. Your phone is a distraction.

4. Don't keep your bedroom too warm.

5. Get seven to eight hours of sleep.

In a 2015 article, "A Recipe for Energy Management Success," Taylor Grayson interviewed Dr. Brian Hainline, chief medical officer at the NCAA. Hainline said, "An often overlooked ingredient to a person's overall well-being is energy management." He further noted that "energy management can be broken into different aspects that all apply to well-being. The most important sector of energy management is often forgotten—not only by college athletes, but everyone: SLEEP. The average person should strive for about seven hours of sleep every night."[1]

To back up Hainline's point, an NCAA study published in 2016 released data showing that student-athletes clearly are not getting enough sleep.

National Comparison Data on Days of Restful Sleep per Week (Enough Sleep to Feel Rested in the Morning)

Number of days	Athletes		Non-Athletes (NCHA-ACHA	
	Male	Female	Male	Female
0–3	52%	57%	55%	60%
4–5	31%	32%	33%	30%
6–7	17%	11%	12%	9%

NCAA Research. (January 2016). *Results from the 2015 GOALS Study of the Student-Athlete Experience.* Retrieved on May 22, 2017.

American College Health Association. American College Health Association-National College Health Assessment (2008–12). *ACHA-NCHA II, ACHA-NCHA IIb.* Hanover, MD. American College Health Association. Retrieved on May 22, 2017.[2]

4. Replace Your Support Services

As you move away from the tremendous support provided by your university and your athletic department, consider how you replace this. Do you need a psychologist, a physiotherapist, a sport medicine doc? These support services you took for granted (though you likely had some of the very best) will now be something you need to seek out, realizing that most health practitioners do not specialize in treating issues specific to high-performance athletes.

5. Consider Coaching

Fischer points out that coaching is a potential avenue (even as a volunteer kids' coach) to fill the "gap" when you retire. He notes that "you see so many players become coaches because they need to be a part of something. You can't wake up every day and say, 'I have nothing to do.' There has to be a purpose in your life."

6. Build an Exercise Plan

Number 1 on this list advised you to create a structure built around physical activity, and within that structure you need to build a plan for how to use the time you allocate for physical activity and training. You no longer have a coach, a manager, or a trainer to tell you what to do and when. You need to build some internal (intrinsic) motivation and keep healthy. Brett Fischer provides a helpful warning to get at it right away:

> I see a lot of former athletes who didn't take care of their body after playing as well as they should have, and ten years later, they aren't where they want to be. When they have a family, and they have kids, they don't have much free time to take care of themselves because they're working more now. They have different kinds of responsibilities.
>
> All of a sudden, now, you have to carve out time to work out. I get up at 4 *a.m.* every day to work out. If I don't do it then, I'll never get to it. I don't like getting up at 4, but I have no choice. I see that more with people who just get finished playing in college. It's just the progression of life and how much you still value the training aspect you were a part of as you were growing up? Some don't and they say they can't get to it and some do.

7. Balance, Balance, Balance

Secret 6 is of utmost importance here. Iglesias explains his approach:

> I preach a balanced life. A life where you try to not let yourself be totally dictated by work, where you're working seventy to eighty hours a week, and then you can't exercise. It's all about healthy living. Money is important, but money is not the end all be all. Life is so much more than how much you make.
>
> You have to look much more introspectively as to where is the happiness? Where is happiness central in my life? My own humble, personal opinion is that the happiest people that I have encountered in my life are those that have really managed balance in their life. Understanding what makes you happy in terms of the lifestyle that you want to live, that's the first step.
>
> The second step is finding out who lives that kind of lifestyle? Try to pick their brain as to how they got to that particular lifestyle. Take a look at that lifestyle, and see if that's an actual fit for you. Just pick the brain of those who are living the lifestyle that is one that you would like to emulate. Pick some ideas from them and then use that as a road map on how to get you there.

8. Replace the Competition

One thing many former athletes miss (and crave) is the competition. But they are not likely to want to compete in their chosen sport, as their form has declined. Thus, a suggested tactic is to find a new pursuit (for example, do a triathlon, join a Dragon Boat racing team) where you can be competitive but in a different arena.

Iglesias concurs: "I'm forty-seven now, and it's been twenty-five years since I've played my last collegiate tournament. That intense, burning desire to compete, I don't know if there's anything outside of actual competitions that truly fulfills you. You go out, you take up golf, you take up bowling, or whatever activities you want along the way, because at some point, you'll never get as good in your sport as you once were, and your time has come and passed."

9. Have Fun When You Exercise!

Exercise is something that is built into our weekly schedule as athletes. We are extremely motivated to work out and improve our physical fitness levels in the hopes that it will improve our athletic performances.

As you transition into a different lifestyle, you may, like many others, struggle to maintain the motivation to work out, and many cannot find the time in their schedule to work out either because of work hours. Regardless of the struggles, it is vitally important for your self-esteem, your overall health, and your confidence to continue to work out and exercise. You may not train like you did as an athlete, but finding ways to enjoy your time exercising is important in keeping a routine steady.

And, yes, fun is the key. Research shows that fun is the #1 reason why people do physical activity. So, instead of going for a daily morning run you despise, join a pickup basketball league or a co-ed soccer team.

10. Take Advantage of All Life Has to Offer

The last (but not least) of our ten steps is to invest in your future!

Working out, eating right, and sleeping well are important but there is much more to life than just those three things. We'd like to offer five additional pieces of advice to be sure you take advantage of more of life's opportunities:

1. Think big, but have short-term goals. Measure your life in two-year spans. Evaluate where you are, and what you want to do every two years during your career.

2. Take calculated risks in life. Try new things. Learn a foreign language. Study Abroad during the summer or winter break.

3. Move around and explore the world while you are young. Living in new places and environments can help give you many different perspectives of life that you wouldn't have seen otherwise.

4. Get out of your comfort zone/bubble. Work at meeting and understanding people different from yourself.

5. Connect with many, because connections can open doors as you experience more in more places.

Iglesias has some useful advice on the keys to success for you to consider when investing in your future and taking advantage of all life has to offer. He says:

> When transitioning out of your sport, you need to stay humble. There's always going to be someone bigger, faster, stronger, and better than you. If you cannot have success, don't look into blaming others, look at yourself in the mirror.
>
> At the same time, that ability to overcome and be resilient, and the ability to overcome adversity is what we have all hopefully developed. It's not about the winning, it's about the journey. The whole point to being a student-athlete is about the journey.

AUTHOR VIEWPOINT—ANDY DOLICH

A Pandemic Playbook for You

After Rudy Gobert of the Utah Jazz tested positive for COVID-19 on March 11, 2020, games, seasons, and tournaments were suspended or canceled throughout the sports world. Many executives and administrators were dazed and confused about how pro, college, and youth sports were going to deal with a global pandemic. There was not a simple solution for keeping millions of fans, players, and workers safe. What were the protocols that they should follow? The lack of teamwork, leadership, and trust forced hundreds of organizations across the country to build protocols from square one. The sports world at large had no pandemic playbook. You need one.

We have seen the unpredictability and virulence of the coronavirus. Thousands of individuals in the business of sports have been furloughed or lost their positions in the past year. Having spent five decades in the world of sports, I have seen unexpected challenges but never the uncertainty of what I call the "new different." To help you navigate this uncertain landscape, consider taking notes on the following foundational elements and including them in your own COVID-19 playbook.

COVID-19 CAREER PLAYBOOK: YOUR FUTURE

Who?

That would be you.

What?

What do you want to do with your life, and how does it sync with the opportunities available? Create a list of every possible job opportunity that you believe may be a fit.

Why?

Think of yourself as a Swiss Army knife and review how many skills, tools, and uses you have. You can't have too many. Identify what skills you are missing and add them to your tool kit. Be absolutely truthful—no BS.

Where?

There are currently 151 teams in the NFL, NBA, MLB, NHL, and MLS. If you are committed to one city or part of the country or the globe, you are shrinking your opportunities. Here's a simple pro sports job-opportunity map.

NFL—twenty-three states, thirty US cities

NBA—twenty-two states, twenty-seven US cities and Toronto, Canada

MLB—twenty-six states, twenty-eight US cities and Toronto, Canada

NHL—nineteen states (including the new Seattle club) and seven Canadian cities (Toronto, Montreal, Ottawa, Winnipeg, Edmonton, Calgary, and Vancouver)

MLS—sixteen states, twenty-two US cities, and three Canadian cities (Montreal, Toronto, and Vancouver)

Don't focus on getting a job just with the teams. They are the ultimate icing on the cake, but think about their venues. These sports homes can hold tens of thousands of the teams' closest friends for a few hours of fun hundreds of times a year. Think deeply about the work force necessary to run these venues, the media outlets that cover them, the corporations that sponsor them, the entrepreneurs that want to pitch them, and the companies that serve them in every category from A to Z.

When?

Now.

How?

Okay, smartie, now you have this information and will continue to learn as a fully awake human being. What are you going to do with it? How are you going to get that position when the competition is tougher than ever? It is said that "notes on paper don't make music." So, back to the beginning. Why did I ask you to take notes on what to include in your COVID-19 career playbook? Simple, now it is time to take those notes and make your own music using what is in your heart, soul, and mind. What do you sound like? Can you bust a move, can you riff, can you solo, can you play in a quartet or a symphony? The spotlight is on you in a world that has changed in ways that no one could have visualized or vocalized. You can't be in the band until someone believes you can play with the combo.

CHAPTER SUMMARY

Investing (as a concept) involves paying into a healthy lifestyle and doing the right things for your future. A healthy lifestyle is the first step in the right direction to a bright future and the rest will follow.

Our experts know that life is a process and the most important part of that process is preparing. Yes, your athletic career may be coming to an end (or already over), but your life isn't. Like most student-athletes reading this book, you have lived only a quarter of your life. If you have good genes, you may still have 75 percent of your life to live. How you want to live is up to you. Maintaining a healthy lifestyle will allow for a life full of opportunities.

Secret 17

Activate Your Student-Athlete Advantage

THE SECRET IN A FEW WORDS

Being a student-athlete is a great opportunity for those who have the privilege to compete. Student-athletes have a different college experience than the regular student does, but there are plenty of advantages that student-athletes can take from their experiences as they transition into life. Many people like to hire former student-athletes—that is no secret. But what are you going to do to give yourself an edge with prospective employers? How are you going to use your student-athlete experience to your advantage?

The real secret is that you need to "activate your student-athlete advantage."

ACTIVATE YOUR STUDENT-ATHLETE ADVANTAGE

Jason Elias is a former student-athlete baseball player who has worked in a variety of roles in the sports industry. During our interview with him, we covered several topics in relation to activating the advantages you have as a student-athlete.

JASON ELIAS

**(former baseball student-athlete at Baldwin Wallace University,
now Associate Athletic Director at IMG Academy)**

I graduated from Baldwin Wallace University [as a student-athlete] and I thought I had a full-time opportunity with FOX Sports Ohio all lined up.

It was a position that ended up being filled internally. I found out a week before I graduated as I walked off the NCAA baseball field for the last time. Even at that moment, I was still under the belief-structure that if I worked hard and competed well, academically, there was going to be some sort of position available, something that I was passionate about. That wasn't necessarily the case. It wasn't until probably almost a year and half later post-graduation that I had then gone to what I was comfortable with, and that was back to school. I was working on an MBA. It was then that I realized the significance of building a network.

MAXIMIZING YOUR STUDENT-ATHLETE ADVANTAGE

I would say most importantly; I don't think most student-athletes coming out of high school realize this enough, and I would even argue that unless they are in a formalized structure within their athletic program in college, they probably don't realize this: You are a part of a very elite fraternity as an athlete. I would say that from my own personal experience, as I was involved in college, I was an athlete, I was a baseball player that used a relationship with an alum . . . to eventually find [my dream job]. There were a couple of stops along the way, but I've traced everything that's happened to me in this industry back to a conversation I had with Jim Tressel [the alum] in 2005. Student-athletes need to understand that it's like being a part of any other group or any other fraternity or niche that you can find out there. It's all about the networking aspect. I think athletes need to understand that they have to be proactive, and they need to understand the power of relationships that they have that they may not even know exist. In many ways, they're unaware of what exists in their back pocket.

There are a couple terms that define a student-athlete, and these terms are also very attractive to a hiring manager. Athletes are resourceful. Athletes understand the meaning of work. Athletes tend to have excellent time management skills. Athletes tend to be adaptable, and collaborative. At times, they're risk takers, which some organizations would look at as a positive thing. Critical thinking skills tend to be very good. If you've been in a locker room, you tend to become more socially intelligent and I think that's an important skill to have. These are all aspects of the competitive and athletic experience . . . and an athlete may not consciously know that they've acquired these skills. The reality is that those particular skills/skill sets are very attractive to a hiring manager, and when you look at a general population of candidates, I can't say that nonathletes necessarily have the specificity of these skill sets.

DIFFERENTIATE YOURSELF

Having the awareness of being a student-athlete plays a significant role, personal awareness. Understanding consciously that these skill sets exist will help those activate their student-athlete advantage. Student-athletes need to know that relationships and awareness of skill sets will be what creates the opportunity. Preparation within that opportunity is going to be what lands you the job. You can get the pick set for yourself through relationships and through skill-building. Once you get open, it's just a jump shot. Now hit the jump shot! You are going to be better prepared to hit that jump shot than the average individual because you've been through the competitive environment.

THE STUDENT-ATHLETE ADVANTAGE IS REAL

It is easy to take for granted the opportunity you have been given to be a member of an intercollegiate athletics team. Think about a regular classroom that holds sixty students. Maybe two are student-athletes, if that. In many classrooms around campuses, there are no student-athletes in that class. Of the remaining fifty-eight students in our hypothetical class of sixty, probably half of them wish they had the opportunity you are getting to play your sport, get an education, and receive all of the intangible skills that we have been highlighting throughout the various secrets presented so far in this book. Are you grateful? Are you activating the tremendous benefits that have been provided to you from your institution? Simply by being a student-athlete, you have an advantage over others as you transition from college to your professional life. But you are missing out on a big opportunity if you are simply satisfied with being a passive member of your team and the university community.

To get the most payoff possible from your experience in college, you have to be an active participant in the opportunities afforded you and be aware of how you can leverage them to your advantage. Jeff Rodin, former student-athlete and now a working professional in Major League Baseball, emphasized this and provides some words of wisdom:

> I would say as a student-athlete, you have a huge advantage. If you're a student-athlete and you work part-time and you're a double major, it forces you to manage a lot of different things and be disciplined. It can be the hardest thing you'll ever do, but it prepares you for life. You might not think you can handle it, but it prepares you and stretches you, allowing you

to grow. Especially at the college and university level, you're talking about a huge transition and foundational-type situation. It's going to set you on a path with the relationships and the experiences that you encounter for the rest of your life. I could not encourage people enough to go through that process and do as much as you can, and get involved in as many different things as you can, because it allows for perspective on what your identity is and what your identity isn't, even more importantly, and creating that self-awareness. It's hard to put everything in perspective and balance that. Balance for me is different than might be balanced for somebody else. For me, when you commit to something, you commit 1,000 percent. You don't just dip your toe in it. It's pretty extreme, but that's also my personality. Do as much as you can, meet as many people as you can, hold yourself accountable, stay humble, and make yourself available to new opportunities because you don't want to miss anything.

WHY EMPLOYERS HIRE FORMER STUDENT-ATHLETES

Employers in both traditional professions and cutting-edge innovative areas are looking for the skills and abilities gained by being a student-athlete. An article in *Entrepreneur* highlights the fact that student-athletes have a strong work ethic, the ability to overcome failure, positive energy, and the ability to handle risks and responsibility. These are skills that other college students have to go out of their way to gain while as a student-athlete they are inherent in your sport participation and competition. Another article suggests that former student-athletes make great employees because they know how to work as a team, are leaders, excel at communication, and are driven. A third article discusses the unique traits of student-athletes, including a competitive nature, handling pressure well, being coachable and willing to learn, having a great sense of discipline, understanding the importance of preparation, seeking and loving challenges, being self-motivated, and understanding the importance of time management. You probably don't even realize you are gaining these skills and that they are specifically sought by employers. A 2014 study, looking at perspectives of employers hiring student-athletes, finds the four most important qualities and skills are a competitive nature, goal orientation, pressure handling, and work ethic.[1]

In a GOALS study done by the NCAA in 2015, student-athletes identified the qualities or skills that have been most positively affected by their student-athlete experience. Take advantage of these skills and develop them to be outstanding!

My college athletics experience has had a positive or
very positive effect on the following skills/qualities in myself

	Division 1	Division 2	Division 3
Commitment to Volunteerism	67%	69%	61%
Leadership Skills	88%	88%	89%
Personal Responsibility	93%	92%	93%
Personal Values and Ethics	86%	87%	86%
Self-Confidence	79%	82%	81%
Study Skills	67%	67%	70%
Teamwork Skills	92%	91%	93%
Time Management Skills	81%	78%	82%
Understanding of Other Races	81%	82%	76%
Work Ethic	91%	90%	91%

Note: Top two scale points on a six-point scale

NCAA Research. (January 2016). *Results from the 2015 GOALS Study of the Student-Athlete Experience.* Retrieved on May 22, 2017.[2]

We asked Dan Butterly, Commissioner of the Big West Conference, to provide us with details about the process of hiring people and how student-athletes have an advantage if they have some experience under their belt. He advised:

> When I get a resume [from a job applicant], I look for if they have the degree. Then I look at their experience. I'm going to look to see what experiences they gained while they were on campus or since they graduated. Then I'm going to look at their references. I want to see who they have associated with, who they are putting on their resume as people who have been influences in their life and will be there for them. That power of "who" is powerful. Those are going to be the key things, but it really comes down to the experience they gained. Once I've got the candidate pool and I've narrowed it down to phone interviews, it really is how they represent themselves on the phone. Can they show confidence without a big ego over the phone? Do they know what they're doing, that they know the league, they know the position, and they know key things I look for in this opportunity? If they can do that, then I'm going to look at an in-person interview. In person, the first thing I'm going to look at is posture. Posture can show confidence. I've had people that come in who are just slouched shoulders and that kind of look grumpy with your slouched shoulders versus head up, shoulders back, and having a good handshake and saying hello, I mean those

are big impacts and student-athletes definitely have a benefit as you can see in some of my answers. They know leadership, they know teamwork, they're driven for success. Those are the type of people that you want in any organization and I think that's a key driver. If I can get a student-athlete who shows the other factors that I'm looking at, then that's going to be my priority hire in many ways.

Brian Sanders, a former student-athlete and now an executive in Major League Baseball, supports Butterly's view and provides further advice on one thing you can do to help you activate that advantage on a resume: "Something that always catches my eye on the resume is some sort of catch phrase, or personal slogan. You have to get someone to give you that interview, and then you have to stand out and you have to compete. Just as you are competing on the field, you have to find a way to compete in the interview process. To stand out, say something a little off the wall, 'what's next?' Not enough young people in the workforce think about 'what's next.'"

HOW TO TRANSLATE LESSONS LEARNED THROUGH SPORT TO YOUR PROFESSIONAL WORK

From the job interview to your day-to-day life in your chosen profession, there are lessons from sport that you can translate to help your efficacy at work. But, and this is key, the ball is in your court. Nobody can activate your student-athlete advantage except you. Since no student-athlete experience is exactly the same as any other, you should be able to add to the list below that shares a few ideas on how to translate your sport experience to advantages in the workplace.

Here are just a few ideas to get you started:

1. *Interviewing:* Student-athletes are often provided training on how to interact with the media. What an amazing advantage in a job interview! Not only do you have on your resume the fact that you were a student-athlete, but you have specific knowledge and practice in an interview setting. Use this to your advantage. Former student-athlete at the University of Iowa Kelsey Cermak provides some useful advice here: "Figure out how to transfer all those skills you gain as a student-athlete onto a resume. Figure out what your weaknesses are and make them strengths. Try to fill up as many holes as possible. . . . I used to do mock interviews once a month during my senior year to prepare for interviews."

2. *Small Talk:* Your experience as a student-athlete is fascinating to most (or many, at least) people. It is a very easy way to start a conversation. Whether you start a conversation about your

experience being a student-athlete or share a cool story from your time competing, most people will be interested. This comes into play at social events for work, at professional conferences, and when building your network.

3. *Creating Buy-In:* You probably do not realize that convincing an athletic team to do something (like practice extra to prepare for the game) with a good attitude is simply a combination of "selling" and "negotiating." This is especially true if you were a team captain or even assistant captain. And, now that you're heading to the work world, how about translating these skills into negotiating your salary, determining your job responsibilities, helping you lead a work team, or even actually informing your selling in the context of your job.

4. *Office Golf Outing or Softball Team:* If you have been around athletics your entire life, it is likely you have some skills in sports even outside the sport you played in college. More and more companies are creating opportunities for employees to be active and part of the office culture. If you can play golf, enjoy being on a recreational softball team, or generally want to keep being a leader on the field—this is an opportunity for you to stand out among your peers at work.

5. *Understanding Your Role:* Very few young employees understand how to lead, how to follow, and how to get out of the way when it's the right thing to do. Athletes understand this concept of changing roles. Moving from high school to college as an athlete, you probably went from one of the best on your high school team to being surrounded by a lot of good athletes in college. Many student-athletes learn to fill the role of starter one week and bench warmer the next—keeping a great attitude in either role. Athletes understand the value of each position on the team as well as the value of those who support the team from the bench.

AUTHOR VIEWPOINT—DR. HEATHER LAWRENCE

Nearly twenty-five years after finishing my athletic career as a college diver, I am still activating my student-athlete advantage. It may sound crazy, but it's true. I am still introduced to new people by friends and colleagues with the phrase "and she was an All-American diver and a member of the US national team." It launches the conversation right into questions about my time as an athlete or allows us to connect over a common interest in sports. I can decide where to take the personal or business relationship from there. This might seem like an example that is years away for you, so let me back up and share with you ten additional examples of activating my student-athlete advantage since college.

1. Graduating college debt free thanks to athletically related financial aid.

2. Using my athletic experience as the focus of my graduate school admissions essay.

3. Being awarded NCAA postgraduate scholarships based on my combined athletic and academic success, which resulted in graduating debt free with a master's degree.

4. Being hired for my first full-time job by the athletics department. Already knowing the coaches and staff I would be working with gave me an advantage over other applicants.

5. Staying calm under pressure while tackling my first real work projects as a young professional. Because I had felt like that in big competitions for years, I knew how to focus on the task at hand and get it done.

6. Seamlessly transitioning to a new culture in a different state for a new job. After being around so many different people through athletics and traveling for competitions over the years, I was quickly comfortable in a new culture. Even when I was uncomfortable, that was okay because athletics had pushed me to that point so many times over the years.

7. Staying active is critical to my ability to function well in other aspects of my life. I wake up at 4:20 a.m. most mornings to work out, a habit I developed in high school and then continued in college due to early-morning practices. Although I know when I need to take a day off to get some rest, I still work out most mornings around 5:00 a.m. and then am ready to tackle whatever the day brings.

8. Exceeding expectations is what I expect out of myself professionally. As a student-athlete, doing the minimum gets you nowhere. The same is true professionally. Taking responsibility for putting in extra work results in professional advancement, just like putting in extra practice in sport results in a higher level of skill.

9. Mental preparation for public speaking or interviews is just like mental preparation for a competition. I have been a keynote speaker in front of more than a thousand attendees, and I prepared for that moment on stage exactly as I prepared for major competitions. Athletes understand the mental prep is as important as the physical prep, and it's no different for big professional moments.

10. Navigating 2020–21 has not been easy for anyone. However, I know my experience as a student-athlete helps me to be okay with the uncertainty of how long pandemic-related restrictions will be in place. It is not very different from wondering if you will be named to a travel squad or the national team or whether your scholarship will be increased the next year. You have to wait to learn what's been decided

and then just live with it and continue moving toward goals. Issues tied to social justice and the political division in the United States are mentally exhausting for everyone, but athletes know how to perform when tired. I have used that grit developed through years of tough training to commit to rising above it all (just as any high-functioning athletic team does) with a focus on understanding others. When the going gets tough, the tough get going.

Lastly, what should you do?

Step 1: Find an employer who also was a student-athlete

Hallie Olson, former swimming student-athlete at Ohio University and now Director of Notre Dame Global Partnerships, in her interview, clearly supports this tactic: "If I'm looking at any resumes and I see that someone was an athlete, that's going to catch my eye, because I know that they've gone through the rigor and they have that work ethic to be successful."

Step 2: Understand what your experience is worth and why it is important

Step 3: Get your foot in the door somewhere . . .

LEVERAGE YOUR CELEBRITY—EDDIE GILL

(former NBA player and TV Analyst for the Indiana Pacers on Fox)

I think student-athletes should really look at doing a better job of leveraging their celebrity. If you're a collegiate athlete anywhere in the country, to some degree, you're a celebrity on campus. You want to start building those relationships with administration. When you go out to do community events, leverage your celebrity as an athlete because those people want to have a conversation with you. My advice to the young players is to embrace that role that you currently have. That doesn't mean you're being overconfident or cocky, but it's just being able to have a conversation with people and be friendly. Build that rapport, you never know what it's going to lead to.

My biggest piece of advice is to leverage your celebrity. I can't emphasize that enough. I've seen it. I'm guilty of it myself. I've done it as a collegiate athlete, and as a professional athlete. We do so many different things that are "mandatory," whether it's by the team, or by the league, or with your association. It's more than just being there. If you can really start forming relationships throughout that entire process, it can make your transition that much easier. If you're a professional athlete, maybe you go back to your university to do something, whether it's on campus or in that community. Those relationships that you build as a student-athlete versus just going through the motions will differ in appearances throughout the community.

CHAPTER SUMMARY

Activating your student-athlete advantage isn't only a thing you do once you graduate just to get your first job, it is something you do for your whole life. Be thankful that you have the ability to activate this advantage for a lifetime of opportunities. Having the student-athlete experience in your pocket allows you to pursue so many opportunities that many people wish they could. Take advantage of the advantages you have because you may just get lucky. Thus . . .

Luck = Preparation meets Opportunity

Secret *18* Create Your Brand

THE SECRET IN A FEW WORDS

Brands are everywhere. We buy them, use them, cheer for them, and, whether you realize it or not, you represent one every day. A brand's image can change from time to time, and brands are created, not found or automatically provided. Many student-athletes, and many people in general, struggle with creating their brand and identity once they start a career. For student-athletes, their identity is no longer as a "player," but has to be created as something different. So the secret is to "create your brand."

CREATE YOUR BRAND

There is a fictionalized story in which, when asked how he created the most famous statue in the world, Michelangelo responded: "I just chipped away all the pieces that weren't David."

Your brand will help define and identify you to important relationships and stakeholders. Importantly, the name on your eventual business card will be much more important than the logo of the entity you are working for.

Branding is a highly developed and sophisticated field that has learned much about how to develop, activate, and grow equity in a brand or a suite of brands. This chapter outlines a multistep approach to brand specific to the context of the student-athlete.

Step 1: Strategies and Tactics

It has been said that if you can't see the finish line at the beginning of a race then you aren't going to get off to a very good start. It is critical to build your brand plan with the proper understanding of the differences between tactics and strategies. First, the definitions:

Tactic:

From the Greek *taktikós:* fit for arranging or ordering, equivalent to arrange, put in order.

Strategy:

A plan, method, or series of maneuvers or stratagems for obtaining a specific goal or result.

A plan for getting ahead in the world.

A particular long-term plan for success, especially in business or politics.

CREATE YOUR BRAND:
HOW DO I GET THERE AND WHERE IS THERE?

How did you get here?

We'd like to offer some insight based on a recent interview one of the authors was conducting. The candidate was asked, "Tell me about yourself. Tell me your story. Tell me how you got here." He said, "By car."

Exactly!

Was he serious? Absolutely serious.

Was he trying to be clever? Absolutely not. The interviewer has a very good wise-guy meter, but it was one of the best responses he had heard and he commented specifically about it in the context of his experiences.

AUTHOR VIEWPOINT—ANDY DOLICH

So, he said he got here by car!

Having spent forty-three years in the front offices of teams in the NBA (National Basketball League), NFL (National Football League), NHL (National Hockey League), MLB (Major League Baseball), NASL (North American Soccer League), NLL (National Lacrosse League), five years as the owner of my own sports consulting business, and two years with Tickets.com, I have learned well that there are a number of simple steps that, when followed, will greatly improve any new job seeker's chances of getting their high-priced athletic footwear in the door.

How did I get from sitting in an Ohio University classroom daydreaming about watching future Hall of Famer Mike Schmidt take ground balls at shortstop at that time? I remember saying, "You know, one of these days, he might be a decent minor league player and hopefully some day when I get out of the Sports Administration Program I might actually work for a team and get paid."

Little did I know back in the 1970s that Mike Schmidt would turn out to be one of the greatest third basemen in baseball history and, not on any kind of equitable level, that I would end up having a fifty-year-and-counting career in sports, and there we were both in Athens, Ohio, dreaming about the future.

In those days before you could graduate you had to do a six-month internship, and mine was with the Philadelphia 76ers.

After three seasons with the 76ers I took a step back to take two forward and joined the Maryland Arrows to the Washington Capitals (NHL) to the Washington Diplomats (NASL) to the Oakland Athletics (MLB) to the Golden State Warriors (NBA) to my own business consulting group to Tickets.com to the Vancouver Grizzlies, who became the Memphis Grizzlies, to the San Francisco 49ers and back to my own sports business consulting firm. That's kind of a compressed time capsule of close to six decades, which never ceases to amuse and amaze me.

If I can do this, so can you. I am the official poster child of possibilities in building a career brand in sports.

One visual reminder of my dream-come-true ride since 1971 after graduating from Ohio University: I have a plaque on my wall, which has every single one of my business cards along the way. I was the beneficiary of a number of informational interviews way back when, as I was going through the internship process at Ohio University, and I show that to everybody that comes through me looking for advice on getting a job in the "high paid, low hour" business of sports, whether it be in the pros or the brave new world of collegiate sports.

I'd say it's not quite as easy as you might think looking at somebody's resume or reading about them or having Googled them. Look at this plaque and spend a few moments seeing the different zip codes while I was also trying to raise a family, find my competencies, and get paid fairly.

When people come to my office they say, "You know, I need to do one of those." It's not complicated. You don't need a patent. Just take your business cards and go into "Frames-R-Us."

In creating your brand, you may be a leader as a student-athlete, and you may continue to be a leader in the next chapter of your life. However, there are many types of leadership. What kind of leader will you be?

YOUR LEADERSHIP DNA: WHAT STYLE WILL YOU USE?

Personal and business leadership skills are defined by the ability to navigate the uncharted waters created by today's society. Implement your leadership skills and keep your brand nimble, focused, and healthy by becoming an expert on the uses of the eight "scopes":

1.   *Microscope:* To view and understand every minute detail of your business.

2.   *Telescope:* To look beyond the given and create road maps to unexplored territories.

3. *Stethoscope:* To listen to the heart of your organization and the people in it.

4. *Proctoscope:* To take you to places that people don't want to go, but necessary to protect the long-term health of the enterprise.

5. *Gyroscope:* To keep everyone centered in times of crisis. In today's world, crisis is the new normalcy.

6. *Periscope:* To give you the ability to stealthily see what your competitors are up to.

7. *Kaleidoscope:* To help you visualize and appreciate the ever-changing business patterns and human interactions of your enterprise. Without diversity we have no teamwork.

8. *Horoscope:* To develop bold plans for the future using a tool of science and symbolism.

Successful leaders who have devoted themselves to their careers share a common thread of DNA. But if you Google "Theories of Leadership" there are only about 8,300,000 links to choose from.

Role models don't always make great leaders. We care more about the latest skinny on *Jersey Shore*'s Snooki and *Keeping Up with the Kardashians* than doing something about the growing epidemic of childhood obesity (or adult obesity, for that matter). We spend more time breaking down player scouting reports for our upcoming fantasy league draft than building up a broken educational system. We live in a world of nanosecond affirmation and even speedier deconstruction. It would have been instructive to have heard what John Wooden thought about the antics of the LeBron James "Decision."

When successful organizations go under the microscope, you will see that there is consistent high-quality leadership and brand mission at all levels.

Successful individuals brand themselves with a DNA strain composed of the Eleven T's. Think of the any industry's best and brightest—these should fit them to a T.

1. *Affinity:* The hours and pressures of the job mean that you can't fake the way you get along with colleagues. The compatibility factor always shines through between leaders and their coworkers when times are the toughest.

2. *Agility:* Today's world calls for incredible changes of pace and direction to keep up with changing market conditions. If you can't go to your left, then work on that move. If you are a winner-take-all negotiator, try enticing your opponents with a carrot instead of beating them with a stick every once in a while.

3. *Creativity:* Business is defined by a herd mentality. A good idea causes the line to form. Leadership shouldn't get stuck in a

"Groundhog Day" thinking. Changing how you approach the business of your business is critical. Look to the outside world of creative business solutions, not just the best practices of your industry.

4.   *Hilarity:* A career is a marathon, not a sprint, whether it is a job at one company or a career made up of many jobs in many places. A career is full of serious goals and objectives, bottom lines, wins and losses, hirings and firings, promotions and demotions, elation and deflation. In the end it is only a game. Many leaders lose their way by weaving a web of woe. Show a sense of humor and a bit of wackiness every once in a while. It will lighten the load for everybody.

5.   *Honesty:* The most respected leaders tell the truth—good, bad, or ugly. Think of the hardest teachers you had in high school or college. They never let you slide as you cursed them under your breath. A few years after graduation you realized they gave you the best education. The same is true with great leaders: They can pat you on the back and kick you in the gut without compromising the organization's view on how to succeed.

6.   *Humility:* One of the many potential hazards that befall leaders is defining themselves by what they do, not who they are. When they lose their way they can take their organizations over the edge. Your business card and title should never control your true sense of self.

7.   *Loyalty:* Leaders ask their staffs to invest their loyalty for the greater good of the organization. When a season, a campaign, a project goes wrong there is usually collateral damage in the form of terminations. Loyalty Street should always be a two-way avenue for the organization's success.

8.   *Mobility:* Mobility is leadership by walking around. Many executives barricade themselves in their office castles with a moat, a closed door, and a fire-breathing executive assistant. The simplest way to lead is to walk around the office every day. The two-minute face-to-face is usually more productive than the ninety-minute conference room agenda-driven meeting.

9.   *Opportunity:* As a leader, everyone is going to want a piece of you. Think of those who mentored or spent time with you when you were coming up! Every young person in your organization who wants to spend a few minutes with you deserves your attention.

10. *Simplicity:* Between multitasking, social media of the day, meetings by the moment, and crisis management, the life of a leader is growing more and more complicated. The great ones

create simplicity without dumbing down the product. If you can't explain what you are up to in two or three sentences, it probably isn't worth explaining.

11. *Unity:* Most sport organizations are split into quarters with ownership, business operations, team operations, and finance existing on different planets. "Ubuntu" is an African term that is generally defined as unselfishness and team unity. The spirit of Ubuntu that teams on the field strive for can become even more powerful if the entire organization lives it.

No one knows which of those eight million-plus leadership styles guarantees success. There are no magic wands, lanterns, or carpets, no silver bullets, secret handshakes, codes, Rosetta Stones, catchy phrases, or best-selling books that guarantee leadership success. It stands the test of time that human beings working together have accomplished far more than the sum of their individual efforts and capabilities. They have committed themselves to something larger than the individual. Leaders live teamwork every day, and the great ones make it happen.

Regardless of whether you go work in sports, education, real estate, medicine or law, these T's can apply to any type of career you pursue. The lessons and concepts are the same.

BECOME AN ETHICAL BEING IN CREATING YOUR BRAND

There are many areas that make up a person's ethical foundation. Here are the top ten in our view:

1. Empower others (do not micromanage: trust others, when trained, to do the job)

2. Maintain a positive attitude especially when the environment is negative (negativity is rarely the answer)

3. Demonstrate high character (make good decisions, think of (all) others, consider your environment)

4. Be willing to lead (do NOT be that critic on the sideline who is first to complain or nitpick, be the one who steps up to help when a leader is needed)

5. Strive to be a leader (leadership is a hard-earned status; do not be in a rush)

6. Remain teachable and coachable (listen to advice you get and be willing to adapt your ways of doing things based on what you hear)

7. Be accountable (take responsibility for your mistakes and stand up for your colleagues)

8. Be fully prepared (never attend a meeting or presentation without being ready for it)

9. Never quit (adapt your timelines, not your goals)

10. Respect your coworkers (treat others, both higher- and lower-ranking than you, as you would like to be treated yourself)

WE ADVISE YOU TO RUN TO CHAOS AND DISASTER!

Most neophytes in the career search process look for the most successful technology brands, marketing agencies, and sports teams they can find and send blind letters to the owner or CEO right after they have won a championship. (Wrong, wrong, wrong.) You want to reach out to the lepers, disasters, car wrecks, and toxic dumps. Find brands, organizations, teams, and properties that people are running away from. That's where you want to be.

Let's give you an example. It is again from the sports industry and is about co-author Andy Dolich, who has thrived for many years in that world. By pure good luck, Dolich's first job in sports was with the Philadelphia 76ers in 1971. Trivia experts would know that this team had records that stand unbroken to this day. In the 1972–73 season when he was Administrative Assistant to the GM, the club went 9–73. That's right—they could not even get into double figures in wins!

In the same season, they had noncontiguous losing streaks of thirteen, fourteen, fifteen, and twenty games. The two longest losing streaks were interrupted by a two-point win which, if they had lost, would have given the club a depressing thirty-three losses in a row. It was a glorious time in that Andy was able to take responsibility for areas that he would have had to wait years to experience otherwise because the organization was in such disarray. He was learning on the job, and fast. Look for chaos, disaster, unrest, change that creates opportunity. That's where you are going to learn and move up the fastest.

· ·

To provide extra advice on creating your brand as you transition out of sports and into a career, we have interviewed experts to help you out.

We interviewed longtime professional sport executive Fred Claire, who provided some valuable insights on brand from his fifty-plus-year career in the sport business, including a very senior role with the Los Angeles Dodgers.

FRED CLAIRE

(Legendary former Executive VP and General Manager of the Los Angeles Dodgers, and cofounder of Scoutables)

In my Dodger days I had a philosophy that I believe works, and it applies to athletes and others: everything we do, everything we say, everything we write, every exchange we have with another person or a group—*how comfortable will you be* when this becomes fully public?

Because it will be public, believe me, particularly for one who lives in the public world. And with technology and social media of today we all live in a public world. So as an athlete or any individual we don't need to create anything or hire anyone to establish our identity. We need to live every minute and every day of our lives in a manner that gives us self-worth and makes our family and friends proud and the universities or schools or companies we represent proud. One doesn't need a "professional" brand; it rings false. Athletes and others should be dedicated and work every day to be the best they can be; to listen to their family and coaches; to be a great teammate; to set a true and proven example for younger people; to inspire others with inspirational acts. We can't change our basic talent, only improve through daily dedication. Along the way we all fall short and we are left to acknowledge shortcomings and always be totally honest and transparent. We are left to get up and continue the journey. At the end, we are not a "brand," we are who those who knew us best with the full disclosure of facts and time know or knew us to be. For all of us there is a legacy. We, and indeed the athletes of today, are writing that legacy *every single day* of our lives.

. . . .

JONI LOCKRIDGE

(former softball student-athlete, former Director of Digital Strategy at the PGA TOUR, now Vice President of Strategy and Operations at iX.co)

WE TALK ABOUT "CREATING YOURSELF, NOT FINDING YOURSELF." WHAT DID YOU DO TO "CREATE YOURSELF" AND WHAT DOES YOUR "BRAND" REPRESENT?

Right or wrong, I believe that the construction of personal brand can be simplified into two tasks: defining who I am, and defining who I am not.

This process requires a willingness and openness to continually evaluate and decide. It's not easy, and it never ends. The idea of a final state of "me" implies that both my own characteristics and the characteristics of the situation and the people around me never change. Knowing this to be untrue, former athletes must recognize that unlike that final buzzer in which the score stands, the act of creating ourselves will span our full lifetime.

HOW DID YOUR BRAND CHANGE AS A STUDENT-ATHLETE COMPARED TO BEING A WORKING PROFESSIONAL?

As a student-athlete, I wanted to be known as the hardest-working individual on the team. I wanted to take more reps than anyone else so I could have that edge that every competitor desires. I thought that if I did this, I could turn my brain off. I could shift from "try," to relax and do, and excel through will power and physical control.

As a working professional, I want to be known as the smartest working individual in the organization. I try to design my time around when my brain can be "on," and my will power now drives my focus more than my feet.

One difference that age has brought—I'm more likely to be able to break or throw away what is already working in order to improve. Considering I work to create digital experiences, this is critical in my job. Had I applied these principles more often as a student-athlete, I would have achieved more success throughout my career.

WITH YOUR ROLE IN THE DIGITAL WORLD, WHAT SUGGESTIONS DO YOU HAVE FOR FUTURE STUDENT-ATHLETES ON HOW TO REPRESENT THEMSELVES ON SOCIAL MEDIA?

I have three suggestions:

First, be smart with your security settings.

Second, remember that your digital personality is a representation of more than just you. Make sure you are willing to accept the consequences for any digital statement you make.

Third, as you work on both your offline and online identity, don't lose your individuality.

Hallie Olson, commenting from her experiences as a student-athlete swimmer turned graduate student turned working professional and now Director of Notre Dame Global Partnerships, noted:

> You are a brand. At peak of what your brand used to be [as an athlete], your entire brand used to be athletics, and now it's not anymore [as a graduate retired athlete]. It [the athlete part of your brand] will always be a part of you, but it's just not something that is at the forefront anymore. Now it's just developing what's the next chapter? What is the next chapter of your life? What are you looking to achieve? Once I started feeling successful somewhere else, when I got a job, or when I was doing things in graduate school where I felt like I was making an impact, that's when I started feeling like I don't have this crisis, I'm not going through this brand-identity crisis anymore.

She went on to describe, very specifically, how she felt about her "brand" as a professional versus having formerly been a student-athlete.

> Being a student-athlete, you are held to a high standard because you're representing your university. When you're in a professional workplace, you are representing a company. When you're

at the professional stage, there are many more expectations and everybody is replaceable. The professional world is more cut-throat. In swimming, we had a three-strike system, if you mess up three times, then you're out. At the professional stage, everybody is replaceable, and you could be gone [fired] in a second if you do something wrong.

In building a brand, Christa Mann, Senior Manager of Communications at MLS and former student-athlete, advised the student-athlete about to become a young professional to "identify yourself for all of the skills that you embody. There will come a day when you are no longer a student, you're no longer an athlete, but you are who you are and it's important to learn who that person is while you are in school. When you are out of school, away from sports, or wherever life takes you, you are still that person."

Finally, Steve Cobb, another former student-athlete, noted: "I think if you are going to create your own brand, you've got to know what a brand looks like in your area of expertise. Create your brand by learning from those people who are in the industry. Find out where you fit. Ask yourself, "What is it that I enjoy, when push comes to shove, why am I here, what's my passion about?" in whatever it is you are doing. I think you develop your brand by realizing what other people's brands are. I'm not suggesting you go and be like somebody else."

CHAPTER SUMMARY

This chapter provides the secret to creating and managing your own brand. Think about what you want your brand to represent, why and how. Think about how you want to be perceived by others. As you create your brand, you will have to decide if you are going to be a leader, and if so, what kind. Your brand will continue to change and shift throughout life, but there will always be a foundation of your brand that we believe will be created after you are no longer an athlete.

Many former student-athletes lose sight of what their brand really is after they finish competing. Many search or try to find their brand instead of creating it. You control your life and you create who you are. Stop searching and start creating. Just as we tell you to create your brand, we advocate for you to "Create yourself, don't find yourself."

Secret *19* Be Fiscally Smart

THE SECRET IN A FEW WORDS

You may think you have a handle on your finances, but you still have a lot to learn as you grow. If you have never had to worry a day in your life about money, you definitely need to treat this secret as extra special. As we've mentioned, being a student-athlete puts a lot of stress and pressure on you in many ways. Once you get out into the real world, you will have new stresses and potentially even more of them, but if you take this secret to heart, you will have less stress financially. Not having financial stress can make so many relationships and aspects of your life better in multiple ways.

This is a REAL secret, one you should pay close attention to and one you probably thought was not about you, a student. Well, you are wrong. It is now that you need to start building very good behaviors and attitudes around money, spending, and saving. Very small amounts saved and not spent can easily translate into very large sums when you're in your sixties or seventies and don't really want to work anymore. Thus, this secret is all about being wise about what you have, limiting what you have to borrow, and seeking to build a few assets (or at least a good credit rating) along the way.

BE FISCALLY SMART

The world is changing right before our eyes economically, socially, and politically. Traditional supply chains and communication methods are declining and new ones emerging every day. Your investment in your four years of college, if you followed the earlier secrets, should have led you to a point where you are graduating (have graduated) with a degree in a field where employment is possible, if not probable.

Along the way, as a student-athlete, you were likely on scholarship (at least partial), which may have reduced the financial stress of your experience by providing support for accommodation, meals, books, sport costs, and more. If you were on a full ride, this may have meant very limited stress here. However, the downside might be that you did not have the chance to develop the ability to manage finances or think about investments or use of assets. So, now is the time! And, these skills will come in handy when you buy a car, get a mortgage, go to grad school, or have children.

As a student-athlete, you are likely to be familiar with studying and following game plans, whether it be as part of a team or figuring out what you are going to do in one-on-one competitions. However, as a student-athlete, your time isn't necessarily your own and strategies for developing a financial plan might not be at the top of your list. You need to understand when to finance a purchase and how. You need to know what to do with extra money. You need to understand debt and payment plans. You need to project and plan for major purchases or expenses that will come.

PERSPECTIVE OF PROFESSIONAL ATHLETE FINANCIAL MANAGEMENT: WHAT CAN WE LEARN?

Bob Boland (Athletics Integrity Officer at Penn State University)

Why so many professional athletes seemingly retire in or quickly develop some form of hardship—financial, social, or medical—and what can be done about this is an important question for the survival of the sport industry. In studying this question, the answer is elusive. The problem of broke and broken former athletes doesn't run exclusively along racial, social, class, or sport lines. The amount earned over a career can positively influence success in retirement, but there remain cautionary tales out there of famed athletes who have burned through or lost giant fortunes. The ability to save certainly can help, but realistically, how does a league or an agent talk about retirement with athletes in their early twenties, whose greatest asset personally and professionally is the confidence to believe they are the exception to all rules. And frankly, athletes would have to save so aggressively that the lifestyle they are seeking in playing professionally would never be in reach. What fun would that be?

Rather, the key to having a successful retirement for athletes, especially at an age when most people's careers are just getting started, lies in lessening the downward slope of their personal lifetime earnings curves. What we have seen help that in the case of successful sports retirees is to look at the transition holistically.

Instead of focusing on spending or savings, [concentrate on] what aspirations does the individual have, what impediments in terms of savings, medical issues, and education does that person possess and figuring out a strategy for having a purposeful, engaged, and meaningful postathletic career. While the ex–pro athlete's earnings may never match their earnings as a pro, they can manage the downward slope of that curve and enjoy their second lives.

The same facts generally hold the key for the postcollegiate athlete, too. Except ideally their earnings curve will look like that of a successful college graduate and peak in their fifties or even later. What factors help the professional person's earnings curve lengthen are easy to calculate. First, education is statistically the most important factor. Yes, I am a college professor and yes, I am deeply invested in myself as I am still paying off my law degree.

Some question the efficacy of this educational debt, and in fairness debt should always be carefully considered, but I pay about as much now for my law degree as I do for either my satellite TV or my monthly wireless data plan, a small cost for something that lets me earn a competitive salary and have portable skills.

Second, while education is important demographically, athletes graduating now are entering into a world where their bachelor's degree isn't as marketable as it once was because so many people against whom they are competing have the same degree. So that puts an extra focus on skills. You need the degree as a symbol, often just to get in the door, but you need skills to be successful.

Too many athletes have an aspiration gap. This seems counterintuitive because an athlete likely has endured years of intense training and practiced unmeasured amounts of self-discipline in getting to their athletic goals, so how can they lack aspiration? New goals, new game. We've found that the way student-athletes are segregated from their communities, their student bodies, their potential competitive sets, means that they struggle to develop postathletic aspirations. Circling back, where does one go to work on aspiration? Usually work or school, and, if you have a degree or a skills gap, getting either a career-making job or profession or advanced degree that provides lifelong earning power can become a vicious cycle.

Boland's perspective is most valuable and his point on needing skills is key for you to consider. Yes, it is true, due to the high demands of the athletic portion of the student-athlete experience, many athletes lag behind their classmates in terms of skill development when it comes time to go on the job hunt. A number of previous secrets address this around using your time wisely to build skills.

A point that is often overlooked is that time management can be just as critical as money management as you build a career game plan. There is no one size fits all equation. Each and every person's situation is unique. Never follow someone else's plan unless you are absolutely sure it fits your financial circumstances and your personality.

Knowing you need a plan is one thing. Coming up with that plan is another. And actually putting your custom plan into action (a plan designed just for you on your reality) is another thing altogether.

BUILDING YOUR FINANCIAL PLAN—WHERE DO YOU START?

- *Assess your current financial situation.* How much do you have in the bank? Do you have a savings/retirement account? Does your employer offer a retirement plan? Will your employer match your contributions? Do you have debt? What's the interest rate on that debt? Do you know exactly where you are financially? Is anyone in your family helping you out financially or paying some of your costs?

- *Know your cash flow.* Do a cash flow analysis. Simply said, how much money do you have coming in and going out? Are you "liquid" (that is, will you have enough money to pay the bills throughout the year)? Yes, cash flow, the dreaded "budget" word. Oh, and if you've never taken an accounting course, do one and learn to do a cash flow statement and analysis.

- *Create a credit rating if you don't have one.* A good tactic here is to start buying things that you can afford (for example, clothes, electronics, computer) with a credit card, pay it off in full, and see your credit rating improve (and ability to borrow money).

- *Have a realistic conversation with your parents and/or spouse to make sure that everyone is on the same financial page.* Consider succession, retirements, death, children, and all factors. Are you still on your parents' payroll or do you have financial freedom? Cutting the money cord to your parents can be a scary scenario but a necessary one.

- *Check reality!* If you think the pros are going to be your ticket to financial independence, just look at the odds.

CREATE YOUR BUDGET

Personal finance isn't something you master at a certain age or after passing a class. You have to work on it over time and adjust as your situation changes. You have to update the documents regularly and track your spending. Financial planning is just like your daily workout or practice. The more you put in, the more you benefit when it's game time.

Your short-term focus may be paying down student loans. But in a few years, it could be buying a house and starting a family, bringing on another unique set of financial circumstances. Perhaps you'll move to another country and be paid in another currency and have to file taxes in a new jurisdiction.

DON'T SPEND MORE THAN YOU EARN!

Former student-athlete Eddie Gill, from whom we've heard a few times, now sends a clear warning to new graduates:

> The first mistake student-athletes make out of college is spending their entire first check on whatever it may be. They think, I got it, well now I have to spend it. If you start that, maybe that becomes a habit for you. I know another check is coming, I'll spend it knowing another one is coming.

A few years back, the Oakland A's had a player who went to salary arbitration. The night before his hearing the media asked him how he felt. "Tomorrow I'm going to wake up rich or richer!" Well, he won his multi-million-dollar arbitration, but there was a major flaw in his plan, which was his lack of a long-term financial plan. Within a year he had spent more than the value of his contract. Within a few years he was out of baseball and had declared bankruptcy. Simply stated, he spent more than he earned and never even thought about creating a financial game plan.

CREDIT RATING

If you don't have one, get started with a credit rating agency. Create a solid rating as soon as you can. Your credit score is more important to your future than how many points you scored as an athlete. All you need is a social security number and a credit card (which you then pay off in full each month, on time) to get started.

PAY OFF YOUR CREDIT CARD DEBT

Once you get started on that credit rating, you have to prioritize paying off your credit card bill in full on time each month so that you don't get charged interest or late fees on an outstanding balance. Yes, there is no point in putting any money in savings while you are paying interest on credit card debt. The best savings accounts pay under 1 percent currently, while the lowest credit cards charge 6 percent, and more likely upwards of 20 percent. The lower your credit rating and the fewer assets you have (common for former/current student-athletes), the higher the credit card interest rate normally is. While it may feel more responsible to start saving, if you already have accumulated credit card debt, eliminate your high-interest debt as fast as you can. Put the maximum amount of money you can toward this debt every month until it's paid off. On other debt, such as mortgages and car loans (which can be as low as 0 percent, at least for an initial period), you can look at the benefit of putting the money in savings versus the costs of carrying that debt.

So, what to do? Well, start by paying off the credit card with the highest interest rate first. As you get them paid off, cancel any cards that charge annual fees. There are so many credit options out there, there's no reason for most people to pay an annual fee.

Seth Etherton, a former student-athlete and MLB pitcher and now Pitching Coach with the Cincinnati Reds, provides some insight and advice:

> Obviously, you want to eliminate debt as fast as you can. Once you finish college, you are financially responsible regardless of your parents helping you out. You need to simplify your life and live within your means. There are a lot of things that we want, but we can't always have them. Determine what is really important to you, and start to make some goals on what is most important from a financial spending perspective.

BUILD AN EMERGENCY FUND

Once you have your high-interest credit card debt paid off, the cards that charge annual fees canceled, and your remaining credit card bills paid on time and, if possible, in full each month, it's time you stay there. Build up three to six months of savings in an emergency fund (in case you lose your job, have a bad investment, etc.). Find the highest interest rate savings account you can, and start putting money there. Today, there are many online savings accounts that pay much higher interest rates than do "regular banks." Don't go crazy with a traditional savings account though, because interest rates are so low these days.

A good rule of thumb for the size of your emergency fund is that it should be equivalent to three months' salary.

PLAN FOR RETIREMENT

This is a challenging goal to tell someone just coming out of college. We debated about it and given its importance to the planning theme that is so strong in the book so far, we have included it.

Retirement planning can seem extremely hard, because you're not sure you'll ever see the money again. It's not fun to take money you could use for entertainment or other discretionary spending now and put it aside for later. But you can't count on social security or pensions. The amount of money that can be made on compounding an investment over thirty years is enormous. Also, retirement savings become another asset you can tap in times of extreme need. The most important thing with retirement planning at your stage is simply to acknowledge it, consider how you might want it to look and get an "idea" of what you will ultimately need to make that happen. It may help you to start investing or saving to get ahead of the curve that is coming. If you have the ability to do so, get an IRA started as soon as you can and consistently contribute to it.

Gill again provides some sound advice: "Once you get your first job, you would definitely want to look into what your company is doing in terms of if they have a retirement savings plan for you. That's the easiest way to save. It depends on the company. There's a lot that will match up to X amount of dollars you put into it, so it essentially is free money for you."

As a start, this can be as simple as building up a small nest egg of dollars in a savings account to move to a larger apartment, save for a down payment on a home, build up dollars for a trip you want to make or bike you want to buy, etc. Perhaps you need to buy a new car for a new job or your family is having a once-in-a-lifetime wedding on a Caribbean island and you want to go. You need some money to cover these things. Get ahead.

OPTIMIZE YOUR TAXES

This may be a bit cart before the salary horse from a job but you need to get some sound tax advice once you start making money to a level where you are paying significant levels of tax. A good benchmark is anything over $30,000 annually. Learn some accounting or get some accounting advice. Once you start thinking about family, homes, children, etc., tax deductions and decisions make a big impact.

START INVESTING

This is the most complex part of a financial plan and can make you debt free or in debt based on the investments you choose. This is another area to seek a trusted professional advisor who has a proven track record. Consistency and diversity are key. As you consider investing, make sure that you have an idea of what your goals are. Obviously there are many different avenues to investing, whether it is high-interest, no-risk savings, high-reward/risky investments, buying real estate, etc.

INSURE WHERE APPROPRIATE

It is probably a good idea to get long term health care insurance as well as disability insurance, along with car insurance and insurance on personal property. These policies are often inexpensive and it is a good hedge against the worst.

Spend a moment and think about how much time you have devoted to your sports and education. Now is the time to bring that enthusiasm, focus, hard work, and teamwork to becoming fiscally smart!

PRACTICAL APPLICATIONS

Most student-athletes don't receive "full rides" and don't have enough time to get a job to pay for tuition otherwise. Therefore, the majority of student-athletes may have some amount of debt from loans that they will have to pay back after they graduate. You'll likely also need to get a car, an apartment in an urban setting, and maybe a new computer and phone. Yes, that new paycheck will get split quickly.

At the end of the day, you should follow the five steps below as a start:

Step 1

Create a checklist of "needs" and "wants." Needs are things like utilities, rent, transportation, clothes, food, necessary travel, and more. Wants are things like a phone upgrade, a new video game, trendy clothes, and trips. Keep these separate and only dip in the "wants" when you have the needs under control, your emergency fund in place, and confidence in future revenues.

Step 2

Start a financial budget template on Excel, Numbers, or other spreadsheet software. Don't do this informally or haphazardly. Build a good and easy to update budget template. Keep all old data so you can track your budget versus reality the year later. Most bank accounts and credit cards now have very detailed online systems with your records that you can draw from.

Step 3

Use technology and apps to help you track your spending, investments, and credit cards. There are many great tools out there now to control your spending (for example, max of $15/week on coffee, how many days you go out for lunch, etc.). Use them if you are not disciplined enough (like many of us are!).

Step 4

Create financial goals for yourself and set yourself boundaries and limits on your spending. Like many of the other secrets in the book, a plan and clear objectives and priorities are needed!

Step 5

Within your means, understand what "lifestyle" you are going to and can afford to live. Be smart. An apartment closer to work where you don't need a car but is a few hundred dollars more may be a better investment than a cheaper apartment far away. Include your extracurricular activities around a balanced and healthy life in these decisions.

CHAPTER SUMMARY

As we tell you to be fiscally smart, don't think it is so easy and that it will all take care of itself. As we mentioned, you need to:

- Build yourself a financial plan

- Create your budget, and spend only what you can afford

- Create a good credit rating

- Pay off your debt and build an emergency fund

- Acknowledge your eventual retirement, optimize your taxes, and start investing

- Insure yourself and be practical

All of these will change as life changes, and it only becomes more complicated if you add a spouse and children to the mix. Educate yourself, and take control of your finances. Don't let them get out of hand or out of sight.

It may not be the first thing on your mind as you are mostly worried about your tuition and when your next meal is, but take some time to learn and think about what is ahead of you or in front of you.

Secret 20 Prepare for the Future by Tracking Trends

THE SECRET IN A FEW WORDS

Since this is The Final Secret, we thought it had better be a good one. In fact, it's kind of a summary secret because it combines elements of Secrets 1, 9, and 12: Create and Follow Your Student-Athlete Plan, Your Major Really Matters, and Face Reality in Sports and Life. Tracking trends may sound boring . . . like some kind of research assignment for a class you didn't really care about. But there's a big difference for this particular research, this quest, because the class is YOU. And if you aren't interested in YOU . . . well, then you should toss this book away.

So here's the secret: If you want to live that life you've possibly imagined . . . the one where you live comfortably and work at a job you like . . . you have to pre- pare for that future and you have to follow the societal and business trends that influence the world around you. Presidential elections suddenly matter because they might influence the creation of new jobs. New inventions matter because they might create entire industries. So, too, popular culture, economic realities, and real-world threats.

No one goes into a big sporting event without some kind of a plan for achiev- ing victory. The reason coaches study game film is to spot the trends the opposing teams employ and to make predictions on what those players (and their coaches) will do in the next game.

You've got to start spotting those trends in life in order to win.

PREPARE FOR THE FUTURE BY TRACKING TRENDS

As this book draws to a close, there is one last secret to share. It's a simple one but something every student-athlete who won't turn pro in sports should learn: how to know who and what is out there . . . and then . . . how to prepare for the future by spotting the road signs, those big neon indicators. You need to come to grips with the fact that the year you graduate, more than a hundred thousand student-athletes who didn't sign pro sports contracts will simultaneously enter the job market with many of them looking for the same jobs you are seeking.

Trends are usually slow moving, but graduation ceremonies happen with perfect regularity every May, June, and December. That means that regardless of what attractive new industry (technology, fashion, electronics, broadcasting, engineering, military, entertainment, social media, and an endlessly changing list) is suddenly emerging, it is one that hundreds of thousands of other graduates will be targeting.

So you need to be quick getting off the blocks and you need to know where to look. In other words, you need to know who "those guys" are. You have to try (and it takes training) to get a step ahead. To know what's coming.

Have you ever participated in a scavenger hunt? Small teams compete to be the first to gather all the items on a list containing a crazed range of objects (for example, a lug nut, a box of Lucky Charms cereal, an Ohio State baseball hat, the front page of the *New York Times*). Some scavenger hunts give vague or mysterious clues, which sometimes simply lead to other clues. A scavenger hunt is usually a fun, competitive race that takes the players on a wild search for the strange objects on the list. Team members have to work together and use their ingenuity to find the items required, and they need to do so with urgency.

That's one way of thinking about spotting and tracking trends. You probably have some rough sense of what is happening in the world but are not sure what it all means. If you're like most people reading this book, politics and big business may or may not have been your thing. You've simply been trying to manage classes, your coaches' expectations, and a social life.

Suddenly, someone tells you that you won't be "going pro" and you have to think about working (ugh!) and earning a paycheck. When that thought kicks in (the whole job thing), you may find yourself racing around (if you haven't lined up a job during your senior year) and trying to match up what you like doing with a company that looks like a good fit.

Think of it this way: You probably like playing sports and you should know that Nike, Under Armour, Warrior Sports, and Sports PT were created by student-athletes (Phil Knight ran track at Oregon; Kevin Plank played football at Maryland; Dave Morrow played lacrosse at Princeton; Lynn Steenberg was a trainer for the football team at Ithaca). You would probably also think that working for a company that creates products for athletes would involve staying close to elite competition and might also be fun.

But what do you really know about Nike, Under Armour, Warrior Sports, and Sports PT? What trends are influencing those brands? What challenges do the CEOs of those companies face? What are the new frontiers in sport apparel or footwear? Where is lacrosse equipment headed in the future? How is technology changing the way sport is played? Why is physical therapy for injured athletes booming as a business?

Naturally, everyone who likes sports can't get hired by a sports company. But everyone can get better at spotting trends and making projections. Famed hockey player Wayne Gretzky once said that he didn't skate to where the puck was . . . he skated to where the puck was going. Translation: the greatest hockey player of the modern era scored more goals by anticipating where he needed to be in order to get the job done (that is, to put the puck in the back of the net). He didn't skate directly at the action. He skated to the place where the action would end up.

If you are only skating toward your collegiate sport, you won't end up where the puck (your career after college) is going. You may talk a good game about your sport, team, or campus, but you won't know what is going on in the world.

TECHNOLOGY AND CAREER MANAGEMENT TRENDS

Dan Butterly, mentioned a few times in the book already, Commissioner of the Big West Conference, provides his insights and advice for current and future student-athletes on the topic of technology trends and tracking changes that will affect your career.

DAN BUTTERLY

(Commissioner of the Big West Conference)

WHAT IMPACT DO YOU SEE TECHNOLOGY MAKING ON THE FUTURE OF THE STUDENT-ATHLETE, AND HOW WILL THAT AFFECT THE WAY STUDENT-ATHLETES WILL NEED TO PREPARE FOR THEIR TRANSITION?

Technology has advanced training, not only in the equipment that is used, but also in nutrition, health, physical fitness, sports medicine, and medical procedures. Student-athletes are dealing with continual changes in technology in their own lives, inclusive of social media, digital content, internet availability.

It is helping to make lives more efficient but is drastically hurting entities such as the retail store industry with regard to how we buy products and services. Also, technology has greatly impacted how we develop interpersonal relationships and how we communicate. For example, managing our personal finances has changed from going to the bank to using mobile devices. Why do you need a financial advisor these days when you can chart, research, and invest all through mobile devices? All college students must evaluate their career fields and look at how technology and innovation will impact their opportunities for career growth. Will you be an innovator, or will innovation take over your career?

WHAT TRENDS HAVE YOU SEEN WITH STUDENT-ATHLETES OVER THE YEARS THAT MAY CONTINUE IN REGARDS TO PREPARING FOR THEIR FUTURE?

Student-athletes continue to be outstanding leaders. That has not changed over the years. There are tremendous traits student-athletes have that many times they undersell on their resume or job interview. Team building, how to deal with adversity, excellent health and wellness, leadership traits, and a zest for success.

One of the great trends I have seen from this generation of student-athlete compared to previous student-athletes is how they venture outside their own sport, come together with student-athletes in other sports, and have created a significant voice and leadership group not only to make the NCAA better, but by leading, to make their generation better too.

When I was an undergrad, I heard student-athletes from other teams often complain about all the great resources football and men's basketball received. Now, many of those same benefits are available to all student-athletes, because of the voice this generation of student-athletes has put forth.

WHAT IMPACT WILL TECHNOLOGY HAVE ON THE JOB MARKET FOR GRADUATING STUDENT-ATHLETES?

Technology is changing the way the world works. I have worked in marketing and sales since I started my career in the early '90s, and the inventory we sold, or mediums we used to promote our brands, are no longer the key mediums. Print, radio, and television have been replaced with the internet, social media, and such digital broadcast channels as YouTube.

This has changed not only marketing and sales, but how businesses do business. Students must always look toward "what's next" and look to be innovators in their field. Soon, streets will be filled with self-driving cars. Social media has changed the "we" to "me." Student-athletes will be key leaders moving forward, as they know how to compete, coach, manage adversity, work within teams, and drive success.

Snapchat is the perfect example of "me" versus the "we." When I was going to school, you were focused on core curriculum, and you focused on your friends. Now you are doing things via social media that we never would have done with an old-fashioned camera. Every statement you make, whether it is written text or photography, is available publicly when posting to social media, whether you make it public or private. Posting on any social medium can have a significant impact on your career, whether that is with a current employer or an employer five to ten years from now.

How that will impact students, not only student-athletes, but students as they go into the working world, as they go into interview space or get the potential to even interview for a position would surprise you. Putting your resume together is one thing and, obviously, having a digital profile on LinkedIn is another. It's very easy for me to hire a background firm to search through your social media accounts to determine if there's anything negative that may impact your job status or the potential of me interviewing you for a job situation here at the Big West Conference, or any place I may be.

I just don't think people nowadays, specifically the high school, early college generation that have grown up with mobile devices, realize the impact that a selfie or a statement that you put up at the age of seventeen or eighteen may have on the future of your job potential.

WHAT TRENDS HAVE YOU SEEN WITH THE JOB MARKET AND HOW STUDENT-ATHLETES CAN BEST PREPARE THEMSELVES FOR TRENDING INDUSTRIES?

In my experience, students can best prepare by taking courses or trying new experiences that challenge them beyond their current major or sport. Life experiences, and finding what you truly enjoy, while developing critical thinking skills, are the fundamental benefits of college. Innovators are working daily to find new ways to change old industry via technology. People are more mobile than ever before.

Look at ways the career field you choose can do business in a new way that our mobile society can engage. If you are an accounting major, take some technology courses and learn how to develop apps or new ways to communicate. If you want to head into the sport field, how can you best engage fans, sponsors, boosters, season ticket holders, etc. so they want to continue to spend hundreds or thousands of dollars to get to your events? In-stadium attendance is trending down, not up, and mobile technology is a key driver.

Chris Dawson is an associate commissioner at the Pac-12 Conference and a former women's basketball player at the University of Virginia. Through her many years in college athletics and her student-athlete experience, she has expertise about the future of student-athletes and what they can do to prepare for the biggest pending changes.

CHRIS DAWSON

(former student-athlete, now Associate Commissioner at the Pac-12 Conference)

I think the biggest potential change in intercollegiate athletics will probably come from the litigation that's still pending. The other things that make it a different world from even when I competed or I would say twenty years ago is the amount of money that's involved, like television money, all the things that people now think you "have to have" to be successful. You have to have a shiny locker room on par with professional locker rooms.

You have to have the next big thing in facilities and I think that there's a financial breaking point that's going to hit and it's already hit some places. In my opinion, the path between athletics as an educational enterprise with a lot of money involved and the legal challenges that come with will be the most difficult thing in the next five to ten years. Student-athletes will have to deal with fewer opportunities across different sports if things get scaled back. Who are the people who are not going to have the opportunity to compete at the Division I level that they have now?

The other aspect for students on campus will be continued pressure to win and perform at a high level academically and athletically all the time. It all depends on the institution, the competitive level, the kind of institution, the preferred major, and the designated major of the student. I think more schools now are aware of the need for mental health services for people.

JOB PLACEMENT

Jim Kahler is a former Division I swimmer at Xavier University who went on to work in the sports industry for many different organizations, including the Cleveland Cavaliers. Kahler is the former Executive Director of the AECOM Center for Sports Administration at Ohio University and is now Director of Sports Gambling Education at Ohio University. He provides his insights in the box below on what you need to consider and prepare for when starting a career and looking for a job. He focusses his advice around the five pillars of job placement.

FIVE JOB PLACEMENT PILLARS

Sports business is like most other traditional industries; however, you need to have an open mind with regard to relocation in order to advance your career. If your end goal is to work for the hometown team you may never get your foot in the door and can find it next to impossible to grow from an entry-level position to the CEO's office. Most sports organizations are small in scale with low turnover rates inside successful companies. To advance your career you need to perform at a level that will get you noticed by your current supervisors, other organizations, and recruiters. When it comes time to make a move, you need to carefully evaluate each opportunity and not let the excitement of being recruited cloud your vision. At an early age I was once given some great advice by a recruiter when she said, "Sometimes in sports you become better known for the jobs you turn down as opposed to the ones you accept."

Over the years, I have developed a rubric for new opportunities, even if it's your first job, that I refer to as the Five Job Placement Pillars. Listed below, in no particular order of importance, are five elements that you need to research and factor in before accepting any new position:

- *Geography*—How will this job meet my needs when it comes to the geographical location? You will need to be able to answer the following questions:

  - If I need to make a trip home in case of an emergency, how long will the trip take me?

  - How expensive is a roundtrip airline ticket?

  - Can I drive the distance in a reasonable time?

  - Are my parents in good enough health to travel in for a visit?

  - Is the location one that would be attractive for family and friends to visit?

- *Organizational Culture*—I know I will end up working long hours in sports, but what's the organizational culture going to be like? Every organization has its own culture and it's incumbent on you to do your research so you will be able to answer the following questions:

  - What's the real goal of the organization that I am going to be working for?

  - What's the management style of the organization—micro or macro?

  - Does the organization consider its employees to be the most treasured possession of the organization? This organizational style is often referred to as the Baseball Team Culture.

  - What are the processes and procedures like with the organization?

  - How does the organization feel about training and developing its employees?

- *Direct Supervisor*—The person who is your direct supervisor will have a tremendous impact on your level of job satisfaction. In challenging times your direct supervisor can become your greatest ally or your worst enemy. So how can you get a read on your new boss during the interview process?

- Do your homework to determine if your supervisor is a developer and someone who enjoys working with their direct reports (that is, employees) or a grinder and someone who is only concerned with net results.

- Take advantage of LinkedIn and see if your new boss has recommendations from former employees or customers.

- Ask yourself if your new boss is going to be with the organization for a while or are they ready to make their next move in the sports business industry, which will more than likely end up with a move to another organization.

- Does your direct supervisor have balance in their life or are they a workaholic?

- How does your new boss define success?

- *Room for Growth*—Will the responsibilities that you are given with your new position provide you with new experiences and challenges? Room for growth doesn't necessarily mean internal growth within the organization as opposed to having the opportunity to develop new skills that will make you more valuable in sports. Some companies talk a good game when it comes to training and executive education. Your direct supervisor might be a great manager and developer but will higher management provide the budget and permission that allows you to attend conferences and networking events?

- *Compensation*—While you will undoubtedly have to pay your dues and be patient in the sports business industry, compensation has to be one of your placement pillars. If you can't afford to live in a great city, sooner or later you will be looking for that next job and you do not want to get the reputation of being a job hopper (someone who takes a new job every eighteen months to two years). Oftentimes energetic and hard-charging employees are willing to take below-entry-level wages and end up expecting a larger-than-life raise after the first year on the job. Please remember if your boss offers you a 10 percent increase after your first year on the job and tells you that you just received the largest percentage increase in the organization that simple math still applies. Ten times nothing (1.1 x a low entry-level salary) will still equate to a low salary unless you find yourself in a sales position that has applicable commissions.

In addition to these five pillars that will help you form the foundation for a good decision you also need to ask yourself what else matters and will drive your final decision. We all have different challenges and situations in life, but I do believe these five basic pillars will come into play every time you make a move in your career. It's also very important to realize that the priority order of your placement pillars will change every three to five years in your life. As you get older, compensation and geography will probably become more important than when you first graduate. You also will be more likely to take a greater risk with organizational culture at the start of your career just to gain experience.

FIVE PLACEMENT PILLARS / RUBRIC

Geography

Organizational Culture

Direct Supervisor

Room for Growth

Compensation

Placement Pillar in Priority Order	Placement Value	Total Score
1.	25–30 points	
2.	20–25 points	
3.	15–20 points	
4.	10–15 points	
5.	5–10 points	
Total Score		

FIVE PLACEMENT PILLARS / SCORING SYSTEM

Letter Score / Total Points	Do Your Homework	Suggestions
A+ / A– = 90–100 points		Accept the offer
B+ / B– = 89–80 points		Proceed with a plan after two years
C+ / C– = 79–70 points		Proceed with caution and a short-term plan
Below 70 points	X	Turn down the offer

While the scoring system that I have outlined above may seem unrealistic, you need to do your homework prior to accepting any new job. Oftentimes the grass will seem greener on the other side of the fence, but you need to be careful and run your current job through the same rubric above before making a change. Early in your career, compensation jumps into a priority position (1–3) when you leave your first job for the second one. Don't let your salary be a bigger issue than it needs to be, as most people tend to let their egos get in the way of continued career development. Don't be in a hurry to leave a supervisor who has a proven track record as a developer of talent or a company that has an excellent organizational culture.

YOUR PERSONAL AUDIT

What have you been given and how does it fit with your life after college?

It's an important question and gives you a reason to conduct a personalized audit. Would you write down any of the following or would you list other things?

- A college degree

- A major (or minor) you selected and liked

- Course specialization relevant to the world you want to inhabit

- A chance to practice and play sports in college (regardless of whether you started, played, or walked on . . . and regardless of whether you played DI, II, III, NAIA, or any other form of organized collegiate sport

- A competitive spirit

- A teamwork orientation (that is, you know what it takes to be a good teammate)

- Physical reliability

- Emotional strength (drawn from hard work and close contests)

- A few inspiring professors

- A happy childhood

- A childhood filled with challenges that you overcame

- A life filled with challenges you are still working on

- Wealth, poverty, or something in between

- The knowledge that your life wasn't easy but you've made the most of yourself

- A vision of what you are still capable of achieving

Your potential and your merit are what matters and both of those lead to a discussion of market forces and market demand. Spotting trends is about knowing what is influencing a market and knowing what employers are looking for in new hires.

You've learned the "college system" (how to register for classes you want, how to get into certain buildings after hours, etc.), so why can't you master the next system?

Lynn Steenberg, the CEO of Sports PT, was mentioned earlier in this chapter and frequently guest lectures at Syracuse University on sport industry leadership. She often tells a story about her father and how he taught her what he called the seven-option rule.

"That was important," Steenberg recalls. "In his business, whenever they were faced with a challenge, my father's business partners would force themselves to come up with at least seven options. I asked Dad: Why the number seven? He said: 'It forces you to think beyond the obvious. It's easy to come up with two or three options. It isn't so easy to come up with seven.'"

Steenberg goes on to say that a lot of times, the first option for many folks is doing nothing. And the seventh option is way at the other end of the spectrum and virtually impossible if not highly improbable. "But then you work to fill in the middle five. It forces you to think broadly."

Spotting trends may be like that. At first you may only see the obvious things or you'll predict things so far into the future you won't be alive to see them happen. But building a capacity to understand how the world works and what is driving the change you see all around you is important because it can shape your future success.

CHAPTER SUMMARY

We've made this chapter's secret sound easy to master, and that is perhaps a disservice to readers. If all of us could spot trends (think of the stock market or gambling), everyone would know what to do next. The truth is that many trends are not that easy to identify and some are extremely hard to put into everyday words. You might sense something but not know how to explain it. You might see something new and believe it is going to be the next big thing. Some days it is, most days it isn't.

But our secret—and it's a valuable one—is letting you know that the most successful people are the ones who have a sense of what's coming next. They have that ability to look around the corner without sticking their necks out. They can correctly guess "fast ball, down and away" or that the player shooting on goal will go "upper left." They are moving to block the shot before it happens.

These prognosticators hold an advantage when they look at what's going on around them. It's the difference between being focused only on self and instead looking at everything else. And that proactive, initiative-taking inspiration is a valuable trait to develop.

Many of us develop that skill early when we know someone will be mad at us before the other person even hears the whole story about how the window got broken. Or the dog got out. Or the door got left open.

But switch this habit from the negative to the positive and try your hand at guessing which business sectors might grow or which companies might be hiring in the future. Which "friends" in your network can really help you and which ones can only talk a good game. Get in the habit of predicting which new social networks or apps will catch on and which will fail. Work on telling the difference between a short fad and a bankable trend.

And don't get down on yourself if you get predictions wrong. All of us swing and miss at a lot of pitches and we do so all the time. But as in sports, you get up, dust yourself off, and try to figure out the next situation.

The End—Your Road Map: It's Not a Secret

Now that you have read our twenty secrets, our final chapter is to ask you to sincerely create and then follow a road map toward personal success. This road map incorporates those twenty secrets and will help you out along your journey.

As you create and follow your road map, you need to keep learning in everything that you do. Always strive to continue to learn because for every one thing you learn, it will open your eyes to three things that you don't know. Your education is something that no one can ever take away from you. As some will say, "Be a sponge and soak everything up."

We believe your career path and life path shouldn't be separate from each other. The two may intersect at the right time and move forward from there, but both paths need to incorporate compatible goals and coexist. Therefore, provide yourself with a road map that gives you guidance to your paths.

To provide you with advice on what to plan and how to navigate through your transition, we interviewed Azure Davey, former lacrosse student-athlete and the former Director of Academic Affairs and Membership at the NCAA.

AZURE DAVEY

**(former lacrosse student-athlete, and former Director
of Academic Affairs and Membership at the NCAA)**

THE PLAN

All strategies and approaches to preparing yourself for life after sport boils down to one master plan—know yourself to the greatest degree possible, commit to learning more about yourself and your abilities, and use that knowledge to determine your next steps.

You must take a hard look at what your interests are, what your skills and abilities are, who you know, what foundational elements you learned along the way and meld it all to create a personalized blueprint. It's not a perfect science—it's meant to evolve and you need to be fluid. However, if you aren't thoughtful about your passions and gifts and refine your pursuit of those passions, you may end up feeling as though you are floating though this transition and the others that will come later in life.

SKILLS TO PREPARE FOR ANY FUTURE CAREER TRANSITION

- *Proactive Thinking and Vision.* Proactively think about where you would like to be in the future and how what you do today may best support that vision. For almost everyone, this vision must be something other than professional sport. Even for those who will go pro, there will be another life, another career. You need to learn about yourself and your personal and professional interests as soon as possible.

- *Flexibility and Adaptability.* The only guarantee in preparing for transition to "real life" is that not everything will go according to plan. Be prepared to both capitalize and pivot when curveballs are thrown your way. Hurdles can sometimes be the best tool to help you define where you want to go.

- *Clear Articulation of Your Skills and Abilities.* One of the most important skills is being able to describe your skill set and articulate why it is valuable. In the case of athletics, what have years of playing a sport taught you and how are those skills transferrable *and* valuable to future employers? Being able to articulate and help others draw the connection is vital. If you can't articulate it, why should you expect others to get it?

PREPARING YOURSELF FOR THE TRANSITION

The day will come that, when asked to describe yourself, you'll need to use labels different from "athlete" or "potential professional athlete." You need to think about what those other descriptions are sooner than your junior or senior year of college. Ideally, you're thinking about those descriptions when you select your school, identify potential co-curricular activities, and prepare for future jobs. The sooner you start using those other descriptive terms to describe yourself, the better. That doesn't mean you don't identify and describe yourself as an athlete—you just need to know what your other gifts, interests, and skills are.

You'll still be an athlete, and chances are many of you will continue to be active throughout life, but knowing that you have other talents and that those talents are just as important as your athlete status is important to transitioning and getting involved in other facets of life.

WHY PREPARATION EASES THE TRANSITION

It's likely that for years you've primarily thought of yourself as an athlete. If you continue with that sole mindset, you might flounder with the next steps. By thinking about yourself in other contexts besides athletics and cultivating those thoughts with action, the transition is less dramatic and your identity and future are open and ready for the next thing—the future you!

Jeremy Foley is Athletic Director Emeritus at the University of Florida. He was the AD there for twenty-five years, and worked in the athletic department prior to becoming the AD. Foley was also a football and lacrosse student-athlete in his days at Hobart College. He provides a unique perspective on how you should become a successful person in life outside of being a successful student and athlete.

JEREMY FOLEY (FORMER FOOTBALL AND LACROSSE STUDENT-ATHLETE, AD EMERITUS, UNIVERSITY OF FLORIDA)

CREATING THE ROAD MAP

You are going to have to create your own road map and you may not find it right away. All of your life, your road map has been given to you, and you have been guided along the way, but now you have to take the lessons you have learned as being a successful student-athlete and take those into the next chapter of your life.

If you transfer what you have learned, continue to evolve, and don't be discouraged, you will be successful. A lot of student-athletes spend time in the past, and the past is gone and done with. Records are shattered, people are replaced, and that is how it will always work. It is important to take those lessons that you have learned from the past with you, but while looking forward.

FIGURE OUT WHAT IS IMPORTANT IN LIFE

The process is this; none of us know what your journey is going to be. I ended up spending forty years at Florida, who knew that was going to happen. You have to let the world come to you, but you still have to put in the work, get your degree(s) and network. I think that a lot of people put too much pressure on themselves to control the game of life. You can't get discouraged because you may not be where you want to be right away, and you can't put false pressure on yourself. Being out in the real world is not going to be as easy as you want it to be. You may not get a job you like right away, and you may not get the job you apply for that you really want, but don't let any of that discourage you. You use the lesson you learned as a student-athlete of getting back up and continuing to work, and keep going.

Throughout my forty years, whenever my alarm clock went off, I never once thought that I "had to go do" my job. I always thought that I "get to go do" my job, regardless of what that day was going to look like, good or bad. My point with that is that if there is something that you really love to do, then go chase it. Regardless of your roadblocks in between, go do it, because I can't imagine having to settle to do something you don't necessarily want to do all the time.

TOP TEN QUALITIES OF A HIGH ACHIEVER

1. High integrity and ethics
2. Outstanding work ethic
3. Ability to listen
4. Ability to make decisions
5. Control over temper
6. Being a people person
7. Loyalty
8. Common sense
9. Toughness
10. Ability to smile and have fun

Too many times, people take shortcuts. The end justifies the means. Winning is the end all be all regardless of the path to get there, and I don't think that is ultimately what it is all about.

Being able to listen to other people makes you a more effective leader. If you aren't listening, people won't give you input. At the end of the day, it's about getting the best input to make the best decision as a leader.

EIGHT ASPECTS OF BECOMING A SUCCESSFUL PROFESSIONAL

1. Learn how to treat people with respect
2. Learn and develop the value of respect
3. Understand the value of people
4. Be known for the having the highest of ethics and personal integrity
5. Be the most honest person you can be
6. Be humble
7. Have a strong work ethic
8. Learn how to lead

You need to be humble. A lot of people that become successful get big egos or it becomes all about them. At some point in time, the success you may be achieving is going to take a hit. You aren't always going to be at the top. People like being around humble people, not I people, or me people.

In staying humble, you have to know that what you are doing is much bigger than you. At the end of the day, this isn't about us. It is all about "the place." At Florida, we are just a part of a great institution. We represent the University of Florida, "we" being the whole department. Every decision we make needs to be made in the best interest of "the place." If the motivation is about ourselves, then we will make bad decisions.

Having a great work ethic is something you can control. I've seen people that have been successful, but at some point in time they stop working because they think they have made it, or they just cruise at what they are doing. I think that the more successful you become, the harder you have to work.

If you want to be really successful, you have to learn how to lead. I think leaders are made, not born. Leading people and motivating people is a key part of being successful. You need to self-evaluate yourself on that level every single day. Leading people changes every day and you have to continue to learn.

I always had a fear of failure. I didn't want to fail because it meant that the University of Florida failed. I used that as motivation, and continued to work harder. As Athletic Director at Florida, the thing that kept me motivated the most was the ability to impact people's lives. I love winning, and I love being in the front row for a lot of special events, but the most important thing to me has been the ability to impact and change people's lives. Changing someone's life is much more important than winning a ring.

That's all, folks (an old line from an old cartoon). Those are the twenty secrets. Finito. No tests. No homework assignments. Just our sincere hope that this book helps you handle the complex process of playing sports in college.

Get busy living. And enjoy your time. Many nonathletes out there would do anything to be you for just one day. Know it or not, you are a hero in someone's eyes. Stay strong.

Afterword

Christopher J. Parker, PhD

NJCAA President and Chief Executive Officer

Life happens whether we want it to or not, so being prepared to succeed is essential. This book has highlighted the life cycle of going from a successful student-athlete to a successful, thriving professional. Employers are actively searching for individuals who possess life skills such as coachability and dependability and a willingness to thrive and succeed during the hardest of times. Therefore these twenty secrets are so important to all student-athletes, those in both the NCAA and NJCAA in the United States, those in U Sports in Canada, and others around the world.

As a former student-athlete, coach, and collegiate-level administrator, I know just how important the direction provided by the authors of *20 Secrets* can be. In my current role with the NJCAA, the second-largest athletic association in the United States, I am tasked with representing our 512 member colleges and providing the best possible experiences for our student-athletes both on and off the field.

In my view, the skills learned as a student-athlete are the same skills necessary to be successful at any given moment, but being aware and staying focused on these skills and success strategies is key. This is one place where this book can help. My advice to a future student-athlete is to not let those skills slip you by, because they can produce positive outcomes in your life. The mentoring, coaching, and education that you can obtain will be the true foundation of your success both in the classroom and on the playing field, but they must translate accordingly.

I highly recommend that student-athletes, as well as coaches and administrators, carefully review the book to ensure that the right track to success aligns for all. Study these secrets, understand these secrets, but most importantly capitalize on these secrets and remember that preparing to succeed is far more effective than the alternative.

Appendix A

NCAA Student-Athlete Success Data

Estimated Probability of Competing in College and Professional Athletics

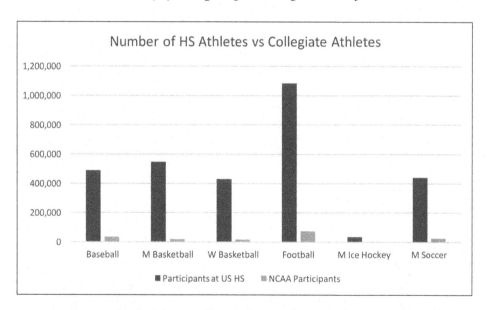

NCAA Research. (2017 March 10). *Estimated Probability of Competing in College Athletics.* Retrieved on May 22, 2017.

(continued on next page)

Estimated Probability of Competing in College and Professional Athletics

(continued from previous page)

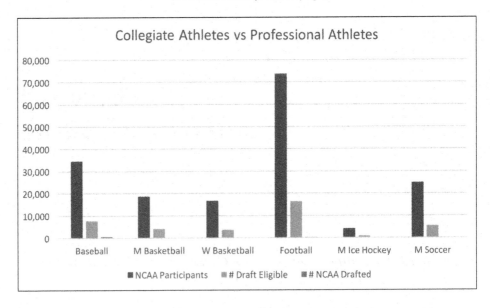

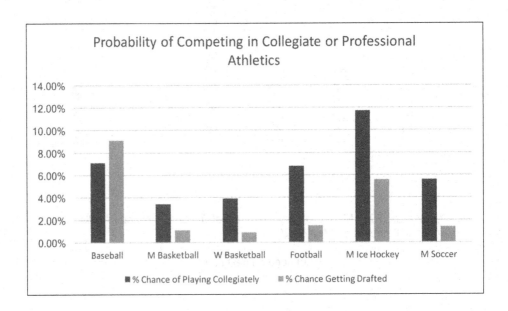

Male Identity by Division (Athlete/Student)

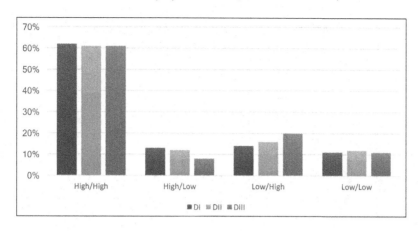

Female Identity by Division (Athlete/Student)

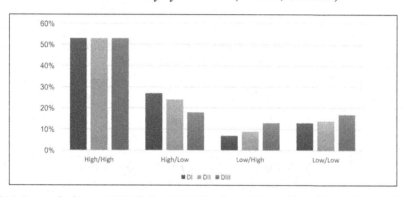

NCAA Research. (August 2013). Do NCAA Student-Athletes View Themselves as Students or Athletes? Retrieved on May 22, 2017.

Estimated Probability of Competing in Professional Athletics

	NCAA Participants	Approximate # Draft Eligible	# Draft Picks	# NCAA Drafted	% NCAA to Major Pro	% NCAA to Total Pro
Baseball	34,554	7,679	1,206	695	9.1%	--
M Basketball	18,684	4,152	60	44	1.1%	19.1%
W Basketball	16,593	3,687	36	35	0.9%	4.9%
Football	73,660	16,369	253	251	1.5%	1.9%
M Ice Hockey	4,102	912	211	51	5.6%	--
M Soccer	24,803	5,512	81	75	1.4%	--

NCAA Research. (March 10, 2017). *Estimated Probability of Competing in Professional Athletics.* Retrieved on May 23, 2017.

Male Opinion of Likeliness of Going Pro

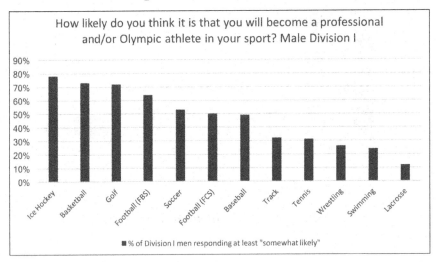

NCAA Research. (January 2016). *Results from the 2015 GOALS Study of the Student-Athlete Experience.* Retrieved on May 23, 2017.

Female Opinion of Likeliness of Going Pro

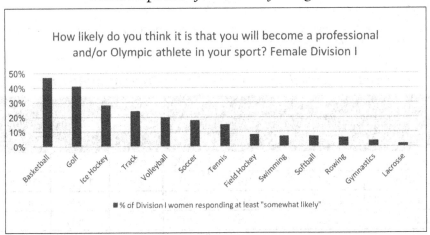

NCAA Research. (March 10, 2017). *Estimated Probability of Competing in Professional Athletics.* Retrieved on May 23, 2017.

Estimated Probability of Competing in College Athletics

	Partici-pants at US High Schools	NCAA Par-ticipants	Overall % HS to NCAA	% HS to NCAA Division 1	% HS to NCAA Division II	% HS to NCAA Division III
Men						
Baseball	488,815	34,554	7.1%	2.1%	2.2%	2.8%
Basketball	546,428	18,684	3.4%	1.0%	1.0%	1.4%
Cross Country	257,691	14,412	5.6%	1.9%	1.4%	2.3%
Football	1,083,308	73,660	6.8%	2.6%	1.8%	2.4%
Golf	146,677	8,676	5.9%	2.0%	1.7%	2.2%
Ice Hockey	35,155	4,102	11.7%	4.6%	0.5%	6.5%
Lacrosse	109,522	13,466	12.3%	2.9%	2.3%	7.1%
Soccer	440,322	24,803	5.6%	1.3%	1.5%	2.8%
Swimming	133,470	9,455	7.1%	2.8%	1.1%	3.2%
Tennis	157,201	8,092	5.1%	1.7%	1.1%	2.4%
Track and Field	591,133	28,334	4.8%	1.9%	1.2%	1.7%
Volleyball	55,417	1,899	3.4%	0.7%	0.8%	1.9%
Water Polo	21,857	1,014	4.6%	2.6%	0.7%	1.3%
Wrestling	250,653	7,075	2.8%	1.0%	0.8%	10%
Women						
Basketball	429,380	16,593	3.9%	1.2%	1.1%	1.6%
Cross Country	222,516	15,958	7.2%	2.7%	1.8%	2.7%
Field Hockey	59,793	6,032	10.1%	3.0%	1.2%	5.8%
Golf	74,762	5,293	7.1%	2.9%	2.1%	2.1%
Ice Hockey	9,514	2,289	24.1%	9.0%	1.0%	14.0%
Lacrosse	88,050	11,375	12.9%	3.8%	2.6%	6.5%
Soccer	381,529	27,358	7.2%	2.4%	1.9%	2.9%
Softball	366,685	19,680	5.4%	1.6%	1.6%	2.1%
Swimming	166,747	12,356	7.4%	3.3%	1.1%	3.0%
Tennis	183,800	8,933	4.9%	1.6%	1.1%	2.2%
Track and Field	485,969	29,048	6.0%	2.7%	1.5%	1.8%
Volleyball	436,309	17,119	3.9%	1.2%	1.1%	1.6%
Water Polo	20,230	1,136	5.6%	3.3%	1.0%	1.3%

NCAA Research. (March 10, 2017). *Estimated Probability of Competing in College Athletics.* Retrieved on May 23, 2017.

The following figures come from *A Study of NCAA Student-Athletes: Undergraduate Experiences and Post-college Outcomes* (Washington, DC: Gallup, 2020). Used with permission from Gallup and the NCAA.

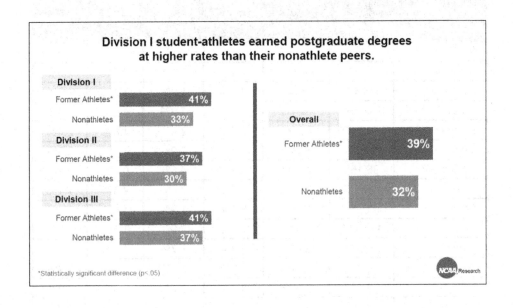

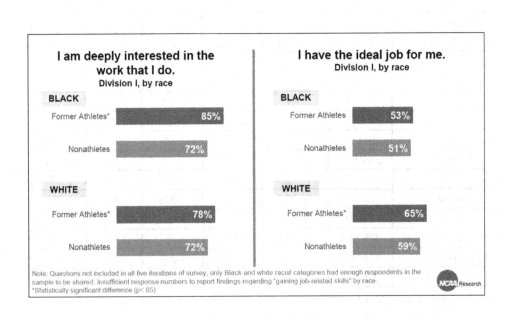

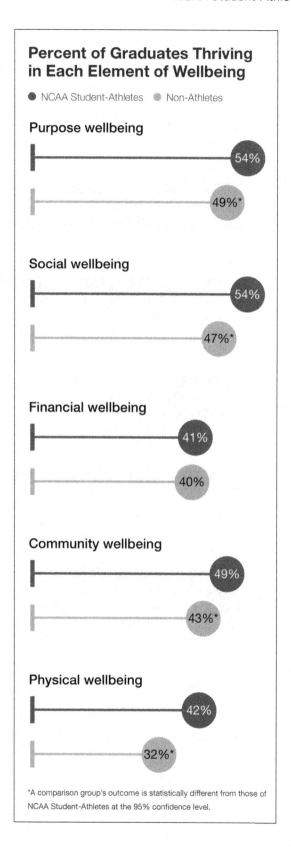

Percent of Graduates Thriving in Each Element of Wellbeing

● NCAA Student-Athletes   ● Non-Athletes

Purpose wellbeing

54%

49%*

Social wellbeing

54%

47%*

Financial wellbeing

41%

40%

Community wellbeing

49%

43%*

Physical wellbeing

42%

32%*

*A comparison group's outcome is statistically different from those of
NCAA Student-Athletes at the 95% confidence level.

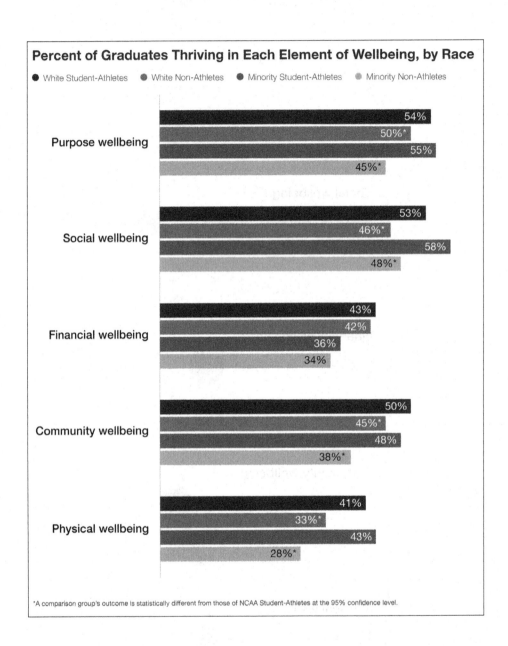

Percent of Graduates Thriving in Each Element of Wellbeing, by Race

● White Student-Athletes   ● White Non-Athletes   ● Minority Student-Athletes   ● Minority Non-Athletes

Purpose wellbeing
- 54%
- 50%*
- 55%
- 45%*

Social wellbeing
- 53%
- 46%*
- 58%
- 48%*

Financial wellbeing
- 43%
- 42%
- 36%
- 34%

Community wellbeing
- 50%
- 45%*
- 48%
- 38%*

Physical wellbeing
- 41%
- 33%*
- 43%
- 28%*

*A comparison group's outcome is statistically different from those of NCAA Student-Athletes at the 95% confidence level.

Length of Time Taken to Obtain a Good Job by NCAA Athletes and Their Non-Athlete Peers

About how long did it take for you to obtain a good job after you completed your undergraduate education?

● I had a job waiting for me when I graduated   ● Two months or less   ● Three to six months   ● Seven months to a year
● More than a year   ● Not applicable because I was not seeking employment upon graduation

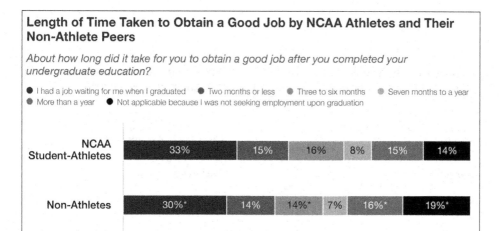

*A comparison group's outcome is statistically different from those of NCAA Student-Athletes at the 95% confidence level.
Note: Totals may not equal 100% due to rounding.

Levels of Student Loan Debt Incurred by NCAA Athletes and Their Non-Athlete Peers

Approximately how much money did you borrow in student loans to obtain your undergraduate degree? (calculated in August 2019 dollars)

● $0   ● $1-$10,000   ● $10,001-$20,000   ● $20,001-$40,000   ● $40,001 or more

Graduated 1975-1989

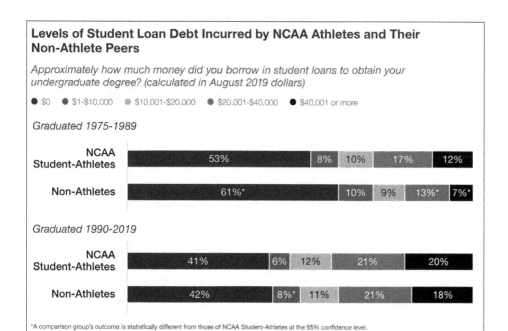

Graduated 1990-2019

*A comparison group's outcome is statistically different from those of NCAA Student-Athletes at the 95% confidence level.
Note: Totals may not equal 100% due to rounding.

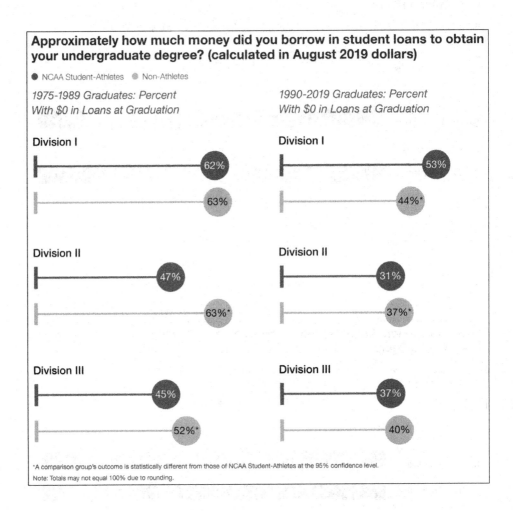

Approximately how much money did you borrow in student loans to obtain your undergraduate degree? (calculated in August 2019 dollars)

● NCAA Student-Athletes   ● Non-Athletes

1975-1989 Graduates: Percent With $0 in Loans at Graduation

1990-2019 Graduates: Percent With $0 in Loans at Graduation

Division I

62%
63%

Division I

53%
44%*

Division II

47%
63%*

Division II

31%
37%*

Division III

45%
52%*

Division III

37%
40%

*A comparison group's outcome is statistically different from those of NCAA Student-Athletes at the 95% confidence level.

Note: Totals may not equal 100% due to rounding.

Advanced Education Attainment Among NCAA Student-Athletes Overall, White Student-Athletes and Black Student-Athletes

NCAA
Student-Athletes

Non-Athletes
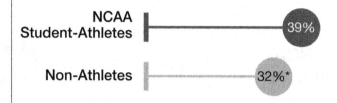

White
Student-Athletes

White
Non-Athletes
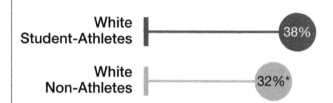

Black
Student-Athletes

Black
Non-Athletes
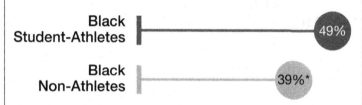

*A comparison group's outcome is statistically different from those of NCAA Student-Athletes at the 95% confidence level.

NCAA student-athletes are 1.3 TIMES MORE LIKELY to earn a postgraduate degree than their non-athlete counterparts.

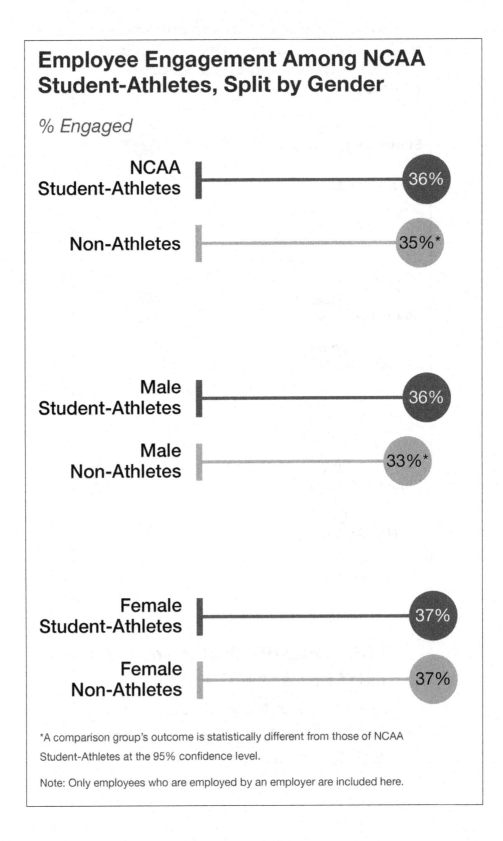

Employee Engagement Among NCAA Student-Athletes, Split by Gender

% Engaged

NCAA Student-Athletes   36%

Non-Athletes   35%*

Male Student-Athletes   36%

Male Non-Athletes   33%*

Female Student-Athletes   37%

Female Non-Athletes   37%

*A comparison group's outcome is statistically different from those of NCAA Student-Athletes at the 95% confidence level.

Note: Only employees who are employed by an employer are included here.

Supportive Undergraduate Experiences Among NCAA Student-Athletes Compared to Non-Athletes

% Strongly agree

● NCAA Student-Athletes   ● Non-Athletes

My professors in college cared about me as a person

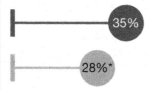

35%

28%*

In college, I had a mentor who encouraged me to pursue my goals and dreams

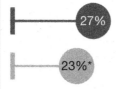

27%

23%*

I had at least one professor in college who made me excited about learning

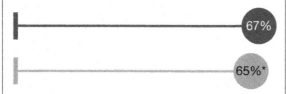

67%

65%*

*A comparison group's outcome is statistically different from those of NCAA Student-Athletes at the 95% confidence level.

NCAA student-athletes are especially likely to have benefitted from meaningful and enriching support experiences with professors and mentors in college.

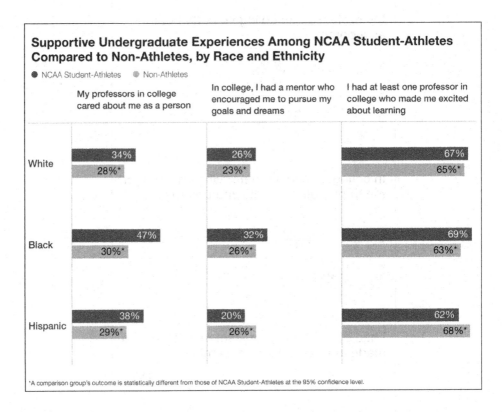

Supportive Undergraduate Experiences Among NCAA Student-Athletes Compared to Non-Athletes, by Race and Ethnicity

● NCAA Student-Athletes   ● Non-Athletes

	My professors in college cared about me as a person	In college, I had a mentor who encouraged me to pursue my goals and dreams	I had at least one professor in college who made me excited about learning
White	34% / 28%*	26% / 23%*	67% / 65%*
Black	47% / 30%*	32% / 26%*	69% / 63%*
Hispanic	38% / 29%*	20% / 26%*	62% / 68%*

*A comparison group's outcome is statistically different from those of NCAA Student-Athletes at the 95% confidence level.

Experiential Learning Among NCAA Student-Athletes Compared to Non-Athletes

% Strongly agree

● NCAA Student-Athletes　● Non-Athletes

I worked on a project that took a semester or more to complete

39%

37%*

I had an internship or job that allowed me to apply what I was learning in the classroom

31%

31%

*A comparison group's outcome is statistically different from those of NCAA Student-Athletes at the 95% confidence level.

NCAA student-athletes (54%) are MORE LIKELY to strongly agree they were challenged academically in college than non-athletes (44%).

Academic and Extracurricular Engagement, Division I

86%[*]

of former Division I student-athletes agreed or strongly agreed they were challenged academically in college, compared with 81% of nonathletes who felt that way.

55%

of former Division I student-athletes worked on a project that took a semester or more to complete, similar to the percentage of nonathletes with such projects (54%).

50%[*]

of former Division I student-athletes held a leadership position in a club or organization, compared with 32% of nonathletes.

*Statistically significant difference (p<.05)

 NCAA Research

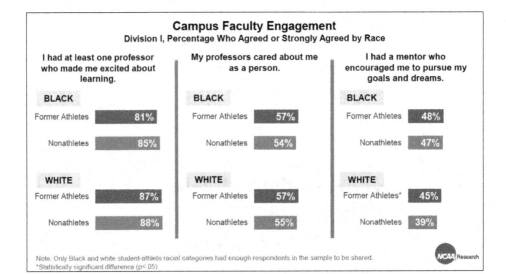

Campus Faculty Engagement
Division I, Percentage Who Agreed or Strongly Agreed by Race

I had at least one professor who made me excited about learning.

BLACK
Former Athletes — 81%
Nonathletes — 85%

WHITE
Former Athletes — 87%
Nonathletes — 88%

My professors cared about me as a person.

BLACK
Former Athletes — 57%
Nonathletes — 54%

WHITE
Former Athletes — 57%
Nonathletes — 55%

I had a mentor who encouraged me to pursue my goals and dreams.

BLACK
Former Athletes — 48%
Nonathletes — 47%

WHITE
Former Athletes* — 45%
Nonathletes — 39%

Note: Only Black and white student-athlete racial categories had enough respondents in the sample to be shared.
*Statistically significant difference (p<.05)

NCAA Research

50% OF STUDENT-ATHLETES strongly agree their education was worth the cost.

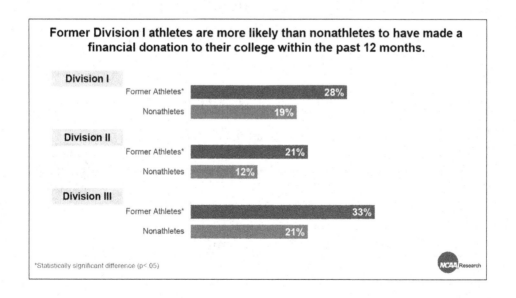

Former Division I athletes are more likely than nonathletes to have made a financial donation to their college within the past 12 months.

Division I
Former Athletes* — 28%
Nonathletes — 19%

Division II
Former Athletes* — 21%
Nonathletes — 12%

Division III
Former Athletes* — 33%
Nonathletes — 21%

*Statistically significant difference (p< 05)

NCAA Research

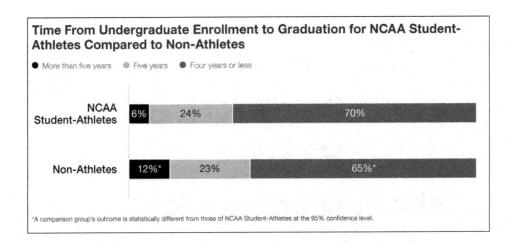

Time From Undergraduate Enrollment to Graduation for NCAA Student-Athletes Compared to Non-Athletes

● More than five years   ● Five years   ● Four years or less

| NCAA Student-Athletes | 6% | 24% | 70% |

| Non-Athletes | 12%* | 23% | 65%* |

*A comparison group's outcome is statistically different from those of NCAA Student-Athletes at the 95% confidence level.

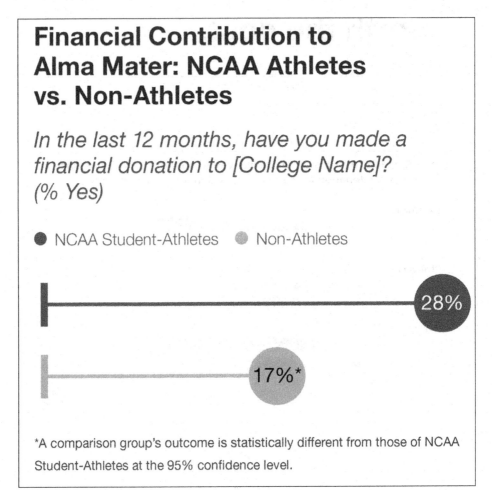

Financial Contribution to Alma Mater: NCAA Athletes vs. Non-Athletes

In the last 12 months, have you made a financial donation to [College Name]? (% Yes)

● NCAA Student-Athletes   ● Non-Athletes

28%

17%*

*A comparison group's outcome is statistically different from those of NCAA Student-Athletes at the 95% confidence level.

Appendix B

Other Resources

Health and Safety Resources from the NCAA website: https://www.ncaa.org
/health-and-safety
NCAA Sport Science Institute: http://www.ncaa.org/sport-science-institute
NCAA Research Center: http://www.ncaa.org/about/resources/research
NCAA GOALS Convention: http://www.ncaa.org/about/resources/research
/ncaa-goals-study

STUDENT-ATHLETE CAREER RESOURCES

NCAA After the Game Career Center: http://www.ncaa.org/student-athletes
/former-student-athlete/careers
NCAA Former Student-Athlete Employment: http://fsacareercenter.ncaa.org
/jobseekers/
Teamwork Online: www.teamworkonline.com
Grit Scale: http://angeladuckworth.com/grit-scale/
Career Personality Test: http://www.humanmetrics.com/personality
/career-choices
LinkedIn: www.linkedin.com
Athletes to Careers: http://athletestocareers.com
Athletes Touch: http://www.athletestouch.co
Athlete Network: https://www.athletenetwork.com

RELEVANT JOURNAL ARTICLES

Bukstein, S. 2016. "Practical Strategies for Thought Leaders in College Athletics and
Higher Education: Developing a 'Meaningful Education and Career Preparation
as Compensation' Model." *Journal of Higher Education Athletics & Innovation*
1(1), https://doi.org/10.15763/issn.2376-5267.2016.1.1.61-72.
Chalfin, P., et al. 2014. "The Value of Intercollegiate Athletics Participation from
the Perspective of Employers Who Target Athletes." *Journal of Issues in Intercollegiate Athletics* (8): 1–17.
Comeaux, E. 2005. "Environmental Predictors of Academic Achievement among
Student-Athletes in the Revenue-Producing Sports of Men's Basketball and Football." *Sport Journal* 8(3).

———. 2007. "The Student(less) Athlete: Identifying the Unidentified College Student." *Journal for the Study of Sports and Athletes in Education* 1(1): 37–44.

Comeaux, E., and C. K. Harrison. 2011. "A Conceptual Model of Academic Success for Student-Athletes." *Educational Researcher* 40(5): 235–45.

Comeaux, E., L. Speer, M. Taustine, and C. K. Harrison. 2011. "Purposeful Engagement of First-Year Division I Student-Athletes." *Journal of the First-Year Experience and Students in Transition* 23(1): 35–52.

Fuller, R. D. 2014. "Transition Experiences out of Intercollegiate Athletics: A Meta-Synthesis." *Qualitative Report* 19(46): 1–15.

Gayles, J. G., and S. Hu. 2009. "The Influence of Student Engagement and Sport Participation on College Outcomes among Division I Student Athletes." *Journal of Higher Education* 80(3): 315–33.

———. 2009. "Athletes as Students: Ensuring Positive Cognitive and Affective Outcomes." In J. D. Toma and D. A. Kramer, eds., "The Uses of Intercollegiate Athletics: Challenges and Opportunities," *New Directions for Higher Education* (148): 101–7.

Gayles, J. G., A. B. Rockenbach, and H. A. Davis. 2012. "Civic Responsibility and the Student-Athlete: Validating a New Conceptual Model." *Journal of Higher Education* 83(4): 535–57.

Harris, H. L., M. K. Altekruse, and D. W. Engels. 2003. "Helping Freshman Student Athletes Adjust to College Life Using Psychoeducational Groups." *Journal for Specialists in Group Work* 28(1): 64–81.

Harrison, C. K., J. Stone, J. Shapiro, S. Yee, J. A. Boyd, and V. Rullan. 2009. "The Role of Gender Identities and Stereotype Salience with the Academic Performance of Male and Female College Athletes." *Journal of Sport and Social Issues* 33(1): 78–96.

Leonard, J. M., and C. J. Schimmel. 2016. "Theory of Work Adjustment and Student-Athletes' Transition out of Sport." *Journal of Issues in Intercollegiate Athletics* (9): 62–85.

Marx, J., S. Huffmon, and A. Doyle. 2008. "The Student-Athlete Model and the Socialization of Intercollegiate Athletes." *Athletic Insight* 10(1).

Melendez, M. C. 2006. "The Influence of Athletic Participation on the College Adjustment of Freshmen and Sophomore Student Athletes." *Journal of College Student Retention: Research, Theory & Practice* 8(1): 39–55.

Miller, P. S., and G. Kerr. 2002. "The Athletic, Academic and Social Experiences of Intercollegiate Student-Athletes." *Journal of Sport Behavior* 25(4): 346–67.

Osborne, B. 2014. "The Myth of the Exploited Student-Athlete." *Journal of Intercollegiate Sport* 7(2): 143–52.

Potuto, J. R., and J. O'Hanlon. 2007. "National Study of Student-Athletes Regarding Their Experiences as College Students." *College Student Journal* 41(4): 947–66.

Watt, S. K., and J. L. Moore. 2001. "Who Are Student-Athletes?" In S. Watt and J. Moore, eds., "Student Services for Athletes," special issue of *New Directions for Student Services* (93): 7–18.

Yopyk, D., and D. Prentice. 2005. "Am I an Athlete or a Student? Identity Salience and Stereotype Threat in Student-Athletes." *Basic and Applied Social Psychology* 27(4): 329–36.

RECOMMENDED BOOKS

A Career in Sports: Advice from Sports Business Leaders, by Michelle Wells and Andy Kreutzer. M. Wells Enterprises, 2010.

Drive: The Surprising Truth about What Motivates Us, by Daniel H. Pink. New York: Riverhead, 2009.

Good to Great: Why Some Companies Make the Leap . . . and Others Don't, by Jim Collins. New York: HarperBusiness, 2011.

Great by Choice, by Jim Collins and Morten T. Hansen. New York: HarperBusiness, 2011.

Grit: The Power of Passion and Perseverance, by Angela Lee Duckworth. New York: Scribner, 2016.

Intangibles: Unlocking the Science and Soul of Team Chemistry, by Joan Ryan. London: HarperCollins, 2020.

Outliers: The Story of Success, by Malcolm Gladwell. New York: Little, Brown, 2008.

Pitch Perfect: How to Say It Right the First Time, Every Time, by Bill McGowan. New York: HarperBusiness, 2014.

Start with Why: How Great Leaders Inspire Everyone to Take Action, by Simon Sinek. New York: Penguin, 2009.

The ONE Thing: The Surprisingly Simple Truth behind Extraordinary Results, by Jay Papasan and Gary Keller. Austin, TX: Bard, 2013.

The 7 Habits of Highly Effective People: Restoring the Character Ethic, by Stephen Covey. New York: Free Press, 2004.

The Captain Class: A New Theory of Leadership, by Sam Walker. New York: Random House, 2017.

The Power of Failure: Succeeding in the Age of Innovation, by Fran Tarkenton. Washington, DC: Regnery, 2015.

The Power of Now: A Guide to Spiritual Enlightenment, by Eckhart Tolle. Novato, CA: New World Library, 1999.

The Subtle Art of Not Giving a F***: A Counterintuitive Approach to Living a Good Life, by Mark Manson. New York: HarperOne, 2016.

The Talent Code: Greatness Isn't Born. It's Grown. Here's How, by Daniel Coyle. New York: Bantam, 2009.

What Color Is Your Parachute? Your Guide to a Lifetime of Meaningful Work and Career Success, 2021 edition, by Richard N. Bolles with Katharine Brooks. New York: Ten Speed, 2020.

Wooden: A Lifetime of Observations and Reflections On and Off the Court, by John Wooden. New York: McGraw-Hill, 1997.

Off Balance: Getting Beyond the Work-Life Balance Myth to Personal and Professional Satisfaction, by Matthew Kelly. New York: Hudson Street, 2011.

Mindset: The New Psychology of Success, by Carol S. Dweck. New York: Random House, 2006.

Appendix C

Contributors to the Book

Contributor	Title	Sport	School
Rod Baker	Assistant Coach and Scout for the Philadelphia 76ers	Basketball	College of the Holy Cross
James Biddick	Student-Athlete Career Development Program Manager at the University of Notre Dame	Field Hockey	New Zealand
Bob Boland	Athletics Integrity Officer at Penn State University	Football	Columbia University
Kevin Brice	Quantitative Analyst for the Los Angeles Angels	Baseball	Pomona College
Kristen Brown	Deputy Athletics Director at Texas A&M University	Basketball	Northern Illinois University
Dawn Buth	Assistant Director of Government Relations at the NCAA	Swimming and Diving	University of Florida
Dan Butterly	Commissioner of the Big West Conference	N/A	N/A
Kelsey Cermak	Assistant Director of Championships and Alliances at the NCAA	Basketball	University of Iowa
Fred Claire	Former GM of Los Angeles Dodgers, cofounder of Scoutables	N/A	N/A
Steve Cobb	Former Director of the Arizona Fall League	Baseball	College of Wooster

Azure Davey	Former Director of Academic Affairs and Membership at the NCAA	Lacrosse	Hamilton College
Chris Dawson	Associate Commissioner at the Pac-12 Conference	Basketball	University of Virginia
Max Dittmer	Principal at CORE Office Interiors	Swimming	University of Iowa
Anson Dorrance	Head Coach, Women's Soccer, University of North Carolina	Soccer	University of North Carolina
Jason Elias	Associate Athletic Director at IMG Academy	Baseball	Baldwin Wallace University
Matt Engleka	Owner of LEJ Agency	Baseball	Ohio University
Seth Etherton	Minor League Pitching Coach with the Cincinnati Reds	Baseball	University of Southern California
Brett Fischer	Staff Physical Therapist with the Arizona Cardinals	N/A	N/A
Jeremy Foley	Athletics Director Emeritus at the University of Florida	Football	Hobart College
Eddie Gill	Former NBA player, now TV Analyst for Indiana Pacers on FOX Sports	Basketball	Weber State University
Kevin Hall	Doctor of Physical Therapy at the Mayo Clinic	Baseball	Wichita State University
Shauna Happel	Assistant Women's Soccer Coach at Mount Mercy University	Soccer	University of Northern Iowa
Kevin Hurd	National Sponsorship Manager at Mike's Hard Lemonade/White Claw Hard Seltzer	Baseball	University of Northern Colorado
Louie Iglesias	Relationship Banker at JPMorgan Chase	Tennis	University of Toledo
Dean Jordan	Managing Executive of Properties and Media, Wasserman	N/A	N/A
Jim Kahler	Director of Sports Gambling Education at Ohio University	Swimming	Xavier University
Immanuel Kerr-Brown	Associate Director of Development at Penn State University	Wrestling	Duke University
Joni Lockridge	Vice President of Strategy and Operations at iX.co	Softball	Furman University

Oliver Luck	Former Executive Vice President of Regulatory Affairs at the NCAA	Football	West Virginia University
Christa Mann	Senior Manager of Communications at the MLS	Soccer	Georgia State University
Nick Manno	Player Personnel Coordinator for the Toronto Blue Jays	Baseball	University of Mount Union
Kerry McCoy	Executive Director and Head Coach, Wrestling, California Olympic Regional Training Center	Wrestling	Pennsylvania State University
Brooks Neal	Director of Corporate Partnerships at the New York Jets	Lacrosse	Syracuse University
Hillary Nelson	Trainer at Positive Coaching Alliance	Softball	Arizona State University
John Nowicki	Senior Manager, Partnerships at Oakland Athletics	Lacrosse	University of Detroit Mercy
Hallie Olson	Director of Notre Dame Global Partnerships	Swimming	Ohio University
Alexis Pinson	Account Manager for the Los Angeles Rams	Volleyball	Arizona State University and Ohio University
Erik Price	Associate Commissioner at the Pac-12 Conference	N/A	N/A
Michelle Pride	Embedded Psychologist, Ohio University Athletics	N/A	N/A
JR Reynolds	Area Scout for the Cincinnati Reds	Baseball	Ohio University
Wally Ritchie	Former MLB Pitcher	Baseball	N/A
Jeff Rodin	Director of Community Outreach and Development for the Arizona Diamondbacks	Baseball	University of Illinois at Chicago
Brian Sanders	Senior Vice President of Stadium Operations for the Los Angeles Angels	Baseball	Chapman University
Drew Saylor	Hitting Coordinator for the Kansas City Royals	Baseball	Kent State University
Glenn Schembechler	NFL Scout	Football	Miami (OH) University
Garrett Shinoskie	Former Director of Athletic Performance at Zone Athletic Performance	Football	Capital University

Bill Shumard	President Emeritus of Special Olympics Southern California	N/A	N/A
Rob Smith	Head Baseball Coach at Ohio University	Baseball	Indiana University
Ryan Sollazzo	Senior Director, Global Corporate Partnerships at Major League Baseball	Football	Florida Atlantic University and Stony Brook University
Terri Steeb-Gronau	Vice President of Division II at the NCAA	Volleyball	University of Alabama at Birmingham
Lynn Steenberg	CEO of Sports PT	N/A	N/A
Colby Targun	Labor Relations at NFL Commissioner's Office	Football and Baseball	Texas State University
Pim Thirati	Assistant Director of Marketing and Digital Strategy at Virginia Tech	Golf	University of Illinois
Mark Trumbo	Assistant Athletics Director for Student-Athlete Engagement, Syracuse University	N/A	N/A
Matt Vansandt	Assistant Commissioner of Championships at the Big South Conference	Track and Field	Augustana College
Steve Watson	Athletic Director at Loyola University Chicago	Basketball	Bowling Green State University
Danny White	Senior Associate Athletic Director, Student-Athlete Services and University Affairs, Virginia Tech	N/A	N/A
Mattie White	Deputy Director of Athletics and Senior Woman Administrator at Indiana University Bloomington	N/A	N/A
Scott White	ER Paramedic at Mayo Clinic	Baseball	Ohio University
Elizabeth Woerle	Assistant Athletic Director for Development at the University of North Texas	Soccer	Drake University
Christina Wright	Assistant Professor of Instruction, and Multicultural Faculty-in-Residence at Ohio University	Track and Field	American University

Appendix D

About the Authors

RICK BURTON is the David B. Falk Distinguished Professor of Sport Management in Syracuse University's David B. Falk College of Sport and Human Dynamics. At Syracuse, Burton serves as the university's Faculty Athletics Representative (FAR) to the NCAA and Atlantic Coast Conference (ACC).

Previously, Burton held a number of industry positions, including Chief Marketing Officer for the US Olympic Committee for the 2008 Beijing Summer Olympics and the Commissioner of the Sydney-based Australian National Basketball League (2003–7). He and coauthor Norm O'Reilly write a monthly column for *Sports Business Journal* and are finishing a new book on the National Hockey League for the University of Toronto Press (2021).

JAKE HIRSHMAN currently works at the PGA TOUR in tournament business and sponsor relations for the Korn Ferry Tour. At the TOUR, he serves as a cochair of an employee resource group and is a member of the Inclusion Leadership Council. Prior to the TOUR, he worked for Learfield IMG College with Purdue Athletics, the Arizona Fall League, the Seattle Mariners, the Arizona Diamondbacks, the Rose Bowl, the Ontario Reign, and the Inland Empire 66ers. Hirshman was a pitcher at the University of Redlands and Ohio University. He earned a bachelor's in business administration from the University of Redlands and two master's degrees (in sports administration and sport science) from Ohio University. In addition to hosting the *Life in the Front Office* podcast, he is coauthor of the forthcoming book *LOL, Loss of Logo: What's Your Next Move?* He is a cofounder and partner of Competitive Advantage Consulting and Sports Business Case Reviews. Additionally, he is an adjunct professor at the University of Florida's undergraduate and graduate sports management programs, as well as the graduate sports business leadership program at Seattle University. Lastly, Hirshman is an advisory board member of the nonprofit Sports Biz Cares, which seeks to create opportunities for individuals from underrepresented minorities and women trying to enter the sports industry.

DR. NORM O'REILLY is recognized as one of the leading scholars in the business of sports. Formerly the Richard P. and Joan S. Fox Professor of Business and Chair of the Department of Sports Administration at Ohio University's College of Business, he is now the founding Director of the International Institute for Sport Business and Leadership at the University of Guelph's Gordon S. Lang School of Business and Economics. He has authored or coauthored fifteen books, fourteen case studies in the Harvard/Stanford series, and more than 145 peer-reviewed journal articles. At conferences, he has won fourteen best paper awards. In 2015, Dr. O'Reilly was awarded the Distinguished Career Contributions to the Scientific Understanding of Sport Business Award by the American Marketing Association's Sport and Sponsorship-Linked Marketing Special Interest Group. In 2016, he was Assistant Chef de Mission for the Canadian Paralympic Team at the Paralympic Games. He was a two-sport university athlete (swimming and Nordic skiing) and was a member of the Ontario University Athletics 1996 championship team in men's Nordic skiing.

ANDY DOLICH has spent more than five decades in the professional sports industry, holding executive positions in the NFL, NBA, NHL, and MLB. He is currently COO of FCF (Fan Controlled Football) and President of Dolich Consulting. As COO of the San Francisco 49ers from 2007 to 2010, Dolich was responsible for generating over $200 million in revenue per season. He served as President of Business Operations for the Memphis Grizzlies (NBA) from 2000 to 2007, where he led the day-to-day functioning of the team's business and marketing programs and the construction and operation of the team's home arena, FedExForum. In his fourteen years as VP of Business Operations and EVP of the Oakland Athletics (MLB), the team set numerous attendance records, won Clio awards for advertising, and appeared in three World Series, including a sweep of the San Francisco Giants in the 1989 Earthquake World Series. Dolich also has held executive-level positions with the Maryland Arrows of Box Lacrosse (NLL), Washington Diplomats (North American Soccer League), and the Washington Capitals (NHL). He began his career with the Philadelphia 76ers (NBA). Dolich received his undergraduate degree in government from American University and a master's in sport management from Ohio University. He serves on a number of sports industry and community-invested boards and organizations. He teaches sports business at Stanford Continuing Studies and is a columnist for the *Ultimate*

Sports Guide, a cohost of the podcast *Life in the Front Office,* and a coauthor of the forthcoming book *LOL, Loss of Logo: What's Your Next Move?*

DR. HEATHER LAWRENCE was a Professor of Sports Administration and Robert H. Freeman Professor of Business in the College of Business at Ohio University prior to joining CrossFit in 2021. Throughout her sixteen years at Ohio, she provided academic leadership to various graduate programs. Dr. Lawrence has extensive international experience in academic programs, such as the Hamdan Bin Mohammed Program for Sports Leadership (Dubai) and other programs at the University of Guelph (Canada), IE University (Spain), SVKM Usha Pravin Gandhi College (India), and Beijing Sport University (China). She has also served as a program delegate to Saudi Arabia. She is an active researcher in sport business, and her book *Event Management Blueprint: Creating and Managing Successful Sports Events* is now in its third edition. Prior to beginning her academic career, Dr. Lawrence worked in various administrative positions within intercollegiate athletics at Southeastern Louisiana University and the University of Florida. Her sport industry responsibilities have included working in NCAA compliance, facility management, construction/renovation management, general administration, and event operations and as a sport supervisor. In her youth, Dr. Lawrence was a USA Diving national team member, NCAA All-American, and SEC champion and was inducted into the University of Florida College of Health and Human Performance Alumni Hall of Fame.

Notes

SECRET 1: CREATE AND FOLLOW YOUR STUDENT-ATHLETE PLAN

1. See Appendix A for NCAA reports supporting the 99 percent figure.

2. Example: J. T. Edwards and M. Washington (2015), "Establishing a 'Safety Net': Exploring the Emergence and Maintenance of College Hockey Inc. and NCAA Division I Hockey," *Journal of Sport Management* 29(3): 291–304.

SECRET 2: UNDERSTAND WHO A STUDENT-ATHLETE IS

1. There exists a vast body of research that shows how college student-athletes take on roles, behaviors, and risk-taking actions different from those taken on by college students in general. A good source is N. R. Mastroleo, N. Scaglione, K. A. Mallett, and R. Turrisi (2013), "Can Personality Account for Differences in Drinking between College Athletes and Non-athletes? Explaining the Role of Sensation Seeking, Risk-Taking, and Impulsivity," *Journal of Drug Education* 43(1): 81–95.

2. See Appendix A for reports on NCAA student-athletes.

SECRET 3: LEARN WHAT NAME, IMAGE, AND LIKENESS MEANS FOR YOU

1. R. Stark-Mason (2020), "Name. Image. Likeness: What Name, Image and Likeness Means for College Sports. And How the NCAA Is Turning to Student-Athletes to Navigate a Path Forward," NCAA, http://www.ncaa.org/champion /name-image-likeness.

SECRET 4: RIDE YOUR SUCCESS WHEEL

1. There is much research on this topic—for more detail, see R. M. Southall (2014), "NCAA Graduation Rates: A Quarter-Century of Re-branding Academic Success," *Journal of Intercollegiate Sport* 7(2): 120–33.

2. E. Comeaux and K. C. Harrison (2011), "A Conceptual Model of Academic Success for Student Athletes," *Educational Researcher* 40(5): 235–45.

SECRET 9: YOUR MAJOR REALLY MATTERS

1. *A Study of NCAA Student-Athletes: Undergraduate Experiences and Post-college Outcomes* (Washington, DC: Gallup, 2020), 11.

2. This table is sourced from a 2015 study by the NCAA on goals. The study comes from NCAA internal documents—shared with the researchers by the NCAA on September 29, 2016, and reproduced by permission.

SECRET 10: TAKE NOTHING FOR GRANTED

1. R. Kuik and S. Potts, "Mental Health and Athletes," Athletes for Hope, http://www.athletesforhope.org/2019/05/mental-health-and-athletes/.

SECRET 13: MENTALLY MOVE ON AS A SENIOR

1. R. D. Fuller (2014), "Transition Experiences out of Intercollegiate Athletics: A Meta-synthesis," *Qualitative Report* 19(46): 1–15.

SECRET 14: IDENTIFY WHO YOU ARE

1. J. Leonard and C. Schimmel (2016), "Theory of Work Adjustment and Student-Athletes' Transition out of Sport," *Journal of Issues in Intercollegiate Athletics* (9): 62–85.

SECRET 15: FIND YOUR OTHER PASSIONS IN LIFE AS YOU PREPARE TO BE A SOPHOMORE

1. "Fast Facts," National Center for Education Statistics, http://nces.ed.gov/fastfacts/display.asp?id=372; "Table 318.10. Degrees Conferred by Postsecondary Institutions, by Level of Degree and Sex of Student: Selected Years, 1869–70 through 2029–30" (2019), Digest of Education Statistics, National Center for Education Statistics, https://nces.ed.gov/programs/digest/d19/tables/dt19_318.10.asp.

2. Bureau of Labor Statistics, "Employee Tenure in 2014," news release no. USDL-14-1714, September 18, 2014, http://www.bls.gov/news.release/archives/tenure_09182014.pdf.

SECRET 16: INVEST IN YOURSELF, YOUR HEALTH, AND YOUR FUTURE

1. Study Source: NCAA internal document shared with the researchers by the NCAA on September 29, 2016; from http://www.ncaa.org/student-athletes/former-student-athlete/recipe-energy-management-success.

2. American College Health Association, *National College Health Assessment* (ACHA-NCHA), Fall 2008, Spring 2009, Fall 2009, Spring 2010, Fall 2010, Spring 2011, Fall 2011, Fall 2012 [ACHA-NCHA II, ACHA-NCHA IIb] Hanover, MD: American College Health Association; (2013-10-31).

SECRET 17: ACTIVATE YOUR STUDENT-ATHLETE ADVANTAGE

1. D. Lavallee (2015), "The Traits of Athletes That Can Predict Workplace Success," *Entrepeneur,* January 16, https://www.entrepreneur.com/article/241857; B. Capaletti (2014), "Why College Athletes Make Great Employees," WorkInSports.com, September 8, https://www.workinsports.com/blog/why-college-athletes-make-great-employees/; V. Ackerman (2013), *Division I Women's Basketball White Paper: Prepared for the NCAA,* June 15, https://www.ncaa.org/sites/default/files/NCAAWBBWHITEPAPER_1_0.pdf; P. Chalfin et al. (2014), "The Value of Intercollegiate Athletics Participation from the Perspective of Employers Who Target Athletes," *Journal of Issues in Intercollegiate Athletics* (8): 1–17.

2. This table is sourced from a 2015 study by the NCAA on goals. The study comes from NCAA internal documents—shared with the researchers by the NCAA on September 29, 2016, and reproduced by permission.